A Goy Who Speaks Yiddish

Stanford Studies in Jewish History and Culture

edited by *Aron Rodrigue and Steven J. Zipperstein*

A Goy Who Speaks Yiddish

Christians and the Jewish Language in Early Modern Germany

Aya Elyada

STANFORD UNIVERSITY PRESS
STANFORD, CALIFORNIA

Stanford University Press
Stanford, California

©2012 by the Board of Trustees of the Leland Stanford Junior University.
All rights reserved.

This book has been published with the assistance of the Research Committee, Faculty of Humanities, The Hebrew University of Jerusalem.

No part of this book may be reproduced or transmitted in any form or by any means, electronic or mechanical, including photocopying and recording, or in any information storage or retrieval system without the prior written permission of Stanford University Press.

Printed in the United States of America on acid-free, archival-quality paper

Library of Congress Cataloging-in-Publication Data

Elyada, Aya, 1977- author.
A goy who speaks Yiddish : Christians and the Jewish language in early modern Germany / Aya Elyada.
pages cm.–(Stanford studies in Jewish history and culture)
Includes bibliographical references and index.
ISBN 978-0-8047-8193-0 (cloth : alk. paper)
1. Yiddish language–Study and teaching–Germany–History. 2. Yiddish literature–Study and teaching–Germany–History. 3. Christian literature, German–History and criticism. 4. Yiddish language in literature. 5. Christianity and other religions–Judaism. 6. Judaism–Relations–Christianity. 7. Christian scholars–Germany–History. I. Title. II. Series: Stanford studies in Jewish history and culture.
PJ5112.E59 2012
439'.10882743–dc23 2012014468

Typeset by Bruce Lundquist in 10.5/14 Galliard

To my beloved family

Contents

List of Illustrations

Preface and Acknowledgments

"*A hun vos kreyt un a goy vos shmuest yidish—zoln zayn kapore far mir*" (A hen that crows, and a non-Jew who speaks Yiddish, they should be my atonement)[1]; in this Yiddish saying, the speaker summons two figures from the world of the inconceivable to serve as his atonement. And to him, apparently, a *goy* who speaks the Jewish language is just as preposterous as a hen that crows like a rooster. But perhaps surprisingly, non-Jews did speak Yiddish, probably from the earliest stages of the existence of this language. And at least from the beginning of the sixteenth century, we also have written evidence for Christians reading, writing, and investigating the Yiddish language and literature.

This book explores the unlikely phenomenon of "Christian Yiddishism," namely the Christian engagement with the Yiddish language and literature during the early modern period. In this context of early modern Christian preoccupation with Yiddish, the term "Yiddishists," which I will use, does not designate admirers or supporters of the Yiddish language, as was sometimes the case in later periods. The Christian authors in this story were persons who took interest in the Jewish language, studied it, and wrote about it for various reasons and motivations, some pragmatic and utilitarian but others nevertheless confrontational or even sinister.

By investigating this unique phenomenon, hardly known in modern historical research, the book aims to contribute to our understanding of Christian attitudes towards Jews and Judaism in early modern Europe, specifically in the German-speaking world. In recent years, growing attention has been given to the complex system of Christian perceptions of the Jew as the archetypical "Other" of early modern Europe. Some of the most interesting aspects of this topic, which still merit investigation, are the diverse and complicated ways in which the Christians of that period understood, defined, and constructed the Jew's "Otherness." Of no less importance are the various motivations that underlay Christian representations of Jewish Otherness, the factors and circumstances that influenced and shaped them, and the functions these representations served in intra-Christian debates.

In addition to its contribution to the field of Christian-Jewish relations in early modern Europe, this book also seeks to illuminate various themes in the field of social and cultural history of language, including the role of language in shaping and defining group identities, images of languages and linguistic stereotypes, language and national consciousness, linguistic domination and social control, and attitudes of majorities toward linguistic minorities. Highly relevant also to our present-day experience, these issues are especially interesting within the scope of the early modern period, with the shifting sands of its complicated and constantly changing linguistic and national landscape. From the mid-fifteenth century, the gradual transition from a dominantly monolingual Latin culture to a multilingual one based on the various European vernaculars brought the linguistic diversity in Europe to the attention of contemporaries. This development evoked a wide spectrum of responses among scholars of the time, who engaged in evaluations and comparisons of the various languages, and debated the question of language and its place in culture and society.

Our story on Christians and Yiddish in early modern Europe starts in 1514, with the publication of the first known Christian treatise on the language,[2] and spans the next two and a half centuries. In order to present the genre of early modern Christian literature on Yiddish in its full spectrum of richness and diversity, the book draws on a wide array of primary sources in German, Latin, Hebrew, and Yiddish, ranging from the scholarly to the popular, and from the theological to the secular. Addressing a broad spectrum of topics and using an interdisciplinary approach, including cultural, theological, and sociolinguistic themes, I hope the book will be of interest to anyone engaged in the fields of early modern European history, Jewish history, social and cultural history of language, Jewish-Christian relations, German studies, and Yiddish studies.

*

It is with great pleasure that I would like to thank both my doctoral advisors, Shulamit Volkov from Tel Aviv University and Michael Brenner from the Ludwig-Maximilians-Universität in Munich, for their professional and personal support during my work on this project. Head of the Lehrstuhl für Jüdische Geschichte und Kultur at the University of Munich, Michael Brenner welcomed me to his group of scholars and students, and provided me with an excellent working environment for my research and academic development. My project has greatly profited from his input, advice, and guidance, and I deeply thank him for that. My great debt to Shula Volkov goes back to my very first steps at Tel Aviv University. In the years that have passed since then, I found in Shula not only a role model of academic excellence but also an inspiring and exemplary teacher. With her insightful criticism, excellent advice, and unlimited dedication she has significantly contributed to my scholarly and personal development, and to the successful completion of this book.

Another debt of gratitude belongs to Chava Turniansky and Richard Cohen from the Hebrew University of Jerusalem, and to Marion Aptroot from the University of Düsseldorf, for their continuous support of my project and their unwavering confidence in its success. Their outstanding scholarly erudition and their commitment to helping young scholars played a crucial role in the advancement and refinement of my work. This book has greatly benefited from their comments and insights, as well as from those of Elisheva Carlebach from Columbia University and Helmut Zedelmaier from the University of Munich. The comments of my father-in-law, Dov Elyada, did much to improve the clarity of the book to a more general audience. Christian Ronning from the University of Munich delivered unfailing help in getting to the bottom of the more opaque and cryptic of the Latin texts I encountered, and Andrea Sinn proved helpful in every possible way. Her friendship and support, as those of my other fellow graduate students in Germany and Israel, have been indispensable in the process of creating this book. Other scholars from various universities and fields of study, including Hans Peter Althaus, Eli Bar-Chen, Ruth von Bernuth, Yaacov Deutsch, John Efron, Michael Heyd, Simon Neuberg, David Ruderman, Winfried Schulze, Erika Timm, and Cornel Zwierlein, have contributed from their experience and expertise at different stages of the project, encouraged me in my work, and were always willing to offer assistance. I thank them all.

Several institutions and foundations, both in Israel and Germany, have provided the financial support for this project. My studies and research in Germany were possible thanks to the generous scholarships of the Hertie Foundation and the Minerva Fellowship Program of the Max-Planck-Gesellschaft. At Tel Aviv University I enjoyed the support of the Pedagogica Foundation, the Dan David Prize, the S. Daniel Abraham Center for International and Regional Studies, and the Goldreich Family Institute for Yiddish Language, Literature, and Culture. The preparation of the manuscript was supported by a generous fellowship of the Yad Hanadiv Foundation. This final stage of the work was undertaken during my stay as a visiting scholar at Duke University; I would like to thank Malachi Hacohen from the History Department at Duke for his hospitality, and for making my time at Duke fruitful and gratifying.

At Stanford University Press, I wish to thank the series editors Steven Zipperstein and Aron Rodrigue for their interest in and support of my project. I am also grateful to Mariana Raykov and Emma Harper, who were very helpful in seeing the book through production, and to Jeff Wyneken for his skillful copyediting. Special thanks are extended to the editor, Norris Pope, for his efficient and highly professional handling of the book's publication, and for his support and helpfulness along the way. Finally, I would like to thank the Research Committee of the Faculty of Humanities, The Hebrew University of Jerusalem, for their assistance in the publication of the book.

Chapters 1 and 8 were published in an earlier version in "Yiddish—Language of Conversion? Linguistic Adaptation and Its Limits in Early Modern *Judenmission*," *Leo Baeck Institute Year Book* 53 (2008), 3–29. The introduction to Part 1, as well as Chapters 2 and 9, were published in an earlier version in "Protestant Scholars and Yiddish Studies in Early Modern Europe," *Past and Present* 203 (2009), 69–98. Portions of Chapter 7 were published in an earlier version in "'*Eigentlich Teutsch*'? Depictions of Yiddish and Its Relations to German in Early Modern Christian Writings," *European Journal of Jewish Studies* 4, no. 1 (2010), 23–42. I thank the Leo Baeck Institute, Oxford University Press and the Past and Present Society, and Brill, respectively, for permission to reuse this material here.

Last but not least, I would like to thank my parents, Mike and Ahouva Lahav, for their unconditional love and support, and for backing me in every personal and professional decision I have ever made. The greatest thanks of all belong to Yishai Elyada, my partner and best friend in the past twelve years, for sharing with me the long and winding road of bringing a new book into the world. Although trained as a neuroscientist, Yishai nevertheless shared my enthusiasm for this project, and was emotionally and intellectually involved in every step of the way. His perceptive comments and suggestions on my work have challenged me to continuously strive for improvement, and his infinite encouragement has been a great comfort at difficult times. Without him, all this would not have been possible.

Note on Spelling and Translations

Throughout this book, I transcribed Yiddish and Hebrew terms, phrases, and titles of works with Latin characters according to the standard YIVO transcription system and the guidelines set forth in the second edition of the *Encyclopaedia Judaica*, respectively. However, when Yiddish or Hebrew words were quoted from Christian sources, they appear in the same transliteration as found in the source. When a certain word appeared in different forms in several sources, the most comprehensible form was selected.

For readability's sake, minor changes and modifications were made in the spelling of some transliterated words (in particular, by bringing Yiddish words closer to the pronunciation of modern standard Yiddish) as well as in the spelling of some of the German words quoted from the early modern sources. Primary sources with bilingual titles in the same edition—Yiddish or Hebrew on the one hand, and German or Latin on the other—are noted only by their German or Latin title.

Unless mentioned otherwise, all translations from German, Latin, Yiddish, and Hebrew are my own.

A Goy Who Speaks Yiddish

Introduction
A Jewish Language in a Christian World

In a famous passage from his autobiographical work *Dichtung und Wahrheit*, Johann Wolfgang von Goethe recalls his impressions as a young boy from the *Judengasse* in his hometown, Frankfurt. Together with the crowdedness and filth of the Jewish quarter, it was "the accent of an unpleasant language" that attracted his attention, leaving "a most displeasing impression" on the young Goethe.[1] Despite this somewhat unfavorable reaction to Yiddish (or "*das barocke Judendeutsch*," as he called it), Goethe, not yet thirteen years old, decided to learn the language. He soon realized that deeper acquaintance with Hebrew was needed, and started taking Hebrew lessons from the rector of the Gymnasium—assuring his tutor that his sole intent was to read the Old Testament in its original language.[2] As for learning the Yiddish language itself, the young Goethe could of course take private lessons from a convert, as he in fact did in the summer of 1761. But he could also make use of the vast linguistic and philological corpus on Yiddish that had been consolidating in the German lands since the beginning of the sixteenth century and that consisted of works prepared by *Christian* authors for a *Christian* readership.[3] These included theoretical depictions and analyses of the Yiddish language, grammars and textbooks, dictionaries, bibliographies of Yiddish writings, literary surveys, and translations from and to Yiddish.

The Christian literature on Yiddish, written and published in the German-speaking world from the beginning of the sixteenth century and into the second half of the eighteenth century, stands as the focal point of this book. The Yiddish that was the subject of Christian works during that period is referred to today as "Western Yiddish" (also known as "Jewish-German" or "Judeo-German"), as opposed to the

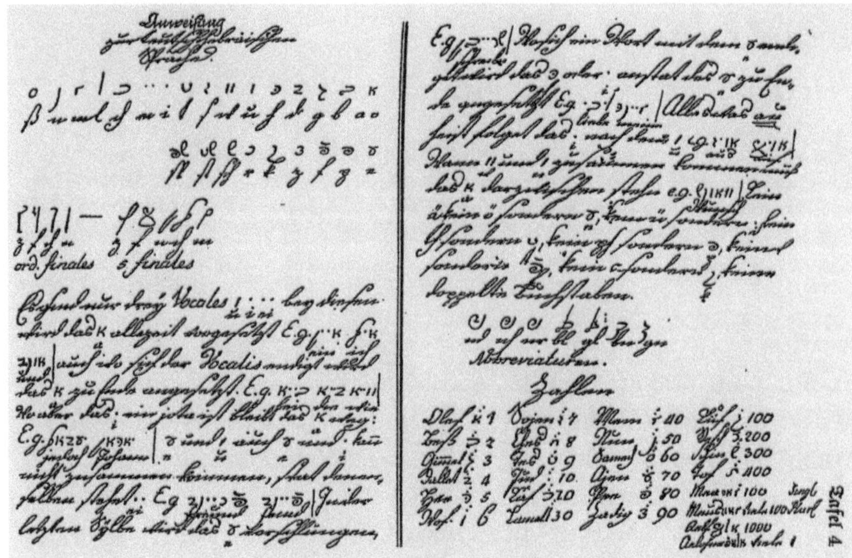

Figure I.1. Johann Wolfgang Goethe, “Anweisung zur teutsch-hebräischen Sprache” (ca. 1760). Reprinted from *Der junge Goethe: Neue Ausgabe in sechs Bänden besorgt von Max Morris*, vol. 1, Leipzig: Insel-Verlag, 1909.

“Eastern Yiddish” of the east-European Jews.[4] In the period under discussion, Western Yiddish served the Ashkenazi communities of Western and Central Europe as the spoken language, and together with *loshn-koydesh* (“the language of sanctity,” namely Hebrew-Aramaic), also as a written language. Unlike Eastern Yiddish, which contains a considerable Slavic component, Western Yiddish was composed almost entirely from German and Hebrew-Aramaic components. Linguistically speaking, therefore, Western Yiddish was much closer to German than modern Yiddish, which developed from the eastern dialects.

The significant lexical and structural similarity with German led to conflicting approaches to Western Yiddish in modern linguistic research. One approach, advocated especially by the German-Jewish scholars of the *Wissenschaft des Judentums* in the nineteenth century, saw Western Yiddish as essentially German in Hebrew letters, with the exception of lexical items derived from the Hebrew-Aramaic component. The other approach, promoted by Jewish Yiddishists at the beginning of the twentieth century, saw Western Yiddish as a language in its own right. According to this view, Yiddish was never identical to German, but already from its early, medieval stages constituted a distinct language. Although the view of Western Yiddish as a type of German can still be found among contemporary scholars, especially those who approach the Jewish language with the tools of German linguistics, it is the view that sees Western Yiddish as a language in its own right that is most widely accepted in present-day Yiddish linguistics.[5]

Until the Jewish eastward migration during the late Middle Ages, Western Yiddish was basically the only existing Yiddish. The eastern dialect that emerged in the new settlements developed between the sixteenth and eighteenth centuries as a fundamentally new variety of Yiddish. Subsequently, this period is characterized by the coexistence of two major Yiddish dialects. The literary language, however, which served both west and east-European Yiddish readers, remained on a Western Yiddish basis well into the eighteenth century. It was only in the later decades of the century that this language was gradually replaced with a literary Yiddish based on the eastern dialects, which eventually developed into Modern Literary Yiddish.[6]

The transition from the western to the eastern dialect as the linguistic infrastructure of literary Yiddish was part of a more profound transformation in the history of German Jewry: the linguistic shift from Yiddish to German from the late eighteenth century onwards. Resulting in the gradual decline of Western Yiddish and its eventual demise as the main language of the German Jews, this linguistic transformation was engendered by the two interrelated processes of Jewish emancipation and acculturation. As a prerequisite for full emancipation, Jews were required to abandon their unique language and replace it with German. This demand was also promoted inside the Jewish community, most notably among the *maskilim* and the economic elite, who supported a certain degree of Jewish integration into German culture and society. For many of the *maskilim*, the transition from Yiddish to German was also a means for reforming and regenerating Jewish culture from within.[7] At the same time, profound and fundamental changes in the intellectual and cultural climate of the German world were being brought about by the Enlightenment, exerting considerable influence on the Christian discourse on Yiddish as well. These changes included the rise of new theories and ideologies regarding language, culture, *Volk*, and nation;

the process of secularization and the decline of theology as a dominant component of European thought; and the emergence of new perceptions of the Jew and his place in German society.[8] All these developments in both the German and German-Jewish contexts brought about a new chapter in the Christian preoccupation with Yiddish. The late decades of the eighteenth century thus mark the concluding point of this book.

Christian Interest in Yiddish in Early Modern Germany

Christian concern with Yiddish should be seen on the one hand as part of a wider interest in Jews and Judaism in early modern Germany, and on the other hand as part of a general interest in questions relating to language and linguistics at the time. Although the Jews constituted only a very small part of the total German population, they attracted attention well beyond their actual number and prominence. From the mid-fifteenth century, Renaissance Humanist scholarship, and later on the Reformation and the Protestant imperative to read the Bible in its original languages, gave rise to what came to be known as Christian Hebraism, the preoccupation of Christian scholars with Hebrew and Jewish studies. In addition to biblical Hebrew, Christian enterprises in Jewish studies also included postbiblical Hebrew, Aramaic, rabbinical literature, and the Cabbala. Another offshoot of Christian Hebraism was the growing interest of Christians in contemporary Jews, their customs, rituals, and way of life, noticeable in the German lands from the turn of the sixteenth century. Driven mainly by curiosity, but not without strong polemical overtones, the most explicit manifestation of this interest was the new genre of Christian ethnographic writing on Jewish ceremonies and everyday life. Anti-Jewish polemics and missionary impulses, which underlay Christian-Jewish relations from the very beginning, continued to play a major role in shaping Christian attitudes toward the Jewish minority throughout the early modern period. With the Reformation, the newly founded Protestant Church reemphasized the importance of winning over converts from Judaism as part of its rivalry with Catholicism and the wish to present itself as the true confession. Reaching an unprecedented scale with the rise of Pietism in the late seventeenth century, the revival of the *Judenmission* in the German territories further enhanced the attention of broader circles in the Christian population to the Jewish minority living in their midst.

The engagement of Christians with the Hebrew language and Jewish texts, their interest in contemporary Jewish culture, and the ever-present ambition to bring about Jewish conversion—these interrelated factors directly contributed to the rise of Christian Yiddish scholarship in early modern Germany, and exerted considerable influence on its main characteristics and on the course of its development. Another driving force that stood behind this new interest was the early modern concern with language, linguistics, and philology in general, and with questions regarding vernaculars, dialects, and foreign languages in particular. Early modern Europe experienced an unprecedented degree of what may be termed "linguistic awareness," leading modern historians to refer to the period from the mid-fifteenth century onwards as the age of the "discovery of language."[9] This period saw a dramatic increase in the study of languages, their structure, history, and the relations between them, as well as in the dealings with issues we would classify today as sociolinguistics, such as the functions of language in the social and religious domains, and the role of language as a marker and definer of group identities. In addition to the pronounced concern of Humanists with the study of the classical languages—Latin, Greek, and Hebrew—an exceptional and hitherto uncommon attention was given to the different European vernaculars. The medieval perception of the spoken languages as lacking grammatical rules and as being inadequate for the realms of scholarship and high culture gradually gave way to a new appreciation of the vernacular. The various European languages became the object of theoretical reflection and linguistic treatment. They underwent a process of codification and standardization, and with the aid of the newly invented printing industry infiltrated new domains, which until then had been under the exclusive reign of the omnipotent Latin. These included the large-scale production of literature in the European vernaculars, their increasing use as vehicles of scholarship and pedagogical instruction, and even the acceptance of vernaculars as languages of administration and international relations. Of special importance, in the Protestant territories, was the penetration of the vernacular into the religious domain, replacing Latin as the language of Scripture, prayer, and the transmission of religious knowledge.

Emerging at the beginning of the sixteenth century among Jewish as well as Christian scholars, the first linguistic treatments of Yiddish appeared at about the same time as those of other European vernaculars. Indeed, it is in this context of the growing attention to vernacular languages, their codification, and their potential as vehicles for the transmission of knowledge that the linguistic and philological interest in Yiddish must be appreciated.[10] Above all, however, the interest in Yiddish should be examined in the light of the specific form that the early modern linguistic awareness took in the German lands, where practically all the linguistic treatises on Yiddish known to us were published. During this period, a significant gap existed between the unsatisfactory state of the German language and its inferior position among the European vernaculars, on the one hand[11]; and on the other, the rising importance of the language in the eyes of many German scholars, especially Protestants, both as the language of Luther's Bible and as a means for defining German identity in the face of political and religious divisions. This unfavorable situation initiated an intensive enterprise of language cultivation in German academic and literary circles; it also exerted considerable influence on the way German scholars perceived and evaluated other languages, including the language of their Jewish neighbors.

Christian Yiddishists and Their Texts

Within the German lands, Christian interest in Hebrew and Judaism, as well as in the rising vernacular, was predominantly Protestant. It is therefore not surprising that early modern Christian involvement with Yiddish, too, was first and foremost a *Protestant* phenomenon. It had its roots in the Reformation era and in the work of reformers, and during the ensuing two and a half centuries was dominated by Protestant scholars.[12] It was also, as noted above, essentially a *German* phenomenon. Although large communities of Yiddish-speaking Jews and Yiddish publishing centers existed in different parts of Europe (such as Poland, Italy, and the Netherlands), Christian interest in Yiddish was almost exclusively confined to the German-speaking world. With very few exceptions, the Christian writings on Yiddish were written by German scholars, and were published in the German-speaking lands (especially in Leipzig, Halle, Basel, Nürnberg, Wittenberg, and Frankfurt am Main). Accordingly, the language that dominates these writings, besides Latin, is German. That the Christian literature on Yiddish was mainly a German phenomenon might be explained by the German roots of the Jewish language. Yiddish originated in the German lands as a result of the encounter of Jews with the medieval German dialects; from its beginning it contained a major German component and was for centuries the spoken language and one of the written languages of the German Jews.[13] The linguistic and territorial proximity of Yiddish and German in the early modern period was well acknowledged by the German Christian authors and played a significant role in their writings on Yiddish. Moreover, the similarity of Yiddish to their own language, and the implications of this similarity from a cultural, social, and national perspective, was probably responsible for the Jewish language attracting the attention of predominantly German-speaking authors.

Most of the Christian authors discussed in this book came from the heart of the academic and ecclesiastical establishment of the time: many held positions as professors of theology, Hebrew, and Oriental languages at the leading German universities; others served as preachers, ministers, and superintendents of the Protestant Church. Hebrew lecturers and censors, professional missionaries, school headmasters, and even a couple of police inspectors also participated in the Yiddish enterprise. About a quarter of the authors who could be identified were converts from Judaism. Although in general there were no essential differences in the literature on Yiddish between the writings of converts and those of born Christians, certain characteristics of the genre were indeed shared mainly by converts (though not exclusively). In particular is the tension inherent in the converts' writing on Yiddish to a Christian audience: on the one hand, they used their proficiency in Yiddish and their intimate acquaintance with its literature in order to position themselves as experts on Jewish matters in the service of their new coreligionists; on the other hand, they attempted to distance themselves from the Jewish language and culture as an indication of their true conversion.

The sources reveal a high level of interaction among the Christian authors, initiated by personal contacts or more commonly by acquaintance with the writings of previous or contemporary authors. References to other authors in the field, long quotations from the works of predecessors, and instances of plagiarism are very common in this literature. This is true for the linguistic presentations of the language, where one often finds the same examples, the same categories and formulations, sometimes even the same mistakes copied from one author to another. It is also true for the main ideas and perceptions regarding the Jewish language, its literature, and its Jewish speakers that come forward in these writings. This is of course not to disregard the differences between the writings of different authors or the development in the Christian literature on Yiddish during the two and half centuries under discussion. Many authors differed, for example, in the question of the close relation between Yiddish and German: some considered Yiddish as no more than German with Hebrew characters, while others emphasized the differences between the two, giving more weight to the Hebraic component in the Jewish language. This basic point of disagreement also led to different opinions regarding how easy it in fact was for German-speakers to learn Yiddish, and most notably, to what extent one could consider Yiddish a language in its own right. Another controversial issue, which had far-reaching implications for the later debates on Jewish integration and emancipation, was the question of why the Jews spoke Yiddish in the first place, and not "normal" German. While some authors related this to the external or objective circumstances of the Jewish experience in early modern Germany (most notably, the fact that Jews were not educated in German schools), others claimed that the Jews deliberately cultivated a language of their own, or that they were simply not capable of speaking "proper German." As far as the entire body of Christian writings on Yiddish is concerned, a diachronic perspective reveals an unmistakable shift at the turn of the eighteenth century towards a more popular literature on the Jewish language. Written mainly in German instead of Latin, the newer literature addressed broader sections of the Christian population and paid more attention to the *spoken* language, in addition to the written one. Eighteenth-century works on Yiddish were also more extensive than those produced during the sixteenth and seventeenth centuries, as elaborated discussions on the nature of Yiddish, its literature, and its Jewish speakers replaced the more strictly linguistic presentations of the earlier period.

Despite the fact that the cultural phenomenon of "Christian Yiddishism" is almost 500 years old, the literature produced during its first 250 years, from the Reformation to the Enlightenment (which twentieth-century Yiddishist Ber Borochov classified as *primitive filologishe shriftn*, to distinguish from the "modern" literature of the nineteenth and early twentieth centuries),[14] has received only limited consideration in modern historical research. Since the writings of early modern Christian Yiddishists deal with the Jews' *language*, they have mainly attracted the attention of modern linguists and philologists of historical Yiddish. The most thorough and comprehensive work on the literature on Yiddish so far is Max Weinreich's *Geschichte der jiddischen Sprachforschung* (1993), which is in fact a later edition of his dissertation from 1923.[15] Most recently, Yiddish scholar Jerold C. Frakes published a history of the scholarly linguistic literature on Yiddish in the sixteenth and seventeenth centuries, entitled *The Cultural Study of Yiddish in Early Modern Europe* (2007).[16] However, both Weinreich and Frakes (despite the latter's claim to present a *cultural* analysis of early modern Christian Yiddishism) are mainly concerned with the linguistic and philological aspects of the Christian writings. Like other modern researchers of Yiddish, they focus on the technical aspects, the means and methods of the research in Yiddish linguistics, while attempting to evaluate the accuracy of the early modern linguistic presentations and hence their reliability as sources in the study of historical Yiddish.

In contrast to the linguistic-philological perspective that characterizes the few existing studies on early modern Christian literature on Yiddish, the present book uses a historical-cultural point of view, which aims to define the place of the Jewish language in the different, albeit intertwined, theological, cultural, economic, and social discourses of the early modern period. An approach of this kind can be found in Sander Gilman's *Jewish Self-Hatred: Anti-Semitism and the Hidden Language of the Jews* (1986), in which the author discusses the discourse on the Jewish languages—both Hebrew and Yiddish—in the German world from the Middle Ages into the second half of the twentieth century. However, not only does Gilman dedicate a very small part of his work to the early modern period; his work also lacks a more substantial historical infrastructure. Thus, although highly interesting, Gilman's work is not always sufficient as far as the historical research is concerned. Other important works in the field, most notably Jeffrey A. Grossman's *The Discourse on Yiddish in Germany: From the Enlightenment to the Second Empire* (2000), explore the cultural phenomenon of Christian Yiddishism in later periods. However, one cannot fully understand the Christian engagement with the Jewish language and culture in modern Germany without a deeper acquaintance with its earlier stages. Indeed, a comprehensive study of the Christian engagement with Yiddish culture in *early* modern Germany, as offered in the present book, is indispensable for a better understanding of the broader theological, cultural, and social discourses on Jews and Judaism, not only in the early modern period but in Germany of the late eighteenth and nineteenth centuries as well.

*

Through depiction and analysis of the Christian texts on Yiddish in the context of their historical background and ideological framework, the book discusses two major questions. The *first* question—Why Yiddish?—relates to the various motivations for Christian preoccupation with the Yiddish language and literature in early modern Germany. In addition to the above-mentioned interest both in Jews and Judaism and in language and linguistics at the time, Christian engagement with Yiddish resulted from the recognition that proficiency in the Jewish language was important and even beneficial for various groups in the non-Jewish population. The existence of a Jewish minority in the German lands, and the fact that interactions between Jews and Christians were relatively common even during the early modern period, certainly played an important role in motivating Christians to acquire the Jewish language. The involvement with Yiddish out of pure interest and as "art for art's sake," as in the case of the young Goethe, was a rare phenomenon in the overall field of Christian Yiddishism. Instead, the Christian authors explicitly and recurrently emphasized the practical uses of Yiddish for Christians, probably in order to promote the dissemination of their Yiddish handbooks and dictionaries, as well as to justify their writing on a Jewish language that, unlike Hebrew, enjoyed neither the status of holiness nor a scholarly value.

The first and second parts of the book are dedicated to the various practical reasons for the Christian interest in the Yiddish language and literature, and accordingly, the different audiences at which the Christian texts on Yiddish were directed. Although a clear-cut categorization of these texts is not always possible, a general distinction can be made between the uses of Yiddish for theological purposes and its uses for more secular objectives, especially in the economic and social spheres.

The Christian occupation with Yiddish for theological purposes, which had a more scholarly orientation, is discussed in the first part of the book. After a general introduction on the place of Christian Yiddish scholarship in the broader context of early modern Christian Hebraism, the following chapters focus on what motivated Hebraists, theologians, and Orientalists to engage in Yiddish. This includes, in the first place, the Christian ambition to utilize the Jewish language and literature for missionary purposes and anti-Jewish polemics, discussed in the first and second chapters. By using Yiddish in both oral and written mission, the missionaries aimed to approach the Jews from a position of familiarity and even friendliness, and to make the evangelical literature accessible to Jewish readership. Acquaintance with contemporary Jewish literature in Yiddish was also considered advantageous for the missionary purpose. Viewed as a valuable source of information about Jews and Judaism, Yiddish literature was considered a useful means for achieving a well-informed and hence effective mission, and especially for repudiating Judaism by turning the Jews' own sources for polemics against them.

The third chapter in this part focuses on the idea that proficiency in Yiddish could serve Christians as a valuable instrument to penetrate the inner Jewish world and expose its secrets, so as to gain a tighter control on this minority. Driven by the conviction that deep hatred of Christ and Christians stood at the heart of Jewish belief and practice, Protestant theologians and reformers sought effective ways of defending Christian religion and society in the face of a perceived Jewish threat. In their eyes, this threat consisted primarily of the blasphemies (*Lästerungen*) and anti-Christian expressions believed to have been present in Jewish literature, prayer, and daily discourse. The image of Yiddish as the Jews' "secret language," used to conceal Jewish affairs from Christian eyes, made familiarity with Yiddish an important tool for Christians, who wished to effectively expose and censor all Jewish blasphemies against the Christian religion and its adherents. Finally, while the above motivations for the interest of Christian scholars in

Yiddish should be seen as part of their concern with Jews and Judaism, the fourth chapter presents the Protestant ambition to utilize the Jewish language for intra-Christian purposes, specifically for supporting theologians in their attempt to gain proficiency in Hebrew and an accurate reading and understanding of the Hebrew Bible.

A more popular orientation characterizes the Christian writings on Yiddish discussed in the second part of the book. Its title, "Yiddish in the Service of Jewish Deception," indicates the common notion of the time, according to which the Jews used their special language for illicit and even criminal purposes. The image of Yiddish as a secret language, which came forward in the Christian discourse on Jewish blasphemies and anti-Christian expressions, is thus extended from the religious domain into the more secular sphere of social and economic relations. The first chapter in this part (Chapter 5) is concerned with Yiddish manuals and textbooks intended for Christian businessmen and merchants who had business interactions with the Jews. Teaching basic Yiddish necessary for conducting business affairs, these manuals aimed not merely to facilitate commercial transactions between Jews and Christians, but rather, as made explicit by many of the authors, to help Christians defend themselves in the face of Jewish deception.

The image of Yiddish as the Jews' secret language was significantly reinforced by the fact that Yiddish was not only the language of the Jewish merchants but also the language of the large Jewish underclass of paupers, vagrants, beggars, and criminals. The association of Yiddish with criminality, discussed in Chapter 6, was nourished to a large extent by the linguistic affinity between Yiddish and *Rotwelsch*, the secret language of the German underworld at the time. The idea of Yiddish as the language of thieves gave rise to "criminological" research on the Jewish language, intended mainly, though not exclusively, for policemen and government officials in charge of the public order. As shown in the last sections of the chapter, civic authorities too, especially bureaucrats and jurists, were encouraged to master the Yiddish language in order to better control the Jewish minority.

Given the ways in which the association between Yiddish and the alleged Jewish subversiveness was depicted in the Christian literature, the conclusion of this part raises the possibility that Yiddish was viewed not merely as a secret language but rather as what we would term today an "antilanguage." The language of an "antisociety," an antilanguage is an extreme version of a non-standard social dialect, deliberately created by socially inferior and marginalized groups antagonistic to the dominant society. In many of the Christian texts, Yiddish is presented as a language of a social conflict, used by the Jewish minority either in the form of passive resistance, in order to maintain and defend their particular social reality, or in the form of an active or even offensive opposition to Christian social and religious order.

As the discussion on the practical uses of Yiddish for Christians suggests, knowledge of the Jewish language and literature was viewed as a necessary tool to exert control over the Jews in the German lands. Knowledge of Yiddish could be translated into a passive or defensive form of control, such as defending Christians against Jewish blasphemy, deception, or criminality; or into an active or even aggressive form of control, such as missionizing among the Jews or using their own sources for polemics against them.

But the interest of Christian authors in Yiddish exceeded the practical uses of the language. By defining and representing Yiddish culture to Christian readers, the Christian authors were in fact taking part in a broader discourse on Jews and Judaism in early modern Germany. It was a discourse that both expressed and helped maintain the existing power relations between Jews and Christians, and the marginal place of the Jews within German culture and society. This form of "discursive" or "ideological" domination becomes especially evident when we examine the ways in which the Christian authors depicted the Jewish language and literature in their works.

The *second* question in the book concerns how the Christian texts depict and represent the Yiddish language. Far from being neutral, matter-of-fact linguistic presentations, the Christian depictions of Yiddish were often shaped by their authors' views of the Jewish culture and religion, as well as by underlying ideological motivations and agendas. These relate to certain issues in Christian-Jewish relations, such as the attempt to define the place of the Jews in German society, but also to intra-Christian discussions and debates, such as Protestant-Catholic polemics or the efforts to standardize and purify the German language.

The various presentations of the Yiddish language in the Christian writings are discussed in the third part of the book. Chapter 7 focuses on the attempts of the Christian authors to define and explain the Yiddish language vis-à-vis its relation to German. The striking linguistic similarities between the two languages on the one hand, and the differences between them on the other, often led to the denunciation of Yiddish as a "corrupt German." However, although the authors formulated their criticism on Yiddish within linguistic categories, *extra*-linguistic considerations relating to the users and uses of Yiddish as a distinct Jewish sociolect within German society decisively shaped the image of the language in these texts. Another important factor discussed is the stance of the authors toward their own German language, to which they compared the German of the Jews. The importance attached to the German language as a major constituent of German national consciousness, and the efforts to cultivate the language and purify it from foreign elements, were central motifs in the discourse on language in early modern Germany; this possible influence on the way German authors perceived the Jewish-German language should not be overlooked.

The Christian concern with the relation between Yiddish and German was also manifested in the discussions regarding the use of Yiddish for the composition of missionary literature, explored in Chapter 8. Although the importance of writing to the Jews "in their own language" was constantly emphasized in the works on missionizing in Yiddish, some of the most important "Yiddish" missionary writings were in fact written in German with Hebrew letters, or at least in a very "Germanized" version of Yiddish, not necessarily suitable for Jewish readers. As we shall see, the attempt of Christian missionaries to "Germanize" the Jewish language resulted mainly from their negative opinions of Yiddish, which they considered not adequate enough for serious theological writings; it also resulted from their wish to avoid what they considered to be a "Judaization" and hence corruption of the German language.

The final chapter of the book (Chapter 9) is dedicated to how the Christian authors depicted the relation between Yiddish and Hebrew. The central argument in this respect was that Hebrew, after being replaced by Yiddish, was no longer the language of the German Jews. In order to establish this point, the authors elaborate on what they refer to as the German Jews' "great ignorance" of the Hebrew language, manifested in the Jews' inability either to speak or to read the language in a satisfactory manner. The chapter attempts to elucidate the complex matrix of motivations that stood behind the Christian discussions on this topic. Apart from the direct theological criticism of the Jews for failing to understand their Hebrew prayers or to read the Bible in its original tongue, the separation between the Yiddish-speaking Jews and the Hebrew language enabled the Christian authors to create a debased image of Jewish-Ashkenazi culture and religion, in contrast to which they could affirm and emphasize their own theological and cultural superiority. The conclusion to this part of the book highlights some of the most important continuities and transformations in the discourse on Yiddish and its relations to both Hebrew and German in the transition from the early modern period to the late eighteenth and nineteenth century.

By exploring why Christians were preoccupied with Yiddish and how they depicted the Jewish language and literature in their writings, I wish to demonstrate that early modern Christian Yiddishism has had implications beyond its purely linguistic and philological dimensions. As part of a broader theological, cultural, and social discourse on Jews and Judaism in early modern Germany, the Christian texts on Yiddish reveal not only the way their authors assumed the unique perspective of language to perceive and define the subjects of their works, but also the way they perceived and defined their own language, religion, and culture in contrast to those of the Jews. A close study of these texts and their underlying ideological motivations provides a further dimension to Christian-Jewish relations in early modern Europe, while shedding light on broader linguistic, theological, cultural, and social concerns in the work and thought of early modern Christian authors and their intellectual environment.

Part I *Yiddish in the Service of Christian Theology*

Introduction

Christian Hebraism and the Study of Yiddish in Early Modern Europe

A major aspect of the new intellectual climate engendered by the Renaissance and later on by the Reformation was the growing preoccupation of Christian scholars with the interrelationship between language and religion, philology and theology. This concern was clearly manifested in the emergence of the so-called Christian Hebraism, a branch of Christian scholarship dedicated to Hebraica and Judaica from the late fifteenth century onwards. Born out of a commitment to the Humanist ideals of a return to the sources (*ad fontes*) and to trilingual education, Christian Hebraism was further stimulated by the ideals of the Protestant Reformation and its theological doctrine of Scripture as the sole source of religious truth (*sola Scriptura*). Searching for the *Hebraica veritas*, the truth inherent in the Hebrew Bible, Protestant scholars devoted much attention to the study of Hebrew, not only for its own sake but mainly for the light it could shed on theological issues, especially on the correct reading and interpretation of the Old Testament.[1]

In this sense, the assertion made in 1750 by the German scholar Wilhelm Justus Chrysander, "It is, after all, agreed that a rigorous theologian must be a philologist,"[2] would not have been exceptional were it not for the interesting fact that these words referred not to the importance of learning Hebrew for theological purposes, but to the importance of learning Yiddish, the Jewish-German vernacular of the time. Moreover, this call to learn Yiddish, made by a Christian scholar and directed at a Christian audience, was not a novelty. Rather, it represented the peak of a continuing interest in Yiddish among Christian, especially Protestant, scholars in early modern Europe, from the beginning of the sixteenth century onwards.

Although the study of Yiddish was secondary to other fields within Christian Jewish studies, such as Hebrew or rabbinical literature, it attracted the attention of some of the most renowned and influential Hebraists and Orientalists in the Germanic world throughout the early modern period. Among the most prominent ones were Paulus Fagius and Sebastian Münster in the sixteenth century; Johann Buxtorf, August Pfeiffer, and Andreas Sennert in the seventeenth century; and Johann Christoph Wagenseil, Johann Christoph Wolf, and Johann Heinrich Callenberg in the eighteenth century. Many of the works published by these and other scholars, either specifically on Yiddish or in which a chapter or appendix on Yiddish was included, saw several editions and were often referred to by other authors. This is true for works which circulated mainly among scholars and also, especially from the late seventeenth century, for works with a more popular orientation. In addition, there were many scholars who did not publish specifically on Yiddish but learned the Jewish language, used it in their works, and commented on it on different occasions. Among these scholars were Christoph Helwig (Helvicus), Johann Andreas Eisenmenger, and Johann Gottlob Carpzov. With the growing attention given in recent research to the reconstruction of the actual learning and working methods of early modern Christian Hebraists, including the inventory of their libraries, their sources of influence, and the various ways in which they acquired knowledge in Hebrew and Jewish literature, one might certainly expect that more cases would come to light of Christian scholars, whose ventures into the fields of Hebraica and Judaica led them to an encounter with Jewish texts in Yiddish as well as with the writings of Christian Yiddishists.[3]

Although closely linked to Christian Hebraism, "Christian Yiddishism" constituted a cultural phenomenon in its own right. Unlike Hebrew, Yiddish was considered neither holy nor ancient by Jews and non-Jews alike. Composed of German and Hebrew-Aramaic elements, it was perceived by non-Jews as a distorted and corrupted kind of German; and as the language of contemporary Jews, it was imbued in the German popular imagination with many of the prevalent Jewish stereotypes of the time, most notably the image of the Jew as a thief and a liar. Consequently, Yiddish was seen mainly as a degenerate language, that of outsiders and thieves. The fact that *Rotwelsch*, the language of the German underworld in that period, contained words adopted from Yiddish nourished the stereotype linking Jews and their language with moral and social corruption.[4]

Among the Jews, too, Yiddish was always considered inferior. While Hebrew was the language of religion and the educated elite, Yiddish was the language of everyday life. Its literature was written mainly for women and children, and also, as the popular Yiddish book *Seyfer brantshpigl* (Basel 1602) put it in its introduction, "for men who are like women and cannot study much."[5] However, neither the low status of Yiddish inside the Jewish communities nor its negative image in non-Jewish eyes deterred Christian scholars, most of them theologians, Hebraists, and Orientalists, from involving themselves with the language and its literature. In fact, Yiddish attracted the attention of German, mainly Protestant, scholars precisely because of these two attributes: that it was a Jewish language, and that it included a significant Hebrew component. Accordingly, proficiency in Yiddish was promoted among Christians, especially among theologians, for three main reasons: to missionize among the Jews, to read Jewish literature in this language, and to use Yiddish as an aid in the study of Hebrew and the biblical text. Each of these reasons presents a different aspect of the relation between philology and theology, and of the attempt of Protestant scholars to use the philological knowledge of Yiddish for their own theological purposes.

One Yiddish in the *Judenmission*

Dating back to the days of the apostles, the long-standing Christian ambition to convert the Jews to Christianity received a new impetus with the Reformation and the beginning of the Protestant movement. In his work *Daß Jesus Christus ein geborner Jude sei* (That Jesus Christ was born a Jew; 1523), Martin Luther presented an optimistic view regarding the possible conversion of Jews to his version of Christianity. Rejecting coercive measures as means for conversion, Luther expressed his hope that "if one treated the Jews kindly and instructed them carefully from the Holy Scriptures, many would become true Christians."[1]

The expected Jewish mass conversion failed to materialize, and in his later years Luther abandoned his optimism and pronounced the Jews severely stubborn and "hard to win over."[2] The hope for Jewish conversion remained nevertheless a constant feature in Protestant thought and practice in the German lands throughout the early modern period. The search for effective albeit non-violent ways to conduct successful missionary work presented Protestant theologians and missionaries with a challenging dilemma: which language would be most suitable and effective when trying to convert the Jews? After realizing that anti-Jewish polemics in Latin, German, or even Hebrew were not useful for missionary work among the common Jewish populace, missionary circles decided to turn to Yiddish, the colloquial language of the German Jews.

Underlying the use of Yiddish in the early modern *Judenmission* was the principle of "linguistic adaptation," alluding to the efforts of missionaries to adapt, or accommodate, the Christian message to the language of the people they hoped to convert. The first example of linguistic adaptation in the history of Christian mission goes back to the miracle of Pentecost as described in Acts 2, in which the Holy Ghost descended upon the apostles, who then began to speak in different languages, approaching each listener in his own tongue. With this story as a guiding paradigm, the principle of linguistic adaptation persisted in missionary thought and practice throughout the centuries as a crucial means for alleviating the difficulties inherent in the process of mission and conversion. This was manifested in the requirement that both the missionary himself and the message he conveyed be adapted to the language of the target audience. Missionaries learned the languages of the peoples among whom they worked in order to enable communication *between* the missionary and the missionized; they produced translations of the Scripture and various missionary writings in the target languages in order to enable the communication *of* the Christian message.[3]

Among the many different forms of adaptation for missionary purposes, such as adaptation in clothing, customs, way of living, social behavior, aesthetics, or art, the linguistic form has always been considered especially powerful and therefore much desired. In the case of Protestant mission among the Jews,[4] this form of adaptation played a particularly important role, for two main reasons. The first reason is that the mission was a *Protestant* mission. With their emphasis on "the Word," on reading and preaching, as the exclusive means to communicate the Christian message, Protestants were confined to using verbal communication in their missionary endeavors, while being excluded from other means of communication such as rituals or visual representations, means used by Catholic missionaries.[5] Therefore, Protestant missionaries were more dependent on language, and hence on linguistic adaptation, than their Catholic counterparts. The second reason for the enhanced importance of linguistic adaptation in the case before us is that this mission was directed at *Jews*. The far-reaching adaptation of missionaries to the rituals and customs of the peoples they wished to convert, as was the case for example with the Jesuit mission in China and India during the seventeenth century,[6] was unthinkable in mission among the Jews. Whereas some pagan customs and rituals could be considered theologically neutral, at least to the extent that they allowed the missionaries to reconcile them with Christian practice, Jewish customs and rituals were overtly rejected by Christian dogma. Any adaptation in this field, therefore, was forbidden, leaving linguistic adaptation by and large the only useful option.

Early Beginnings and Pietist Revival

The high point of mission in Yiddish in the German lands was between the end of the seventeenth century and the second half of the eighteenth century. Already in the sixteenth century, however, first attempts had been made to offer the New Testament to the Jews "in Jewish clothing" (*veste judaica*). In 1540 the convert Paul Helic (also: Helicz) published in Cracow the first known Yiddish translation of the New Testament, probably translated by the convert Johann Harzuge.[7] The first Jewish printers in Poland, Helic and his two brothers opened their business in 1534, just a few years before the conversion of the three brothers to Catholicism.[8] The titles they produced included the first Yiddish books ever printed, and they continued to publish in Hebrew and Yiddish after their conversion.[9] In the Latin dedication to his Yiddish New Testament, Helic outlined the missionary intentions underlying his translation. Accusing the rabbis of keeping the Jews blind to the Christian truth, the recently converted Helic expressed the hope that his translation of the New Testament into "the vernacular language, that is Theutonic"[10] would reveal the truth of Christianity to his former coreligionists, and would thus help to bring about their conversion. Although Helic dedicated the work to Piotr Gamrat, the Bishop of Cracow and an ardent Catholic, this Yiddish New Testament was, ironically, a translation of Luther's Bible rather than of a Catholic one.[11]

Half a century later the Protestant reformer and professor of Hebrew and theology at Strasbourg, Magister Elias Schadeus, published another Yiddish translation of Luther's New Testament. This translation comprised a selection of five books (the Gospels of Luke and John, Acts, and the Epistles to the Romans and to the Hebrews), which the reformer considered "the best and most useful" for Jewish readers.[12] Schadeus elaborates on the decision to publish this translation in the introduction to another of his works, *Mysterium* (1592), where he explicitly promotes the use of Yiddish as part of a "friendly" missionary approach and adds an appendix instructing Christians how to read and write the "German-Hebrew script."[13] Apart from the New Testament, the Hebrew Bible too was translated into Yiddish for missionary purposes. In 1544 two Yiddish Bibles were published: one by the convert Paulus Aemilius in Augsburg, and the other by the Protestant reformer and Hebraist

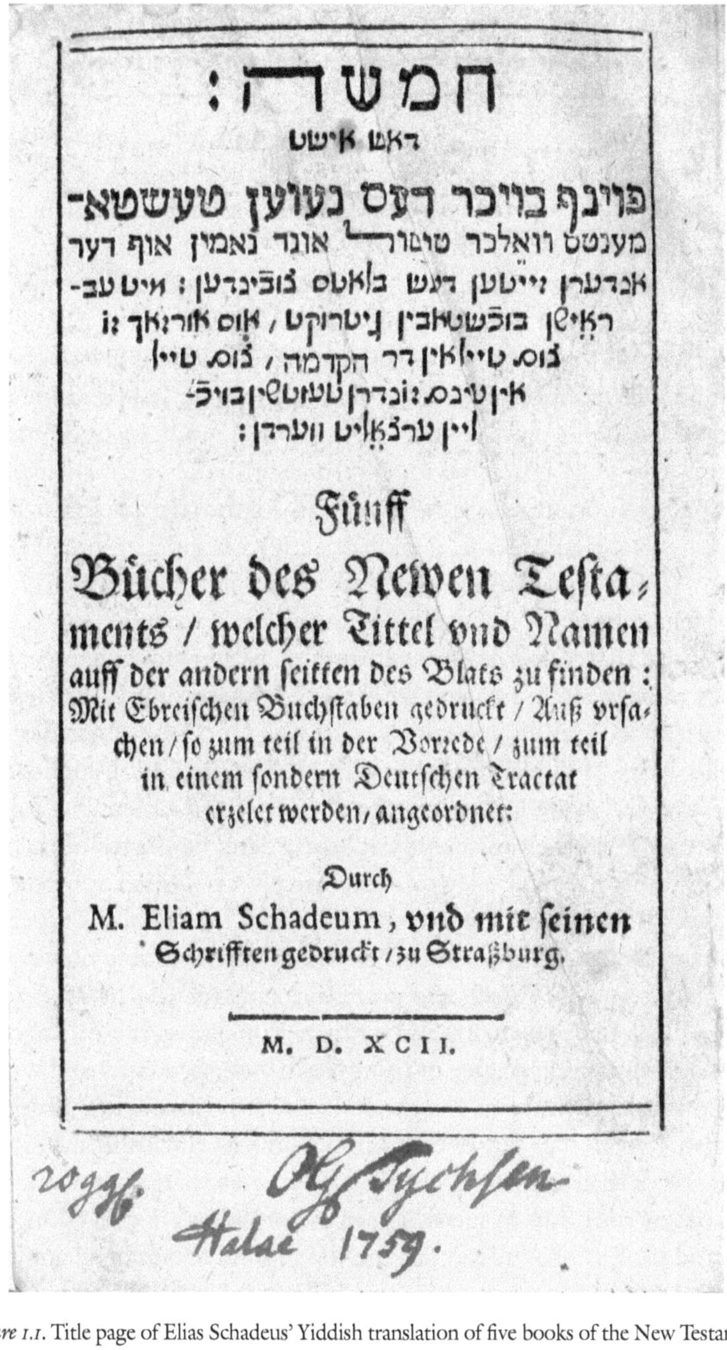

חמשה:

דאש אישט

פֿוינף בויכר דעס נעוען טעשטא-
מענטס וועלכר טיטל אונד נאמין אוף דער
אנדרען זייטען דעש בלאטס צו פינדען: מיט עב-
ראישן בוכשטאבין גדרוקט, אויז אורזאך זו
צום טייל אין דר הקדמה, צום טייל
אין איינם זונדרן טייטשן בויכ-
לין ערצאלט ווערדן:

Fünff

Bücher des Newen Testa-
ments / welcher Tittel vnd Namen
auff der andern seitten des Blats zu finden:
Mit Ebreischen Buchstaben gedruckt / Auß vrsa-
chen / so zum teil in der Vorrede / zum teil
in einem sondern Deutschen Tractat
erzelet werden / angeordnet:

Durch

M. Eliam Schadeum, vnd mit seinen
Schrifften gedruckt / zu Straßburg.

M. D. XCII.

20936 O G Tychsen
Halae 1759.

Figure 1.1. Title page of Elias Schadeus' Yiddish translation of five books of the New Testament (Strasbourg 1592). *Source*: Sammlung Tychsen, Harald Fischer Verlag.

Paulus Fagius in Constance. Fagius' Bible was probably translated by the convert Michael Adam, who was also the Yiddish translator of the historical book *Yosifon*, published by Christoph Froschauer in Zurich in 1546.[14] This Bible was published in two editions, with two different titles and introductions: one in German, written by Fagius and addressed to the Christian reader; the other in Yiddish, probably written by Adam and addressed to the Jewish reader.[15]

During the following century, however, these early endeavors to use Yiddish as a linguistic tool for missionary work among the Jews were apparently no longer pursued. Although the hope for Jewish conversion did not disappear from Protestant writings on Jews and Judaism, little was done in practice to evangelize the Jews.[16] Instead, authors were now usually content with denouncing the Jews for their blindness and stubbornness (*Verstockung*). Many of the relevant authors used Yiddish sources in order to demonstrate Jewish superstition and blasphemy,[17] but they published their anti-Jewish polemics in Latin or German, rendering them inaccessible to most Jewish readers.

Only at the end of the seventeenth century, with the rise of the Pietist movement and its emphasis on the responsibility of individual Christians to actively assist in the conversion of the Jews, did missionary work in Yiddish begin in earnest. The theoretical foundations of this project were laid in 1699 by the jurist and Orientalist Johann Christoph Wagenseil from Altdorf. An ardent supporter of the missionary cause, Wagenseil wrote extensively on Jewish subjects and was one of the prominent Hebraists and Yiddishists of his time.[18] In the introduction to his Yiddish textbook and anthology, *Belehrung der Jüdisch-Teutschen Red- und Schreibart* (Instruction in the Jewish-German manner of speaking and writing; Königsberg 1699), Wagenseil emphasized the importance of using Yiddish for both oral and written mission. If one wishes to win the Jews over to Christianity, Wagenseil claimed, "one has to put oneself on the same level with them, . . . and make use of their German dialect." As opposed to Schadeus' work from the sixteenth century, Wagenseil's call to use Yiddish as part of an assertive and professional mission to the Jews found an attentive audience, and was translated into practice by his disciples in the following years. Already in 1700 Christian Moller published a new Yiddish translation of the entire New Testament, followed by missionary works in this language, most notably by Caspar Calvör (1710), Philipp Nicodemus Lebrecht (1719), and Johannes Müller (1728).[19]

Another prominent disciple of Wagenseil was the theologian and philologist Wilhelm Christian Justus Chrysander, who became the most important Yiddish grammarian of his time. Like Wagenseil himself, Chrysander did not publish missionary literature in Yiddish, but enthusiastically advocated using this language when conducting mission among the Jews. Alluding to the miracle of Pentecost, Chrysander emphasized that "since the miraculous gift and extraordinary impartation of the capability to speak in untaught languages has ceased, so must the [Christian] love pledge to obtain this useful tool through industrious study,"[20] a goal he sought to facilitate with his own work. As professor in Helmstedt, and later in Rinteln, Chrysander offered Yiddish courses and published a Yiddish textbook as well as a theoretical tractate on the importance of learning Yiddish—all in the name of the missionary cause.[21]

In 1728 Wagenseil's missionary vision in general, and that of mission in Yiddish in particular, was given an institutional framework with the establishment of the Institutum Judaicum et Muhammedicum in the Prussian city of Halle. The institute was founded by Johann Heinrich Callenberg, a devoted Pietist and professor of philosophy and Oriental languages at the University of Halle, with the outright aim of spreading Christianity among Jews and Muslims.[22] The missionary activities of Callenberg's institute concentrated on three fields. The first was the publication and distribution of missionary literature in Oriental languages, especially in Yiddish. Thanks to a vast network of helpers and sympathizers stretching across and beyond the continent, missionary publications were taken to the remotest places and almost immediately distributed among the Jews, usually free of charge or at a very small price. The second field of activity was the training of well informed and highly qualified missionaries to work among the Jews. Some of these trainees were later employed by the institute as "traveling missionaries": they were to travel among the Jewish populations, first of Germany and Eastern Europe and later of Northern Europe and the Levant; initiate conversations on religious matters; and distribute the books published by the institute. Since advanced linguistic skills were considered a prerequisite for any missionary fieldwork, the training of would-be missionaries, usually young students of theology at the University of

Halle, included instruction in the different target languages, especially Yiddish. For this purpose, Callenberg established a Yiddish course in 1729—the very first at a German university.[23] The founding declaration of the Yiddish *collegium* encouraged the students "to learn the Oriental languages, and especially to take root in the Jewish-German language, which is very simple, so that they would be able not only to read and understand it, but also to write and speak [the language]. This would prove very useful, and would contribute so much more to promoting the conversion of the poor Jews."[24] Among the more famous missionaries educated at the institute and in the Yiddish language one should note Stefan Schultz, who eventually succeeded Callenberg as director of the institute, and Oluf Gerhard Tychsen, who later became a renowned Orientalist and an ardent Yiddishist.[25] Like other activities of the institute, the Yiddish *collegium* in Halle outlived Callenberg himself, and many years after his death the Yiddish courses at the institute, under the instruction of Schultz, still enjoyed good attendance of students.

Callenberg also composed and published a Yiddish textbook (1733) and a Yiddish-German lexicon (1736), both specifically designed to aid missionaries in their interactions with Jews.[26] By this he hoped to promote the study of Yiddish as a missionizing tool among his students and also among others who wished to take part in the missionary effort. As Callenberg himself noted, the publication of these linguistic works was meant to draw "Christians, especially students of theology, to the learning of the Jewish-German language, which is indispensable for a thorough instruction of the Jews."[27]

Finally, in addition to actively propagating the Christian faith, the institute, in its third field of activity, offered baptismal candidates and converts further instruction in their new religion, and provided them with initial material support.

From the establishment of the institute in 1728 until his death in 1760 Callenberg regularly informed the institute's donors and supporters of its multiple missionary activities. This took the form of voluminous journals, in which Callenberg published his own reports and those by the institute's traveling missionaries on their encounters with Jews in different places, as well as letters sent from collaborators and sympathizers from all over the Protestant world. After Callenberg's death his successors continued to publish the journals until the dissolution of the institute in 1792. These journals constitute an invaluable source for the ideas, notions, and intentions that lay behind the eighteenth-century Protestant mission to the Jews, and also for the way it was carried out in practice, the challenges it faced, and the impact it achieved.

The Advantages of Yiddish as a Missionary Language

That linguistic adaptation was indispensable for a successful mission among the Jews was a recurrent and much emphasized theme in early modern writings on this topic. After asserting that "Jews do not read anything which is not written according to their manner," or that "one cannot get very far with the Jews unless one is familiar with *their own language*,"[28] the authors emphasized the importance of adapting the Christian message to the Jewish manner of speaking and writing. By this they hoped to achieve two goals: to bring the Christian teachings to the Jews in a language they could understand, and to overcome or at least lower Jewish resistance to missionary efforts by presenting the Christian message via a more familiar and friendly medium.

One of the basic assumptions of the advocates of mission in Yiddish was that all previous endeavors to convert the Jews had been unsuccessful simply because they addressed them in languages they did not understand. An oft quoted statement regarding this point was made in 1699 by Johann Wagenseil. Referring to traditional anti-Jewish polemics in Latin and German, Wagenseil argued that those writings "have indeed proved very beneficial to the Christian church," but not "to the Jewish synagogue," for they were written in languages the Jews could not read. Regarding oral mission, Wagenseil reminds his readers of the uselessness of disputing with Jews in German, "for they are not used to the pure *Hochdeutsch*, and do not understand, what is being said."[29]

Compared to non-Jewish languages, Hebrew was considered much more adequate for the task. However, as acknowledged by the missionaries, proficiency in Hebrew was usually confined to the Jewish educated elite, whereas large sections of the Jewish population in the German lands did not have sufficient knowledge of this language.[30] But by using Yiddish, one was able to reach out to a very broad Jewish public, both geographically and socially.

Although missionary writings mention "our Jews" (*unsere Juden/Iudaei nostri*) as the main target for missionary efforts in Yiddish, mission in this language was by no means confined to the Jews in the German lands. The arch-missionary Johann Callenberg, for example, emphasized the pan-European character of Yiddish. He addressed his Yiddish missionary writings "to the entire European Jewry," including in the first place the Jewish populations of Central and Eastern Europe, as well as other communities of Yiddish-speaking Jews dispersed throughout the continent.[31] Promoting Yiddish to the status of a Jewish lingua franca, Wilhelm Chrysander further expressed the belief in the missionary potential of Yiddish in a somewhat exaggerated, though quite revealing statement: "With Yiddish one could get along in the entire world."[32]

Yiddish was considered advantageous for achieving not only geographical breadth but also social depth. In statements echoing Luther's call to use the vernacular in order to reach out to ordinary people, missionaries stressed the importance of Yiddish translations of Scripture and other missionary works for the benefit of Jewish women and uneducated men, who could not read Hebrew.[33] The importance of bringing the Christian message to the lower strata of Jewish society lay undoubtedly in their large numbers, but also in the assumption that poor and uneducated Jews might be easier to convince than their wealthier or more educated coreligionists. As put forward in a letter addressed to Callenberg by one of his supporters, advocating the publication of missionary writings in Yiddish: "The simple folk and the women are, as is known, easier to sway than the supposedly wise. And one can never know, if the beloved God would not perhaps act even more powerfully through such people, and a converted wife would make a believer out of her unconverted husband."[34]

Overcoming Jewish Resistance: Missionaries and the Jews' Special Language

The second goal the missionaries hoped to achieve by approaching the Jews in their own language was to overcome Jewish resistance to missionary efforts. It was a consensus among early modern theologians and missionaries that the Jewish heart was stubborn and difficult to convert, and the fact that the Jews used a language of their own was perceived as part of the problem. As the unique language of a religious and social minority, which was in many ways marginalized and even isolated from the dominant Christian society, Yiddish both expressed and helped sustain the distinctiveness of the Jewish minority and its separation from the rest of society. As is usually the case in such forms of social dialects,[35] Yiddish enjoyed a high degree of intimacy and casualness and drew a distinct line between Jews and non-Jews, effectively functioning as a means of inclusion and exclusion. On the one hand, Yiddish served to create a special bonding and solidarity among the Jews, a kind of members-only club to which those who did not speak Yiddish did not have access. On the other hand, because non-use of Yiddish was such a straightforward identifier of non-Jews, the unique language of the Jewish minority served to protect it from outside influences, primarily from the influence of Christian mission.

These social attributes of Yiddish, which rendered it an obstacle for Jewish conversion, did not go unnoticed among Christian missionaries and theologians. In fact, some raised the possibility that the Jews adhered consciously and deliberately to Yiddish in order to resist Christian influence. Thus, for example, alongside the voices claiming that Jews *could* not read German,[36] there were also voices claiming that they *would* not read this language. According to some of the authors, the Jews rejected German as a "*Goim und Heyden Sprache*" (a Gentile and heathen language), or were even repulsed by this language, which they considered "*loschon tome*" (an impure language).[37] Christian authors also noted that the Jews designated the Latin alphabet as *galkhes* (the language of the priests), a term that expressed their aversion to this kind of writing and that was meant to clearly distinguish between non-Jewish texts (*galkhes bikher* or *galkhes sforim*) and Jewish ones.[38] Referring to the Jews' reluctance to read German, or indeed anything written in a non-Jewish language, Wagenseil pointed out that the Jews felt averse even towards Hebrew books, which included Latin translations and were read from left to right, according to the "Christian way."[39]

In addition to this rejection of non-Jewish languages, some authors related the Jews' unwillingness to read anything that was not written "according to their manner" to the fact that they did not wish to expose themselves to the influence of non-Jewish books. In the German introduction to his Yiddish translation of the Bible, Paulus Fagius claims he would have preferred to see the Jews read the Bible in other versions; but "I know unfortunately only too well this poor people's stubbornness, that they do not read anything which is not written according to their manner, and that their Rabbis forbid them to read books other than theirs, on pain of punishment."[40] Seventeenth-century convert Christian Gerson further stressed this point, informing his Christian readers that the Jews "do not let their youngsters study any language, so that they would not read Christian books by these means, and be led away from Judaism."[41] Instead, they read Jewish books in Yiddish, which were designed to strengthen them in the Jewish faith and therefore obstructed their way to conversion.

Put to good use in Christian hands, however, the unique language of the Jews, which they used in order to *resist* conversion, could be turned against them, as a means *for* conversion. First, it would bring the Christian message to the Jews in a pleasant and familiar language—a language that could lend the foreign and intimidating Christian teachings a friendly and even intimate Jewish touch, which would melt the barriers and help the message penetrate their stubborn hearts. Second, by using Yiddish, Christian missionaries hoped to blur the lines between themselves and the Jews and thus gain access to the closed Jewish world, a necessary prerequisite for a successful mission.

Proficiency in Yiddish served Christian missionaries in all stages of the missionary process. Before starting their conversion attempts, missionaries were advised to prepare themselves for the task by reading missionary literature in Yiddish, as well as Jewish literature written in this language. Although usually condemned by Christian scholars as being risible (*lächerlich*) and full of superstition,[42] Yiddish literature was nonetheless recommended to missionaries as a source of information about Jews and Judaism. This could assist them in repudiating Judaism by turning the Jews' own sources for polemics against them. Already in the beginning of the seventeenth century, the Lutheran theologian Christoph Helwig recommended his German translation of the Yiddish *Mayse-bukh* to Christians who wished to show the Jews "to what harmful and deceitful works they are being directed by their rabbis," and "put their deceitful works in front of their noses."[43] The same idea, albeit expressed in much more pleasant formulations, was restated almost a century later in the writings of Pietists and their supporters, who stressed an acquaintance with Jewish sources, both Hebrew and Yiddish, as a prerequisite for a well informed and hence effective mission. Wagenseil, for example, claimed in his *Die Hoffnung der Erlösung Israelis* (The hope of Israel's redemption; Leipzig 1705) that "just as one cannot help a sick person as long as one does not know what he lacks . . . so it is in the spiritual healing, too, that one must get to the bottom of the problem, so that it would be solved from the root."[44]

In the second stage, when going out to spread the Christian message among the Jews, the missionaries intentionally used their competence in Yiddish to conceal, or at least obscure, their Christian identity for as long as possible. The missionary Stefan Schultz, for example, boasted that he spoke Yiddish so well that the Jews he met at an inn took him to be "a born Jew."[45] Furthermore, the intimacy and casualness associated with Yiddish helped the missionaries establish comfortable and friendly relationships with Jews, as a means to pave the way for the edifying talks.[46] In some cases, missionaries used Yiddish to attract the attention of Jews and lure them into conversation. We hear, for example, of missionaries sitting in taverns and inns who, when a Jew entered the room, would start speaking Yiddish with each other, or pretend to be reading a Yiddish book. The Jew, who believed them to be Jews, or was simply attracted by the two strangers speaking his mother tongue, approached them. By the time he realized his mistake, the missionaries had already seized the opportunity and started a conversation on religious matters, or had given him some of the missionary writings they carried with them.[47]

In case they managed to strike up a conversation, the missionaries were advised to mix specifically Jewish terms and expressions with their Yiddish in order to lower potential resistance on the side of the Jewish interlocutor. As Chrysander pointed out,

> There are words [in Yiddish] that, according to the Jews' liking, embody something beautiful, appealing, fruitful, and moving, which, in German translation, does not have so much sweet attractiveness and prettiness [*so viel süsse Anzüglichkeit und Nettigkeit*]. If one therefore stooped down to use such words, which are common among the Jews, and which are associated with some connotations [*Neben-Errinnerungen*], one would be

> able not only to bring them to clearer terms of what one wishes to have, but also they are thereupon easier to direct, with more confidence in our understanding and with more agreeability [*Annehmlichkeit*].[48]

Illuminating examples of such terms can be found in Callenberg's Yiddish lexicon for missionaries from 1736. Thus, for example, he translated the phrase "convert to Christianity" to the phrase "gather oneself under the wings of the *Schechina*" (the holy presence of God in Jewish tradition). With this he hoped to avoid the derogatory connotations of *meshumed*, the Yiddish Hebraism for "apostate," which translates as "one who is destroyed."[49] Practicing how to converse with Jews in Yiddish, especially "in such Jewish expressions," was part of the missionaries' training in Halle; it was hoped that "in this way the conversation with the Jews would henceforth be on the whole easy and blessed."[50]

Between Adaptation and Deception: Missionary Literature in Yiddish

The strategies employed to overcome Jewish resistance to missionary efforts were also used in the missionary writings in Yiddish, including translations of the Old and New Testaments, the Catechisms, and various anti-Jewish polemical works.[51] The fact that the works were written in Yiddish and contained Jewish terms and phrases was meant to attract Jewish readers and help them understand, and eventually accept, the Christian teachings. The missionaries maintained that since these works were written for the Jews "according to their common Jewish-German manner of reading and writing," or translated for them into a familiar language, accommodated to their way of reading, they would surely read them with pleasure and would not remain unaffected.[52]

Many Jews, however, upon realizing that these were Christian works, persisted in their refusal to read them. The solution adopted in some cases was to hide the name of the author and place of publication, or any other external markers that could betray the Christian origin of the work. Paulus Fagius, for example, published his Yiddish translation of the Bible (1544) in two editions, with two different titles and introductions: one in German, the other in Yiddish, addressed respectively to Christian and Jewish readers. Unlike the German edition, the Yiddish one contained no details regarding the translator and publisher of the work. Moreover, the anti-Jewish introduction of the German edition was replaced in the Yiddish edition by a Jewish-friendly one, which addressed the readers in the first-person plural in order to give the impression that it was a Jewish work. In other missionary works in Yiddish, which included an additional title and introduction in Latin meant for Christian readers (as in many of the tracts published by the Institutum Judaicum in Halle), missionaries were advised to remove the Latin-character sections before giving the works to Jews, as not to discourage potential readers.[53]

That the line between adaptation and deception was indeed a very fine one is well demonstrated in the most renowned missionary work in Yiddish, *Or le'eys erev/Dos likht kegn abend tsayt* (Light at evening; Halle 1728), by the Protestant preacher Johannes Müller. This was the first work published by Callenberg in Halle,[54] and in many ways it served as a model for the other works that followed in that it truly epitomized the entire concept of adaptation—and deception—in the missionary literature in Yiddish. Written in a friendly and affectionate manner and adjusted entirely to Jewish perceptions,[55] the work discussed the imminent redemption of the Jewish people without revealing its Christian message until the very last pages. In the title page no indication was given regarding the place of publication or the identity of the publisher. Callenberg later noted that the author had asked to remain anonymous, "for otherwise the Jews, immediately when seeing on the cover that a Christian prepared this booklet . . . would not even consider it worth reading."[56] To further create an impression that this was a Jewish work, the name which eventually appeared on the title page was "Johanan Kimhi," a Hebraicized version of the author's real name, Johannes Müller.

Especially interesting in this respect is the one-page introduction to the work, which like the work itself seems to be Jewish in both form and content. Addressing his Jewish readers in the first-person plural, the author promises that the book will prove from Jewish sources that Israel's redemption is at hand. Just before listing the chapters of the work, the author makes the following remark: "Now in these times not only has Israel, for our many sins, been in exile for so long, but it is also consorting with many priests, who have learnt the Holy Tongue, and who [now] wish to convince the Jews from verses [Scripture] that there is no hope for Jewish redemption from this bitter exile." And that is why, Müller continues, rabbi Menahem (his main character; literally: "one who comforts") searched the Bible and other Jewish sources diligently and found proofs for the coming redemption of the Jews, which he delivers in this book.[57]

The Christian practice of using Jewish sources to prove Christian precepts was not new in Müller's day. Especially since the rise of Christian Hebraism from the late fifteenth century onwards and the Protestant call to read the Bible in the original Hebrew, Christian scholars used their proficiency in Hebrew to prove to the Jews their allegedly mistaken understanding of their own sources, as Müller himself did in this work. However, Müller presents his work as if it were a *Jewish* answer to the Christian Hebraists. By this he attempts to create a pretended alliance with his Jewish readers: if Hebrew has become a tool in the hands of Christians for anti-Jewish polemics, here, in Yiddish, his readers would find comfort (*nekhomes*) and reassurance. In other words, Müller was using the high degree of intimacy and solidarity produced by the use of Yiddish in order to convey the message that even if works in Hebrew could not always be trusted, for they might have been written by Christians, works in Yiddish were safe, for they had surely come from inside the Jewish community.

Just how effective this tactic was can be seen from the following anecdote published in Callenberg's reports. One of Callenberg's assistants, himself a convert from Judaism, was approached on the street in Halle by a local Jew, who tried to question him regarding the identity of the author of *Or le'eys erev*. At some point the Jew told the convert that the Jews suspected that he, the convert, was the author. The Jew explained that a Jewish rabbi would never have written this work, since the message is Christian; on the other hand, the Jew argued, "a true Christian [from birth] could not have written it either. If it were written entirely in Hebrew, I might have believed it; but not like this. Because no Christian, however well he may be educated in Hebrew, can combine German and Hebrew in writing, and in such a correct manner, as here."[58]

The missionary endeavors in Yiddish in general, and the missionary literature in this language in particular, provoked a wide range of reactions among the Jews, from willingly reading such works to tossing them into the fire.[59] But apart from these extreme reactions, it seems that the overall Jewish stance was one of bewilderment as well as concern that these Christian works in the Jewish language would eventually succeed in their mission. As put forward by the above-mentioned Jew in his conversation with Callenberg's assistant, "our people . . . are afraid, and not without a reason, that when simple folk were to obtain this book [*Or le'eys erev*], they would be easily convinced by it since it is the language of Jacob, but the hands are those of Esau."[60]

The importance of Yiddish for the missionary cause persisted beyond the attempts to convince Jews to convert to Christianity. Once a decision to convert had been made, a Jewish candidate for baptism had to go through a long process of learning and instruction in the Christian religion, which usually had to be done in Yiddish. Among the reasons for the publication of Yiddish missionary tracts in Halle was the demand for such writings among preachers who instructed Jews wishing to convert. Callenberg relates that he received complaints from preachers arguing "that they could not give these persons [the Jews who wished to convert] anything to read, for the latter have learned to read nothing but their Jewish [language]."[61] The theologian and *Generalsuperintendent* in the Lutheran church of the Principality of Grubenhagen (in present-day Lower Saxony), Caspar Calvör, recounts in the introduction to his missionary work *Gloria Christi* (Leipzig 1710) that the first step in writing this book was made when a Jew who wished to convert came to him to learn the Christian precepts. "I found it advisable," Calvör recalls, "to compose the main teachings of Christ in Yiddish, for this Israelite to read."[62]

This learning process, and the role Yiddish played in it, did not end with conversion either. Although instruction in German and the Latin alphabet was usually part of the convert's initiation process, in most cases the act of *religious* conversion did not mean an immediate *linguistic* one; Yiddish works, as well as Yiddish-speaking instructors, were still needed to aid the process of conversion and ease the convert's adjustment to the new religion. Faced with the ever-present danger of converts relapsing from Christianity, Callenberg and his missionaries provided former Jews, some of them baptized years before, with missionary writings in the Jewish language. The issue of converts' instruction was also raised in the manifesto calling for the establishment of a Yiddish *collegium* in Halle, as one of the arguments in favor of this proposition: "Especially since the number of baptized Jews that walk about here in Halle markedly grows . . . , and that are in grave need of instruction in the Christian doctrine, and also heartily demand it; but since there are no subjects [missionaries] present, who can converse with them in their tongue and expressions, they had to do up to now without such instruction."[63]

The efforts to convert the Jews thus led to an unprecedented Christian, mainly Protestant, interest in Yiddish in the first half of the eighteenth century. In addition to professional missionaries trained in the Jewish language, we often hear of private initiatives of clergy and even laypeople, who studied Yiddish privately in order to effectively converse with their Jewish neighbors on matters of religion and thus expedite their conversion.[64] Missionary impulses were not absent either from other Christian considerations for learning Yiddish, such as the ambitions to read Yiddish literature and to expose Jewish secrets. In these cases, however, other arguments in favor of learning Yiddish were focused on, adding new dimensions to the role of Yiddish in Christian-Jewish relations in early modern Germany.

Two "From the Jews' own books"
Yiddish Literature, Christian Readers

Mastering Yiddish was also recommended to the Christian *Studiosis Theologiae* to enable them to read Ashkenazi Jewish literature in this language. During the early modern period, a rich corpus of Yiddish literature was published in the Holy Roman Empire, including both religious and secular works, such as biblical translations and paraphrases, ethical books on morality and proper conduct, prayer books, medieval epics and romance, poems, fables, and drama.[1] While Hebrew was the language of Jewish scholarly literature, works in Yiddish were meant primarily for the larger segments of the Jewish population, including Jewish women, children, and less educated men, who could not read Hebrew and lacked the training required to fully understand complicated rabbinic texts. The fact that this was the targeted reading public of this literature influenced both its content and style. As Yiddish scholar Chava Turniansky explains, these were mainly popular works, and their authors, who drew their material primarily from Hebrew sources, "removed the theoretic and abstract passages, omitted the intellectual speculations, avoided the arduous deliberations and the complicated ideas, and concentrated on the practical, concrete, simple and easily comprehensible elements, and especially on those which were presented as appealing narratives."[2]

To be sure, this literature was by no means held in regard by the Protestant scholars, who sharply criticized it for both style and content, declaring it ridiculous, foolish, and distasteful (*lächerlich*, *albern*, *abgeschmackt*). Due to their peculiar and ridiculous expressions (*seltsamen, lächerlichen Redens-Arten*), it was argued, Yiddish works would awake mainly scorn and laughter among Christian readers, and could thus serve them as a source of amusement (*Belustigung*) or even as an "*Anti-*

Melancholicum."[3] An exception to this general disparagement of the literary quality of Jewish works in Yiddish can be found in Wagenseil's introduction to his *Belehrung der Jüdisch-Teutschen Red- und Schreibart*, a Yiddish primer with an extensive anthology of Yiddish texts from the year 1699. Although in other instances Wagenseil, too, sharply criticizes Yiddish literary works, in one passage he nonetheless chooses to compliment it, recommending Yiddish literature as a "felicitous amusement" (*eine treffliche Erlustigung*), not in a disparaging manner but rather out of appreciation of its literary qualities. Referring in particular to Yiddish "books of history . . . that include both true and invented stories," Wagenseil asserts that

> one can drive away one's cares, heavy thoughts, and sadness by no better means than Judeo-German books, and they have the advantage that they contain no evil prattle that corrupts good conduct, but rather things that delight and also instruct in virtue and honesty which one absorbs so well that one cannot easily forget them, which is not the case with the stories and myths of other peoples.[4]

Even if Yiddish literature could be considered harmless amusement to *Christian* readers (although as noted by one of the authors, it should be taken "with a grain of salt"),[5] it was nevertheless denounced by Christian scholars as harmful and damaging to *Jewish* readers. The Jews, so ran the argument, spent their time reading this idle literature instead of the Bible. Even more problematic were the popular religious works in Yiddish, which often included adaptations from the Talmud and other rabbinical works, because they led the Jews away from God's word and strengthened them in their erroneous faith. Some authors even accused contemporary rabbis of encouraging the reading of Yiddish literature among the common, uneducated Jews, in order to keep them in ignorance and prevent them from being exposed to the Christian truth revealed in Scripture.

In a report from 1734 one of Callenberg's traveling missionaries recounts how he confronted the owner of a Jewish bookshop, in which Yiddish adaptations of popular German *Volksbücher* such as *Till Eulenspiegel* and *Claus Narr* were offered. In response to the shopkeeper's assertion that these books were meant for Jewish women, so that they would be able to amuse themselves and to pass the time on Sabbath, the missionary argued: "Is that what Sabbath was meant for? I assumed, that on Sabbath one is supposed to study (the [Jewish] law). . . . This is a grave sin on the account of the men, and especially of the rabbis, that the poor people are not instructed," and that "on Sabbath one gives the women and children such books in the hands, which are no good for them, but rather do damage, and spoil them."[6] A similar critical stance toward secular literature in Yiddish is found already two centuries earlier in the "Jewish" introduction to Fagius' and Adam's Yiddish translation of the Bible from 1544. In the introduction, written in Yiddish and addressing the Jewish reader,[7] the author advocates his Bible for the benefit of Jewish "wives and young women who all know well how to read Yiddish, but who pass their time by reading worthless books such as *Ditraykh fun Bern*, *Hildebrant* and others like them which are nothing but lies and invented things. These wives and young women could use their free time to read this *Khumesh* which is nothing but pure truth."[8]

Yiddish adaptations of secular German literature, particularly epic poetry and chivalric romance such as *Dietrich von Bern* or the *Artusromane*, were not approved by Jewish rabbis and scholars either. Denouncing such *galkhes bikher* (Christian texts) as obscenity, filth, and frivolity, Jewish authors lamented the great popularity of these works among the broad Jewish populace.[9] As a substitute for leisure-reading on Sabbath and holidays, they offered their coreligionists *Jewish* works in Yiddish, which were considered pious and edifying. Yet these works, too, encountered vehement opposition from Christian scholars, who directed their criticism at both the cultural and religious value of the Jewish works.

In 1612 the Lutheran theologian and professor of Hebrew at the University of Giessen, Christoph Helwig (Helvicus), published a German translation of numerous stories from the widely read *Mayse-bukh* (Book of stories; Basel 1602), a compilation of about two hundred and fifty stories based largely on Talmudic and midrashic tales, which advocated itself as the "Yiddish Gemara." In the introduction to his translation Helwig explains that the Jews hold the stories in the *Mayse-bukh* in the highest regard. They believe the stories are true and holy, and read them on the Sabbath and Jewish holidays as a means to honor and sanctify these days. However, Helwig maintains, any reasonable person would immediately recognize that these are nothing but foolish and risible fables, invented by the rabbis in order to keep the Jews in their ignorance and superstition. As far as Helwig is concerned, the Yiddish *Mayse-bukh* is a decisive proof that "the poor people are led by the nose and fooled by the rabbis," and that "all the lies, as crude as the rabbis devise them, are pure sanctity for them."[10] From a Christian perspective, the danger in this situation is clear: "For it is undeniable, that still in our time such lies hold back many among the Jews, so that it is all the more difficult for them to convert to Christianity, because they consider these [lies] to be true, and get therefore noticeably [more] stubborn in their superstition."[11]

Another target for Christian criticism was the *Tsene-rene* by Jacob B. Isaac Ashkenazi,[12] the most popular book of traditional Yiddish literature. Especially popular among Jewish women for reading on the Sabbath and holidays, it included paraphrases of biblical texts accompanied by elaborate commentaries from a large variety of Jewish sources. Johann Jacob Schudt, an eighteenth-century Lutheran Hebraist and schoolmaster at the Frankfurt Gymnasium, referred to the *Tsene-rene* in his ethnographic work *Jüdische Merckwürdigkeiten* (Jewish curiosities; 1714–18), in which an entire chapter was dedicated to the language of the German Jews.[13] Emphasizing that the Yiddish book was meant for Jewish women and uneducated men, Schudt condemns the *Tsene-rene* as a work in which one finds "pure scum [*sentina*] and an accumulation of all the distasteful Jewish fables and perverse commentaries of the Rabbis."[14] Schudt wonders why it has not yet been translated "into our German" (*in unser Teutsch*), claiming it could serve the Christians as a source for great entertainment and a good laugh, "in that surely, [even] someone in the height of fever, when he hears this being read, would have to laugh from the bottom of his heart."[15] Twenty years later, one of the Pietist missionaries in Halle reported that he had once discussed this "women's Bible" (*Weiberchomesch*) with a couple of Jews. Referring to rabbinical commentaries included in the book, the missionary complained to his Jewish interlocutors that "[this exegesis] is so foolish [*läppisch*], that it seems to me that your scholars are working diligently to keep the poor women in their ignorance and blindness, and wish to ensure that the light of the Holy Bible remains concealed from their eyes."[16]

In their critical discussions on the Yiddish literature that drew its material from Jewish rabbinic sources, it seems that the Christian authors chose to ignore not only the fact that the Jewish audience of this litera-

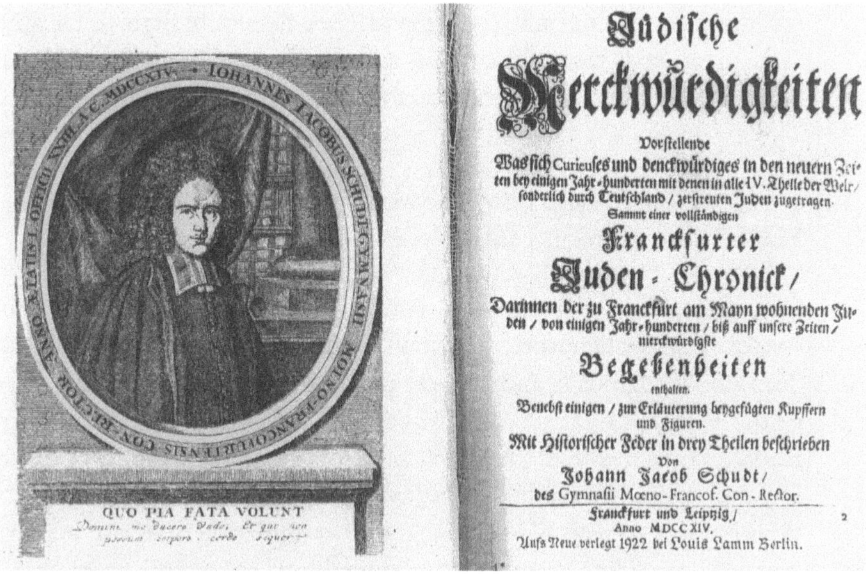

Jüdische
Merckwürdigkeiten
Vorstellende
Was sich Curieuses und denckwürdiges in den neuern Zei-
ten bey einigen Jahr-hunderten mit denen in alle IV. Theile der Welt/
sonderlich durch Teutschland / zerstreuten Juden zugetragen.
Sammt einer vollständigen
Franckfurter
Juden-Chronick/
Darinnen der zu Franckfurt am Mayn wohnenden Ju-
den / von einigen Jahr-hunderten / biß auff unsere Zeiten /
merckwürdigste
Begebenheiten
enthalten.
Benebst einigen / zur Erläuterung beygefügten Kupffern
und Figuren.
Mit Historischer Feder in drey Theilen beschrieben
Von
Johann Jacob Schudt/
des Gymnasii Mœno-Francof. Con-Rector.
Franckfurt und Leipzig/
Anno MDCCXIV.
Aufs Neue verlegt 1922 bei Louis Lamm Berlin.

Figure 2.1. Title page of Johann Schudt's *Jüdische Merckwürdigkeiten* (Frankfurt 1714–18)

ture constituted a reading community at a time in which illiteracy was prevalent in the general population, but also the important contribution of this literature to German-Jewish spiritual and cultural life, and the motives that stood behind the encouragement this literature gained from Jewish rabbis and scholars. Many of these rabbis were of the opinion that since large publics among the German Jews could not read Hebrew, it was better that they pray and study in Yiddish than stray from the religion altogether because of the language barrier. In this sense the Yiddish literature does not testify to Jewish ignorance and cultural inferiority, as the Christian authors presented it, but quite the contrary—it testifies to the Jews' aspiration to educate and enrich themselves, within the existing limitations. It is more probable, however, that the Christian authors understood perfectly well the social and educational function of Yiddish literature within Ashkenazi Jewry, but simply objected to the very necessity of its use. Since fortifying the foundations of traditional rabbinic authority was not by any means a laudable cause in the eyes of Christian scholars, it is no wonder that they rejected Yiddish literature, together with other manifestations of Ashkenazi Jewish culture. After all, as is clear from the support of the same authors in Yiddish missionary literature, when it suited their goals they did not hesitate to take the same position as that of the rabbis and recommend writing in Yiddish for what *they* considered beneficial for the Jews.

"To slay Goliath with his own sword": Yiddish Literature and anti-Jewish Polemic

Despite making no attempt to conceal their contempt for this "despised" Yiddish literature, Christian authors repeatedly demonstrated deep knowledge of it and actively promoted its reading among their fellow Christians. They emphasized how important and useful such reading could be, and they took practical measures to make Yiddish literature more accessible to non-Jews by offering their readers instructions on how to read Yiddish, including grammatical rules and reading exercises; providing them with bibliographical lists and chrestomathies; and in some cases translating Yiddish works into German and Latin.[17] The prevalent notion, so well expressed in Chrysander's assertion from 1750, was that "not everything in them [the Yiddish books] is unhealthy; rather, they have a lot in them, that a Christian philologist and theologian can use . . . if he knows how to extract the quintessence."[18] Indeed, Christian authors made use of Jewish works in Yiddish wherever it suited their purposes.

Jewish literature in Yiddish was recommended to Christian readers as a source of information about actual Jewish beliefs and practices. This would prove helpful in conducting missionary work from a position of acquaintance, as well as in repudiating Judaism by using the Jews' own sources for polemics against them. As Chrysander, for instance, noted, reading Yiddish literature would be very beneficial for Christians in that "one makes for oneself, from their own books, a more accurate and complete notion of the condition of present-day Jews, . . . their teachings, . . . customs, prevalent prejudices, motivations, most common/base sins, blasphemies . . . etc. Consequently, one would be more skilled to missionize them . . . and would be able to better choose the most convenient means for winning them over."[19]

The Christian use of Jewish sources in anti-Jewish polemics was a medieval practice, which entered a new phase with the work of Protestant

Hebraists and their unprecedented expertise in Hebrew and Aramaic. Incorporating the field of Yiddish literature brought new advantages for Christian scholars. While Hebrew and Aramaic literature admitted these scholars mainly to the confined world of the Jewish elite, works in Yiddish gave them access to the religious and cultural world of the greater part of the Jewish population in the German lands. Moreover, as Yiddish literature was in many cases less sophisticated than Hebrew literature, in the sense that it did not necessitate formal education and did not contain complicated teachings, it also became beneficial to less educated Christians who wished to get to know the Jewish world and prepare themselves to dispute with Jews from a more knowledgeable position.

The appreciation of the Yiddish literature as a window to the closed Jewish world is well reflected in the genre of polemical ethnographies of Jews and Judaism.[20] Offering their readers detailed depictions of contemporary Jewish customs and way of life, the authors of such ethnographies used to emphasize that the information was taken "from the Jews' own books" (*aus ihren eigenen Büchern*) in order to give their work an aura of authenticity and reliability. Johann Buxtorf, the most renowned seventeenth-century Christian Hebraist, is a case in point.[21] Professor of Hebrew and censor of Jewish works in the city of Basel (one of the main centers of Yiddish printing at the time), Buxtorf was well acquainted with Jewish literature in the vernacular. He published the first-known bibliography of Yiddish books,[22] and made extensive use of Yiddish popular literature in his work, particularly in his widely read *Synagoga Judaica: Das ist Juden Schul* (1603), one of the most important ethnographic depictions of early modern Jewish life. Written in German instead of Latin, the *Juden Schul* was a popular work, intended to reach out to a broad readership of German-speakers. It was published in numerous editions, and as historian Stephen G. Burnett notes, "was the standard work on Judaism for a century after Buxtorf's death, shaping subsequent Christian ethnographies of the Jews and later anti-Jewish polemics."[23]

In *Juden Schul* Buxtorf quotes extensively from several Yiddish books, including prose narratives (*mayses*), morality books (*muser-sforim*), and books of customs and correct conduct (*minhogim-sforim*). In addition to the aforementioned *Mayse-bukh* one should also mention Moses Henochs Altshuler Yerushalmi's *Seyfer brantshpigl* (Basel 1602), one of the most famous ethical books in the vernacular, and Simon b. Judah Levi Ginzburg's *Minhogim-bukh* (Venice 1593 [1589]), the first printed version of Yiddish books of this kind, based on the Hebrew book of customs by Isaac Tyrnau.[24] Incorporating materials from rabbinic literature, translated into the vernacular in a simplifying manner, these works were designed to make the principles of Jewish belief and practices more easily accessible to less educated Jews. Thus they also proved very useful to Buxtorf, who wished to make these same principles more easily accessible to less educated Christians and provide them with effective counter-arguments in disputations with Jews. As Burnett argues, Buxtorf's translations from Jewish popular religious literature, incorporated in his work, were especially effective for clergymen, who could use them as "ready-made sermon illustrations" when conducting mission among the Jews.[25]

By exposing their readers to Yiddish literature, or drawing upon Yiddish works in their own anti-Jewish treatises, Protestant authors aimed not only to equip Christians with useful and reliable arguments for disputations with Jews, in order "to slay Goliath with his own sword,"[26] but also to strengthen the Christian readers in their own faith. In some cases, this was due to the fact that certain Yiddish texts included biblical teachings and sayings, which were considered edifying for Christian readers as well. In most cases, however, Christian authors expressed the opinion that Yiddish literature could benefit Christian readers because it so well reflected the degenerate religious and cultural state of contemporary Jews. The underlying assumption was that the encounter of Christians with Jewish literature, which was considered ridiculous and superstitious, would surely make them rejoice in their own true belief (as opposed to the Jews' error and blindness) and would serve as a warning, confronting Christians with the consequences awaiting those who abandon God's word.

Such an argument can be found, for example, in Wagenseil's introduction to his publication of a Jewish translation of the Psalms into Yiddish, where he notes: "Whenever observing the blindness of the eyes and the eclipsed understanding with which the Jews are afflicted, a pious Christian reader would hopefully take the opportunity to thank God for granting him and other true believers the grace to understand, through his beloved Son and Apostles, many secrets included in the Holy

Psalms."[27] Another example can be found fifty years later, in the work of Wilhelm Chrysander from 1750. Listing the different benefits a Christian could gain from reading Yiddish literature, Chrysander mentions that it can motivate Christians "to develop an appetite for Christian books, which deliver the religious doctrines and obligations more thoroughly, clearly and tidily . . . , and to thank God more heartily for the bright light he bestowed upon us," and put them in position "to compare deficient and feeble teachings of the Jews with more mature treatises of the Christians."[28]

Three Blasphemy, Curses, and Insults
Yiddish and the Jews' "Hidden Transcript"

The ambition to use the acquaintance with the Yiddish language and literature for anti-Jewish polemics and missionary purposes discloses a Christian understanding of Yiddish as the *private* language of the Jews, used inside the Jewish communities to discuss intimate internal matters. Another, more consequential notion of Yiddish assumed it to be their *secret* language, deliberately used to conceal Jewish affairs from Christian eyes. From a sociological perspective, "privacy and secrecy both involve boundaries and the denial of access to others; however, they differ in the moral content of the behavior [or information, for that matter], which is concealed."[1] Unlike privacy, which is taken to be simply a withdrawal from the public order and is therefore seen as not threatening to others, secrecy is understood to operate in disregard of or opposition to that order and is imbued with negative associations of furtiveness, evil, and various forms of deceit. Regarded as an intentional and illegitimate concealment of information, "to think something secret is already to envisage potential conflict between what insiders conceal and outsiders want to inspect or lay bare."[2]

The notion of Yiddish as the Jews' secret language should be seen against the backdrop of the broader discourse on Jews and secrecy in early modern Europe. As historian Elisheva Carlebach argues, attribution of secrecy was an essential ingredient in shaping perceptions of Jewry throughout medieval and early modern Europe, and played a prominent role in constructing the Jew as the quintessential Other in Christian society.[3] The conviction that Jews were saturated by deep hatred of Christ and Christians, but lacked the power to openly express it, nourished the belief that hidden malicious intent stood at the heart of every Jewish belief and practice, thus creating a sense of fear and danger in the face of a perceived Jewish threat. Between the sixteenth and eighteenth centuries Jewish secrecy was a recurrent motif in numerous works on Jews and Judaism. The authors, many of them former Jews, capitalized on these prevalent perceptions and promised to reveal the covert and subversive aspects of Judaism to their readers. Seeking to align themselves with their new coreligionists while distancing themselves from their former ones, converts to Christianity used their intimate acquaintance with the Jewish world to position themselves as the ideal exposers of its secrets.[4]

As the languages of the Jews, Hebrew and later on Yiddish constituted an important pillar in the myth of Jewish secrecy. During the Middle Ages, the consolidation of the Christian perception of Hebrew as the secret language of the Jews was accompanied by the belief that Hebrew possessed magical powers.[5] As the association between Jews and magic began to disintegrate in the German lands in the first half of the sixteenth century, Hebrew, too, began to lose its alleged magical qualities. It nonetheless retained its secretive attributes, and the belief that Hebrew as well as Yiddish functioned as secret languages of the Jews persisted throughout the early modern period.[6]

The Jews' language needed to be exposed as a secret in itself, together with other aspects of Jewish secrecy such as rituals and customs. Even more fundamentally, it needed to be exposed for the access it could provide to further secrets of the Jews, or what we would call the "hidden transcript" of this minority, concealed in their books and daily discourse. As political theorist James C. Scott asserts, every subordinate group creates a hidden transcript, a "discourse that takes place 'offstage,' beyond direct observation by powerholders," in contrast to a public transcript, which is the subordinate discourse in the presence of the dominant. The subordinated, according to Scott, are not free to speak their minds in the presence of power. Behind the scenes, though, they are likely to create and defend a social space in which resistance to domination may be voiced and the existing power relations challenged.[7] In the case of the Jews in early modern Germany, as was well observed by contemporary Christian authors, their distinct language supported the existence of such a hidden transcript, as that language helped them establish the social space in which resentment to the dominant Christian culture could be safely expressed. Moreover, as some of the authors emphasize, the fact that the Jews used a distinct language allowed them to employ their hidden transcript not only "behind the scenes" but in the very presence of Christians not proficient in the language.

Yiddish Literature and anti-Christian Polemic

From their privileged position of knowledge of Hebrew and Yiddish, either as birthright or as the product of scholarly training, converts from Judaism and Christian Hebraists alike promoted the notion that the Jews' secret language and the content it helped conceal posed a genuine threat to the Christian order. From a theological perspective, this threat took the form of blasphemies (*Lästerungen*) and anti-Christian expressions believed to have been present in Jewish literature and prayer. These accusations against the Jews, which played an important role in the attacks on the Talmud in the thirteenth century,[8] persisted throughout the early modern period. As traditional accusations of ritual murder and desecration of the host started to lose ground from the sixteenth century onwards, blasphemies and anti-Christian propaganda came to be considered the main danger from the Jews. The category of what was considered blasphemous and anti-Christian in Jewish literature had a very broad definition, ranging from Jewish tenets that did not coincide with Christian ones, through subtle anti-Christian polemics, and up to outright disparagement of Christianity.[9]

While Hebrew prayer books and elite rabbinic culture traditionally stood in the focal plane of Christian scrutiny and censorship regulations, certain Hebraists also turned their attention to the more popular but—to Christian eyes—less conspicuous layer of Jewish culture that proliferated in the realm of Yiddish literature and oral tradition, and in which anti-Christian elements, or what could be considered as such, were not unusual. Elements of anti-Christian polemic existed in popular Yiddish works such as the *Mayse-bukh*, and especially in the genre of historical chronicles, including works originally written in Yiddish as well as translations from Hebrew into the vernacular. A prominent example is the *Toledot Yeshu* (The life of Jesus), a highly unflattering "counter-biography" of Jesus that circulated in the Jewish world from the Middle Ages and was often cited by Christian polemicists as decisive proof for Jewish subversiveness. *Toledot Yeshu* was especially popular in Ashkenaz, where it circulated in both Hebrew and Yiddish variants.[10]

As part of their endeavors to expose Jewish anti-Christian sentiment from their own experience as former Jews, converts to Christianity described their personal encounters with Jewish anti-Christian writings in the vernacular, such as Yiddish variants of the infamous *Toledot Yeshu*. According to convert Samuel Brenz, the Jews read unpublished, handwritten versions of this book secretly on Christmas Eve, together with eating garlic (*Knoblauchfressen*) and other activities which were meant to debase the holy night.[11] A less common example was the *Bukh der fartsaykhnung* (Amsterdam 1696), described by one convert as "attacks and mockery against the New Testament . . . rendered in an accessible manner, in order to arm the common Jew with arrows against the Christian teachings."[12] Other authors, most notably theologians and Hebraists, concentrated on denouncing the "blasphemous" and anti-Christian expressions embedded in Yiddish prayer books and biblical translations. In his introduction to a German translation of a Yiddish prayer book for Jewish women, *Gebet-Buch derer heutigen Jüdinnen* (Schweidnitz and Leipzig 1734), Johann Jacob Rambach, a Lutheran professor of theology from the University of Giessen, explicitly stated that a central goal of this translation was to address what he perceived as the need for Christians to become acquainted with Jewish blasphemies and anti-Christian sentiments. The Jews, he argued,

> let their hatred to our savior, to the Christians, and to the Christian religion show very clearly also in their prayers. . . . And although one can find a prayer for the Christian authorities in their so-called "thick prayer book" [*dicken Tephilla*], printed in Frankfurt in 1688, . . . it is there more for appearance than for devoted use . . . ; in their common prayer books, on the other hand, which they use in their synagogues and at home, you find nothing like that.[13]

Rambach's last remark is especially interesting as it points out the gap between the Jews' public and hidden transcripts. It was not from the Jews' official prayer books that one could learn about their true intentions and deliberations, but from the ones used behind the scenes, in the private sphere of the Jewish home and among the Jewish women, where Yiddish served as the primary language. With the same ambition of penetrating Jewish "off-stage" discourse, Wilhelm Chrysander recommended that Christians learn the Yiddish handwriting, noting that "in the handwritten Jewish-German *Selichot* [special prayers recited in the weeks preceding the Day of Atonement] the passages against the Christian religion, omitted from the printed [versions], still stand."[14]

A popular target for accusations of blasphemy and anti-Christian propaganda was the first complete Yiddish version of the Bible, translated by Jekuthiel ben Isaac Blitz and published by Uri Fayvesh ben Aaron ha-Levi in Amsterdam in 1676–79.[15] Already in 1686, the Lutheran theologian and distinguished professor of theology at the University of Kiel, Christian Kortholt, vehemently attacked Blitz's translation in his *De variis scripturae editionibus tractatus*, a survey of the various editions and translations of Scripture into different languages. Denouncing the Jewish translator as a "blasphemous impostor," Kortholt condemned the Yiddish Bible for what he considered to be a deliberate distortion and dislocation of the words (*prava & insulsa verborum traductione*)in a way that corrupted the holy text, especially the verses that bear witness to the expected coming of Christ. And if that was not enough, Kortholt continued, the translator shamelessly integrated extensive passages of Jewish apologetics and anti-Christian polemic into the text.[16]

In the following generations, Blitz's translation continued to invoke the wrath of Christian scholars, who repeated and elaborated Kortholt's accusations. In 1728 the Lutheran theologian and Hebraist Johann Gottlob Carpzov fiercely attacked Blitz's translation for what he considered the "confused and foolish apologetic of Jewish faithlessness and refutation of Christian truths" incorporated into the Yiddish text.[17] To demonstrate this claim, Carpzov extensively quoted from Blitz's discussion on Isaiah 7—not without disgust and anger, as he emphasizes, but also with the justified cause of bringing the "virulence and derision" of the anti-Christian expressions to the attention of his readers.[18] Twenty years later, Wilhelm Chrysander recommended this Yiddish translation to Christians who wished to explore "the Jews' finest objections [to Christian interpretation], and the common manner, in which they misinterpret the most pertinent sayings of the Old Testament," since it contained "falsifying perversions" (*verfälschende Verdrehungen*) that deviated from the Hebrew text, and was accompanied by "poisonous blasphemies and hostile assaults against the Christian religion."[19]

Blitz's translation also came under scrutiny in Johann Schudt's *Jüdische Merckwürdigkeiten* from 1714, where the author related to this "foolish, tasteless, vicious Jewish-German translation of the Old Testament" as part of his discussion of Jewish life in Holland. Vehemently attacking Amsterdam's authorities for a lack of adequate censorship in their city, Schudt considered this Yiddish Bible a decisive proof of the unwelcome results of the "overly extensive freedom of the Jews in Holland," where "the Jews have their own printing shops, and there they may freely publish their blasphemous books at their liking . . . , in which they blaspheme and disgrace Jesus and our faith."[20] As an example of the way the Jewish translator allegedly falsified and misinterpreted "the clearest prophecies of the Lord Messiah," Schudt cited Blitz's translation of Isaiah 7:14, a central point of controversy between Jews and Christians over the centuries. Relating to the second part of the verse, "*hinneh ha-almah harah ve-yoledet ben*" (The virgin will be with child and will give birth to a son), Schudt sharply criticized Blitz for translating the word *almah* not as a *Jungfrau* (virgin) but rather as a *junge Frau* (יונגי פרויא, young woman), thus deliberately pulling the carpet from under one of the most important Christian tenets.[21]

The charge that the Jews falsify the biblical text in order to conceal the places that refer to Christ is of course a very old one. As historian Joshua Trachtenberg explains, already "Jerome and other early Church Fathers frequently complained that the Jewish teachers consciously and deliberately perverted the meaning of the original text," and "medieval scholars did not hesitate to impute to Jews even the crime of tampering with the text of the Bible in an effort to destroy its Christological meaning."[22] In light of this notion, Christian authors viewed the "problematic" places in Yiddish Bibles not simply as the outcome of some unavoidable translation fallacy, and certainly not as a legitimate alternative to their own interpretation, but as a strategic mistranslation, ideologically motivated by anti-Christian impulses. The Jews, according to this view, used the medium of translation in order to manipulate the holy text, and hence as a weapon in the war they waged against Christian tenets in their secret vernacular.

The desire to detect, collect, and expose anti-Christian elements in Jewish sources gained a most sinister expression in the work of Johann Andreas Eisenmenger, professor of Oriental languages at the University of Heidelberg. In his *Entdecktes Judenthum* (Judaism unmasked; 1711 [1700]), spanning more than two thousand pages, Eisenmenger promised his readers a "thorough and truthful account, how the stubborn Jews dreadfully blaspheme and dishonor the Holy Trinity, God the Father, Son, and Holy Spirit, abhor the Holy Mother of Christ, the New Testament, the evangelists and apostles, derisively scathe the Christian religion, and utterly despise and curse all of Christendom."[23] To achieve this goal, Eisenmenger diligently collected numerous passages from the Talmud and many other Jewish works, which to his mind supported these allegations. The passages were cited in the original Hebrew, Yiddish, or Aramaic and accompanied by German translations. Although Eisenmenger did not blatantly falsify his sources, he nevertheless managed to create a distorted presentation of Jewish beliefs and practices. Supporting traditional anti-Semitic charges such as the blood libels and poisoning of wells, this work is often seen as a remnant of medieval anti-Jewish polemics; yet it also exerted considerable influence on modern anti-Semitic discourse.[24]

In addition to almost two hundred books in Hebrew and Aramaic, Eisenmenger used for his discussion no fewer than thirteen books in Yiddish, including the *Tsene-rene*, *Mayse-bukh*, *Seyfer brantshpigl*, *Minhogim-bukh*, and other popular books of stories, prayers, and customs. One of the Yiddish books that received special attention was Salman Zvi Hirsch of Aufhausen's *Yudisher teryak* (Jewish antidote; Hanau 1615), probably the first Jewish apologetic book ever to appear in print. The book was published as a response to the accusations raised against the Jews the year before by Samuel Friedrich Brenz, a Bavarian Jew who had converted to Christianity in 1610. Like other anti-Jewish works written by converts, Brenz's *Jüdischer abgestreiffter Schlangen-Balg* (Jewish cast-off snakeskin; 1614) explicitly purported to expose the anti-Christian elements allegedly hidden in Jewish religion and culture.[25] Despite Eisenmenger's disdain for not very educated converts, he nonetheless made extensive use of their works, particularly when he could not find proof for his allegations in Jewish sources.[26] In different places in his work, Eisenmenger cited anti-Jewish charges from Brenz and other converts followed by Hirsch's vehement denials as they appeared in his *Yudisher teryak*, which Eisenmenger cited in the original Yiddish alongside a German translation. Referring to Hirsch as "*gottlose[r] Lügner*" (godless liar) and to his *Yudisher teryak* as "*Lügen-Buch*" (book of lies), Eisenmenger used this Jewish apologetic work against its grain: by presenting Hirsch's refutations of the anti-Jewish charges as "detestable lies," he not only exploited them in order to *support* the convert's accusations, but at the same time demonstrated that the Jews indeed desired to conceal their true nature and to deceive the Christians regarding the genuine content of their hidden transcript.

Anti-Christian Yiddish Oral Culture

The fact that Yiddish literature enjoyed considerable popularity among Ashkenazi Jews, and that it was mainly confined to the private sphere of the Jewish home, made the ability to read Yiddish a valuable instrument for Christians who wished to penetrate the inner Jewish world and expose its secrets in order to gain a tighter control on this minority. But Christian authors were not content with exploring Yiddish literature only. They also tried to penetrate the Yiddish oral culture to find out what the Jews said among themselves about Christians and Christianity.

The claim that a considerable gap existed between the Jews' public and hidden transcripts was central to many works written by converts from Judaism, who considered it their mission to bring this gap to the attention of Christians. One of these converts was Dietrich Schwab from Paderborn, whose *Jüdischer Deckmantel* (Jewish cloak; 1619) was often cited by later authors.[27] "Many simple Christians," Schwab wrote, "believe that the pleasant and friendly words of the Jews are pure honey, not noticing the deception that lies beneath these smooth words, and the poison hidden beneath the honey. . . . They speak peace with their neighbor, but the evil is in their hearts."[28] Jewish duplicity, according to Schwab and other converts, was even more conspicuous in the face of power. When dealing with the authorities, claimed Brenz in his *Jüdischer abgestreiffter Schlangen-Balg*, the Jews "place themselves, but only on the outside, as obedient subjects [*Unterthanen*]; but secretly they curse and imprecate their authorities/masters [*Herrschaften*] . . . their mouth is full of cursing, falseness, and deceit."[29]

During the early modern period, former Jews and Christian Hebraists ardently collected popular Jewish sayings intended to mock and insult Christianity and its adherents.[30] Unlike the charges regarding the existence of anti-Christian elements in Yiddish literature, those regarding the existence of such elements in Yiddish oral culture could not be refuted or verified. Nonetheless (and maybe precisely because of this fact), they constituted a very popular theme in works on Jews and Judaism, diligently transmitted from one author to the next.[31]

Jewish anti-Christian expressions, recorded in Christian sources, may be divided into two categories. The first category comprises curses and other forms of verbal aggression, such as insults and epithets invectively used to express hostility and contempt toward the speaker's antagonist. At its simplest level, Jewish verbal abuse documented by Christian authors takes the form of individual lexical items, derived to a large extent from Hebrew. These plain, direct insults include words such as *Kelef* (dog), *Mamser* (bastard), *tippisch* (fool), *chasir* (pig), *chammor* (donkey or "ass"), and the like.[32] A more complex form of verbal violence is the ritualized curse, or *klole* (from the Hebrew *kelalah*), where the speaker does not merely express his disdain of another person but attempts to actively invoke some misfortune upon the maleficiary. Thus, although closely related to common swearing, cursing tends to be more malevolently intended, as it deliberately aims to offend and discomfort the enemy.[33]

In their representations of Judaism, Christian authors mentioned various examples of Jewish maledictions (*lästerliche böse Wünsche*, *Verwünschungen*), ranging from the common though highly potent "*Jimmach Schemo*" (May his name be blotted out) to the more creative "*Daß dich Mamser der choli hannophel erstosse*!" (That the falling pestilence [epilepsy] will afflict you, bastard!). Like other subtypes of what the American linguist James Matisoff termed "psycho-ostensive expressions," Yiddish insults and ill wishes were "intended by the speaker to be accepted as the direct linguistic manifestation of his psychic state of the moment"; in our case, one of hostility and anger. They were also a convenient and conventionalized way of letting off steam—"releasing bursts of psychic energy that might otherwise remain hopelessly bottled up."[34] With their function as a relief valve for aggressive feelings of anger and frustration, Yiddish swearing and cursing were no different from similar phenomena in other cultures. Moreover, despite the impression conveyed by the Christian sources, Jewish speech acts of this kind were not inherently anti-Christian, and could be directed at both Christians and fellow Jews alike.

An exception to this rule are certain curses (*kloles*), which under specific circumstances were not simply manifestations of anger or hostility but constituted an integral part of a Jewish ritual, bearing therefore far-reaching theological implications. For example, the words *kapore* (atonement) and *mise meshune* (strange or unusual death; sometimes translated as a quick, sudden, unnatural or painful death). As eighteenth-century convert Gottfried Selig noted in his Yiddish-German lexicon from 1792, these expressions were commonly used among Jews for cursing, wishing someone a sudden and unnatural death (*Du sollst die misso meschunne uiber bau seyn*) or that this someone will serve as atonement for their sins and die in their place (*Du solt mein kapporo werden*).[35] According to some authors, however, these curses were specifically used against Christians on the Jewish Yom Kippur (Day of Atonement), as part of the *kapparot* ritual. In his study of the depictions of Yom Kippur in Christian polemical ethnographies on Jews and Judaism in early modern Europe, historian Yaacov Deutsch showed that the Jewish custom of *kapparot* (the custom of discharging one's sins on a rooster, whose life is promptly sacrificed in return for the effecter's atonement) appears in almost all Christian descriptions of the holiday. In many descriptions we also find the charge that Jews, especially poor ones who did not have the money to buy a rooster, would transfer their sins to unsuspecting Christians, while uttering the words "*Wär' capporo miso meschunno*."[36] The Christian authors would then translate it for their readers, usually adding elaborated meanings as they saw fit; for example, "be a sacrifice for me through a quick death. Go to hell in my place, as atonement for my sins."[37] This claim also appears in other polemical works against Judaism, especially in books that list Jewish insults and prayers against Christianity. Although not all the descriptions of the *kapparot* ceremony mention this procedure, and some authors even cite it as a false accusation, we still find this claim as late as the mid-eighteenth century; for example, in Wilhelm Chrysander's *Unterricht vom Nutzen des Juden-Teutschen* (Course on the use/usefulness of the Jewish-German [language]; Wolfenbüttel 1750), where the author emphasizes how important it is that Christians learn not only to read and write Yiddish but also to speak and understand it. With this charge of ritual curse as a prominent example, Chrysander illustrates his claim that the ability to understand Yiddish can protect innocent Christians from the threats posed to them by their Jewish neighbors.[38]

The second category of anti-Christian expressions consists of what Yiddish scholar Max Weinreich refers to as *lehavdl loshn*, or differentiation language. According to Weinreich, there is an entire group of Yiddish lexemes intended to designate objects and persons that are not Jewish. The principle behind these terms is one of differentiation, of emphasizing the notion that "'theirs' is different from 'ours.' And since 'ours' is a priori better than 'theirs,' there is in the word that designates 'theirs' always an element of derogation or disparagement."[39]

Christian documentations of Jewish discourse include detailed and well illustrated inventories of derogatory Jewish references to Christians.[40] In addition to *goy* and *orel* we also find the popular designation *sheygets*, for non-Jewish boys, and its feminine form *shikse*, derived from the Hebrew word *sheketz*, "a detestable thing." In an unusual moment of candidness, Eisenmenger shares with us that he too was once called *sheygets* by some Jews who failed to recognize who he was, but asserts that this term is usually reserved for young boys. The authors also discuss the designation *shabes sheygets/shikse* (and the more common *shabes goy/goye*) for Christians working in Jewish homes. Other references comprise the curse words mentioned above, such as *Kelef* and *Mamser*, which function in this case not as spontaneous insults in a moment of anger but as references on a regular basis. "When it is going well for us Christians," writes Eisenmenger, "you [Jews] say: *baavonos horabbim haben die* כלבים *Kelofim groß* מזל *massal*, that is, on account of our many sins the dogs have great fortune." And Brenz notes, "when a Christian has many kids, so they say: *Er hab viel Mamserim* [bastards], that is, [he has] many sons of prostitutes."[41]

Jewish designations for Christian religious figures and sacred objects constitute the other major theme in the works discussed. Thus for example we hear that the Jews refer to Jesus contemptuously as the *Thola* (from the Hebrew word *talui*, the hanged one), designating Christian religious hymns as *Thola Lieder* and the sacrament of the Lord's Supper as *Thola achlen* (songs of the hanged one; eating the hanged one).[42] In some cases the derogatory effect is achieved by introducing a certain sound change to an existing word in a way that mocks it, as in replacing *talmidim* (disciples, referring to the apostles) with *tashmidim*. As

Eisenmenger explains to his readers, the term derives from the Hebrew word שמד (*shmad*), meaning "to destroy" or "to exterminate." From the same root, Eisenmenger continues, the German Jews have also created the Yiddish verb *schmadden*, meaning to baptize. Referring to a convert, they would therefore say, "*er habe sich schmadden, das ist vertilgen lassen*" (he let himself be destroyed).[43] In other cases, such as the derogatory reference *tifle* for a church (from the Hebrew *tiflah*, tastelessness), the deformation is based on the existence of two similar-sounding but semantically different Hebrew words: *tefillah* (in Yiddish: *tfile*, prayer); and *tiflah* (tastelessness). Another popular example is the substitution of the Hebrew word *Kelef* (dog) for the German *Kelch* (chalice), the cup for the wine used in the Mass. When a Jew buys a chalice that was stolen from a church, Eisenmenger tells us, he prides himself in front of other Jews, saying, "*ich habe einen Kelef aus einer Tuma gekinjet*, that is, I bought a dog from the impurity (namely the church)."[44]

Like the insults or psycho-ostensive outbursts of the first category, the differentiating words, too, served to give vent to the emotional attitude of the Jewish speaker toward his subject matter. With their main function of clearly distinguishing between Jews and non-Jews, however, these words were necessarily directed toward Christians. Moreover, they were not the result of some momentary psychic state of the speaker, but common currency in the Jewish vernacular of the time, deeply entrenched in Ashkenazi culture. The uses of the *lehavdl loshn* vocabulary thus went beyond the more strictly psychological function of the swearing and cursing of the first category. Instead, this form of swearing served the important social function of maintaining the boundaries of the Jewish community, and of enforcing its collective identity vis-à-vis Christian society.

Anti-Christian Expressions and the *shund-shriftn* Tradition

Within the corpus of Yiddish textbooks and manuals intended for Christian audiences, the issue of anti-Christian sayings in Yiddish oral culture gained a central position in what came to be known as "anti-Semitic works on the Yiddish language," or as Ber Borochov refers to them, "*shund-shriftn vegn yidish-taytsh*,"[45] published during the eighteenth and early nineteenth centuries. Seeking to ridicule and denigrate the Jews and their language, these works focused on the vulgar strata of Yiddish as spoken among common Jews, and included many instances of slang, coarse and offensive expressions, cursing, and abusive language. At the same time, these authors used their writing on Yiddish for "exposing" Jewish secrets and anti-Christian sentiments.

The most renowned work of this genre is the *Jüdischer Sprach-Meister* (Jewish language master/tutor; circa 1714).[46] Hiding behind the initials J.W., the author declares himself on the title page as "one who formerly spent many years among this [the Jewish] people but now loves God from the bottom of his heart and willingly serves his fellow man." The work aims to teach Christians the spoken language of the Jews by means of a lengthy dialogue in Yiddish (written in Latin characters) with a parallel German translation. The dialogue is between two Yiddish-speaking Jews, a simple Jew named Joune (Jonah) and a corrupt rabbi, Rebbe Jtzick (Isaac). Using a very crude and lowly kind of Yiddish, replete with slang, curses, and blatant sexual terminology, the two discuss the origin and nature of various Jewish beliefs and customs, including Jewish holidays and dietary laws, sexual practices, and ritual cleanliness. The result of this hybrid work, a language-teaching manual drawing upon the tradition of Christian ethnographies on Jews and Judaism, is an especially denigrating presentation of Jewish language and religion, aiming to expose the absurdity and inferiority of Jewish religious as well as linguistic practices.

In the introduction, J.W. advocates his work both for pleasure (*Lust*), "due to the ridiculous turns of speech, which are in vogue among the Jews," and for utility (*Nutzen*), in order to "discern their harsh curses, foul invective, and abusive ill-wishes" (*schwere Flüche, schändliche Schelt-Worte, lästerliche böse Wünsche*). The Jews, according to J.W.,

> wish to pass themselves off as the Chosen People Israel and to say without any timidity that they surpass all other nations in their life and conduct just as in their respectability, temperance, humility, honesty, and other such attributes. Yet they curse, slander, and scold one another, not taking it as any sin, although the Lord God, through Moses, expressly forbad that. Since they do not consider it a sin to carry on in such a way amongst themselves, how much less do they hesitate to insult a Christian in various similar ways, as daily experience teaches.[47]

Two other works that need to be mentioned here are *Kurtze und gründliche Anweisung zur Teutsch-Jüdischen Sprache* (Brief and thorough instruction in the German-Jewish language; 1733) by the pseudonymous PhilogLottus, and *Jüdischer Sprach-Meister, oder Hebräisch-Teutsches Wörter-Buch* (Jewish language master/tutor, or Hebrew-German dictionary; 1742) by a certain Bibliophilus.[48] Recommending his Yiddish-German dictionary as an easy instruction to the expressions Jews use among themselves in their "*Hebräisch-Juden-Teutsch*," Bibliophilus elaborates on the usefulness of such knowledge for Christians. One of the main benefits he stresses is that such knowledge would enable Christians to understand what the Jews say about them in their presence, or indeed straight to their faces, safely encrypted in the form of an unintelligible language. In a special appendix, "Of the Jews' sacrileges and blasphemies against Christ our Savior, his Holy Mother, and against all Christians," Bibliophilus provides various examples to illustrate this point; many of them, as he notes, are from his personal experience. He mentions for instance that the Jews refer to a Christian as *Sched*, which he translates as *Teufel* (demon). Thus they "greet" Christians with the words "*sched willkomm*" (welcome, demon) instead of "*seyd willkomm*" (welcome).[49] Another derogatory term the Jews use to denote a Christian, according to Bibliophilus, is *Kelef* (dog). Bibliophilus tells us that he once visited a house of a Christian where two Jews were also present. Upon his arrival one Jew said to the other, "*Diesen Kelef habe ich haijom auch schon in dem Mokom geroenet*, that is I have already seen this dog today in town."[50] The Jews' language, in other words, did not only reflect their duplicity and cunning but also served as an avenue for communicating anti-Christian feelings of animosity and contempt to other Jews present, without running the risk of exposing these feelings to their Christian interlocutor.

The overt and covert anti-Christian elements embedded in early modern literary and spoken Yiddish can be interpreted as a defensive strategy, intended to protect the Jewish community from the influence of Christianity. In a reality in which converting to the dominant Christian religion and culture was not only an ever-present option but actively advocated by Christian missionaries, it is perhaps not surprising that the Jewish minority developed internal resistance mechanisms to maintain its existence as a distinct group.[51] One way of achieving this goal was via a "counter-conversion literature"—polemical works in Yiddish intended to strengthen common Jews in the Jewish faith, and in some cases even equip them with adequate answers to Christian polemics. Another means was the *lehavdl loshn* vocabulary found in early modern spoken and written Yiddish. This defensive mechanism seems to have been especially effective in its oral version: in every utterance regarding Christians and Christianity the Jewish speaker in fact reasserted the demarcating line between himself as a Jew and the non-Jewish surroundings, both for himself and for his Jewish audience. The fact that the Hebrew component is so strongly represented in the *lehavdl loshn* vocabulary is of special importance in this respect, and not only for suggesting that the language of differentiation was intended to be concealed.[52] By referring to Christian persons and entities in words derived from the Hebraic rather than the Germanic component of Yiddish, the Jewish speaker was demonstrating his own solidarity with the Jewish community, while distancing himself from the Christian subject of his speech. The differentiation, in other words, was achieved already by the speaker's choice of linguistic source, in addition to the derogatory semantic of the designations he used.

The impression conveyed by the Christian sources, however, is that the authors did not perceive the Jews' hidden transcript as stemming merely from the wish of the Jewish minority to distinguish itself from its non-Jewish surroundings and maintain its separate existence, or even from the need of Jewish speakers to give vent to their emotions and attitudes. Rather, the overall presentation is one of an outright Jewish attack on Christian religion and society, stemming from a deep and indelible hatred of the Jews toward Christians and Christianity. The choice of the Christian authors to present Jewish oral and literary culture as a menacing threat to the Christian social and religious order may have resulted from the wish of the authors to sensationalize the more latent elements of Ashkenazi Jewish culture. Having promised to "expose" the hidden layers of Jewish culture to their readers, they now had to make good on their promise. Another possibility is that the authors were in fact right to view the anti-Christian insults and curses in Yiddish culture as nothing short of deliberate acts of aggression, meant to actively, even physically offend their Christian objects. Recent scholarship on premodern Jewish-Christian relations has already suggested that deep hatred of Christianity and anticipation of its total destruction constituted a central feature of Jewish-Ashkenazi religious ideology, even before—and long after—the atrocities of 1096.[53] According to medieval historian Israel Yuval, the curses against the Christians that were integrated into Ashkenazi chronicles and liturgical texts should not be seen simply as a spontaneous emotional response to actions taken by the Christians toward the Jews, but as a manifestation of a full-fledged messianic doctrine, in which the motif of vengeance against the Gentiles takes center stage.[54]

Given the long tradition of hostility to Christianity among Ashkenazi Jewry and the fact that Christian scholars were well aware of this tradition, it is probably no wonder that the latter were highly suspicious of all literary and oral manifestations of Jewish-Ashkenazi culture, including those in the vernacular. But even if one is reluctant to view the anti-Christian elements in Yiddish culture as resulting from a religious ideology of animosity and vengeance, one should not underestimate the strong—and highly negative—impression they must have made on Christians at that time. As studies on swearing and cursing in early modern Europe have demonstrated, this kind of verbal act, "which will probably seem trivial to most readers now was taken very seriously indeed by contemporaries."[55] With the understanding of language as being no less forceful than action itself, these acts did not merely signify a "breach of decorum" or a general lack of culture on the side of the swearer, but were viewed as possessing the power to undermine social, political, and religious institutions. Offensive language was perhaps the "weapon of the weak," but it was nonetheless a weapon, and the aggressiveness it communicated as well as the damage it was believed to invoke were perceived as a real, tangible threat to mainstream society.

The anxiety about the subversive power of language resulted in recurring attempts of early modern rulers and legislators to discipline the tongue, especially in cases of insults by inferiors to their social superiors and of blasphemies against God and the church. The courts, writes Peter Burke in a study on foul language in early modern Italy, took such cases very seriously "and expended a good deal of effort on what we might call 'mere words,'" treating them as deliberate acts of aggression rather than as "symptoms of chronic badmouth."[56] Both verbal offenses, that of blasphemy and that of insults up the social ladder, were closely associated with political crimes such as treason and sedition, and were believed to endanger the unity and stability of society. The religious offense of blasphemy in particular carried with it a grave transgression, since it implicated the entire community and not just the blasphemous person. It was therefore viewed as an even greater threat due to the fear of divine punishment to society as a whole.[57] Given the status of the Jews in early modern Germany both as a subordinate minority and as the adherents of a religion that refused to recognize and accept Christianity as the true faith, it is perhaps not surprising that the anti-Christian expressions embedded in their vernacular were encountered with such vehemence on the side of Christian authors, who perceived such expressions both as blasphemous and as dangerous acts of resistance and insubordination on the part of the Jewish minority.

Four *Ancilla theologiae*

Yiddish as a *Hilfsmittel* for Theological Studies

The motivations for Christian interest in Yiddish discussed so far should be seen as part of Protestant concern with Jews and Judaism in the German lands. Another consideration relates to the Protestant ambition to utilize the language for intra-Christian purposes, specifically for supporting theologians in their study of Hebrew and the biblical text. An accurate reading and understanding of the Hebrew Bible was central to Protestant theology, but mastery of Hebrew and deep understanding of the biblical text were not easy to acquire, particularly as Protestant scholars strove to achieve these goals without the mediation of Jews.[1] For Christian Hebraists, who looked for ways to assist their coreligionists in these difficult tasks, Yiddish came in very handy, for several reasons.

Hebrew via Yiddish

The fact that Yiddish is composed of both Hebrew and German gave rise to the rather odd pedagogical notion that it could serve German-speaking Christians as an aid, or *Hilfsmittel*, for learning Hebrew.[2] The Reformer and Hebrew professor Paulus Fagius, for example, encouraged the study of Yiddish among his students, not as an aim in itself, as he himself noted, but as a linguistic intermediary between German and Hebrew in order to facilitate their study of the holy tongue.[3] In 1543 in the city of Constance, Fagius published the first four chapters of Genesis in Hebrew, with a facing Yiddish translation, for the benefit of his students who did not possess a Hebrew Bible. In the introduction to this work, Fagius made clear that he attached the "Jewish-German translation [*germanica Iudaeorum interpretatione*], so that they would easily and clearly learn and understand not the method of reading Jewish-German, but the Hebraisms of the Holy language. And also because this effort seemed to some . . . in this way to assist the study of the Hebrew language."[4]

Two centuries later, Yiddish was still considered a useful bridge to learning Hebrew. Among his reasons for Christians to learn Yiddish, eighteenth-century Christian Hebraist Wilhelm Chrysander included the fact that it contained many Hebrew words and expressions and could therefore serve as "a continuing recitation of the Hebrew [language]."[5] Another reason noted by Chrysander was that learning Yiddish would enable Christians to read Hebrew manuscripts written with "Jewish-German letters."[6] Here Chrysander was in fact repeating a notion advocated at the beginning of the seventeenth century by the great Christian Hebraist Johann Buxtorf. In the dedication epistle to his highly influential *Thesaurus grammaticus linguae sanctae hebraeae* (Grammar of the holy Hebrew tongue; Basel 1609), Buxtorf mentioned this point as one of the main reasons for the inclusion of a tutorial on Yiddish in the work, stressing that "I examine the method and use of Hebrew-German [that is, Yiddish] script not merely for the sake of books written among the Jews in the German [Yiddish] language, but rather because older Hebrew manuscripts use practically the same script." Buxtorf reemphasized this goal at the beginning of the appendix on Yiddish, where he explained that many of the older Hebrew manuscripts, which contained "many esoteric things that would without doubt cast special light on Hebrew history," were not written in the biblical square script but rather in "German characters," that is the Ashkenazi semicursive, the same one that served for writing Yiddish.[7] Promoting the knowledge of the Yiddish script among Christian scholars was therefore a prerequisite for gaining access to many Jewish secrets and mysteries, which according to Buxtorf were still waiting to be unveiled.

Central to the idea that Yiddish could ease the difficult task of learning Hebrew was, on the one hand, the recognition that both languages share an alphabet and a sizeable amount of vocabulary, and on the other hand, the assertion that for anyone who knew German, Yiddish was much easier to learn than Hebrew.[8] Another, quite original argument supporting the "Hebrew via Yiddish" method is found in an anony-

בראשית

בראשית

Figure 4.1. First page of Paulus Fagius' *Prima quatuor capita Geneseos hebraice* (Constance 1543)

mous work from 1733, entitled *Kurtze und gründliche Anweisung zur Teutsch-Jüdischen Sprache*.[9] Elaborating on the benefits of Yiddish for the *Studiosis Theologiae*, the pseudonymous author, "PhilogLottus," focused on the idea that Yiddish can serve "as an aid [*Hülffs-Mittel*] to supplement the Holy Tongue."[10] Like his predecessors, he explained it by pointing to the linguistic affinity between the two languages, but also to what he considered to be the "entertaining effect" of Yiddish. As noted in a previous chapter, Yiddish literature was often considered by Christians to be highly amusing, not only for its content but to a large extent for the language in which it was written. Johann Wagenseil, for instance, noted with regard to the Yiddish historical poem *Das Vintz Hanß Lied* that because of its "peculiar turns of speech" (*seltsamen Red-Arten*) this poem would arouse "more laughter than pity" among Christian readers; whereas the anonymous author J.W. recommended a Jewish dialogue in Yiddish that he had published "first of all for pleasure, due to the ridiculous turns of speech, which are in vogue among the Jews."[11] As far as PhilogLottus was concerned, the "amusing quality" of the Yiddish language made it all the more adequate to supporting the study of Hebrew, as it could insert a "playful" (*spielend*) element into an otherwise tedious and difficult task. "The dead languages," according to PhilogLottus, "are very difficult to learn and to memorize, and the Hebrew is no exception. Here the Jewish [language; that is, Yiddish] can make a good contribution. Since it sounds somewhat ridiculous, one reads some pages with delight in idle hours, and thus internalizes it better, and much livelier, than what one studies with much trouble and all the much too artificial rules."[12]

Illuminating the Biblical Text: Yiddish Lexicographical Tradition

Knowledge of the Yiddish language and literature was further recommended to the *Herren Theologis* for illuminating difficult words and obscure passages (*dunckeln Orten*, *loca obscuriora*) in the Hebrew Bible. For Christian and especially Protestant Hebraists, who "considered the Bible to be the 'effective cause' of the Christian faith, preoccupation with the individual words of the Hebrew Bible was a significant philological task with important theological ramifications,"[13] and many of them did not hesitate to turn to Jewish sources for guidance and assistance. For the most part, these included the works of the great Jewish grammarians and commentators of the Middle Ages, such as David Kimhi, Rashi, and Abraham ibn Ezra. But Yiddish literature apparently was not considered a bad option either.

The practice of using Yiddish as an aid for the study of the Hebrew Bible was common among Ashkenazi Jews already during the Middle Ages. Closely connected to the teaching method of the *kheyder* (religious primary school for Jewish boys), the oral tradition of explaining Hebrew religious texts by giving a Yiddish equivalent for each successive word took the form, in its early written stages, of Yiddish glosses in Hebrew manuscripts, intended to clarify difficult terms in the biblical text and the commentaries. As Yiddish scholar Jean Baumgarten explains, "the Yiddish glosses are found interlinear (above the line), between the columns of the folio manuscript, or in the margins. . . . In addition to word definitions, there are also explanations of entire phrases, interpretive glosses, and aggadic commentary, which constitute the earliest traces of biblical commentary in Yiddish."[14] In the course of the sixteenth century, the medieval tradition of Yiddish glosses further developed with the publication of printed glossaries, concordances, and biblical lexicons. Here one should note *Mirkeves ha-mishne* of Rabbi Anshel, a Hebrew-Yiddish biblical concordance first published in Cracow around 1534[15]; and the two biblical dictionaries by Moses ben Issachar Sertels: *Seyfer be'eyr Moyshe* (Prague 1604–5), which includes terms from the Pentateuch, and *Seyfer lekakh tov* (Prague 1604), which includes terms from the Prophets and Hagiographical books.[16]

Christian Hebraists drew upon the existing lexical apparatus in Yiddish, originally prepared by Jewish authors for the Jewish reading public, for their own purpose of reaching a deeper understanding of the Hebrew Bible text. Sebastian Münster, the most important Christian Hebraist in the first half of the sixteenth century and one of the earliest Christian Yiddishists,[17] incorporated Yiddish translations, labeled as "the Jews say" (*Iudaei dicunt*) or "in German" (*Germanice*), in his Hebrew and Aramaic dictionaries in order to better illuminate the meaning of certain words. Münster acknowledged that he had borrowed the Yiddish words from two Jewish manuscripts: a fourteenth-century German-Jewish version of *Arukh*, an Aramaic dictionary composed in Rome around 1100 by Rabbi Nathan ben Yehiel, which included Yiddish glosses; and a Yiddish translation of the Bible attributed to a certain Rabbi Shlomo, of which we have no further information.[18] Already before Münster, Johannes Reuchlin, the father of Christian Hebraism in the German lands, was also well acquainted with the Jewish tradition of Yiddish glosses. He had two volumes of biblical manuscripts in his possession, in which the difficult Hebrew words were rendered in Yiddish. Yiddish translations of the definitions and explanations were also included in the first Hebrew book he is known to have acquired—a medieval Hebrew lexicon that one of his teachers, a certain "Calman the Jew," copied for him in 1486. Together with the Hebraist Conrad Pellikan, Reuchlin translated into Latin the *Kleyne orukh* of Asher ben Jacob Halevi, a fourteenth-century abridged dictionary of terms from the Talmud that included Yiddish glosses.[19]

Seventeenth-century Christian Hebraists continued to use Yiddish lexical treatises in their own works, a practice they explicitly recommended their readers to follow. "To the *Herren Theologis*," wrote Johann Wagenseil in the introduction to his *Belehrung der Jüdisch-*

Teutschen Red- und Schreibart, "the expertness in the German-Hebrew dialect would prove very beneficial, and would give them a good instruction, [how] to correctly interpret many obscure expressions and difficult words that are found in the Hebrew Scriptures of the Old Testament." Noting himself as an example, Wagenseil explained that whenever he came across an obscure word or phrase in the Hebrew Bible, he first consulted the book *Be'eyr Moyshe*, "which explains in German [Yiddish] all the obscure expressions and difficult Hebrew words, chapter through chapter."[20] Johann Buxtorf, one of the most important authorities on Hebrew education in the seventeenth and eighteenth centuries, also recommended Yiddish biblical dictionaries such as *Seyfer be'eyr Moyshe* and *Seyfer lekakh tov* as "a book not unprofitable for Germans" (*Liber non inutilis Germanis*), drawing on this genre in his own work.[21]

If Yiddish translations of Hebrew words were considered valuable for providing Christians with a relatively easy and convenient access to the Jewish understanding of the biblical text, they were also considered valuable because of the linguistic affinity between Yiddish and Hebrew. As the eighteenth-century author PhilogLottus rightly noted, Christian scholars at that time considered what was termed "Oriental languages" a useful tool for biblical philology and exegesis. In addition to Hebrew, the group of Oriental languages included mainly Aramaic, Syriac, and Arabic. The underlying assumption was that since these languages were related to Hebrew, they could assist the reader in correctly translating and interpreting difficult words in the Hebrew text.[22] This practice, the author asserted, was indeed very beneficial; but using Yiddish for this very purpose would be of even greater utility. After all, he claimed, Yiddish was "a daughter of Hebrew" (*eine Tochter der Ebräischen*), and hence especially suitable to fulfill this important function.[23]

Illuminating the Biblical Text: Yiddish Translations and Commentaries

In addition to the Yiddish lexicographical tradition of biblical glosses and dictionaries, the centuries-old Jewish practice of explaining every word of the holy text through a Yiddish equivalent gave rise to another

Ashkenazi literary tradition—the so-called *taytsh-khumesh*, a literal translation of the Bible, in which a Yiddish word or phrase literally translates each corresponding word or phrase in the Hebrew original.[24] Christian Hebraists and theologians were usually very keen on sharply criticizing Yiddish biblical translations for their strict adherence to the literal meaning of the text, and condemned them as "Jewish superstition."[25] However, it was precisely this method of word-for-word translation that made biblical texts in Yiddish highly valuable to the very same Hebraists and theologians, who used them for gaining an accurate understanding of the literal sense of the Hebrew text. Thus, despite the fundamental bias against them, Yiddish translations of the Hebrew Bible were nonetheless recommended to Christians as useful tools for clarifying difficult words and passages in the holy text; and where nothing better could be found, as substitutes for Hebrew dictionaries and lexicons.[26]

An example of this ambivalence can be found in the words of Christian Hebraist Elias Schadeus at the end of his Yiddish tutorial from 1592. Referring to the fact that "how the Jews otherwise translate, namely word-for-word, is found in a number of books printed in German [Yiddish]," Schadeus mentions his plan to publish a Yiddish version of the book of Job, "translated word-for-word by the learned and experienced Rabbi Elia Levita." However, as Schadeus immediately makes clear, this is "not so much for the sake of Jewish translation as for the many passages and words in that text that are difficult to understand."[27]

Of course, not all Jewish biblical translators could be trusted as much as the great Hebrew grammarian Elia Levita. The Yiddish Bible of Jekuthiel Blitz (Amsterdam 1676–79), for example, was sharply criticized by Christian scholars, not only for integrating alleged blasphemy and anti-Christian polemic into the translation but also for distorting words, phrases, and even entire verses in the holy text.[28] No wonder, therefore, that Blitz's version was not considered useful for Christians for better understanding the literal meaning of the biblical text, but rather only as a means to get familiar with the "distortions and evasions" (*Verdrehungen und Ausflüchte*) of the Jews.[29] In some cases, general skepticism was expressed as to whether the Jews were at all capable of producing a decent literal translation of the Bible. Eighteenth-century author Johann Christoph Bodenschatz, for example, claimed in his *Kirchliche Verfassung der heutigen Juden* (The religious condition of contemporary Jews) from 1749 that due to insufficient proficiency in the Hebrew language,

> only very few [Jews] know their Bible well, can read it and . . . translate it into German . . . , but without the slightest thoroughness, and even less so with any minimal skill. Of the [Hebrew] Grammar very few among them have any knowledge, through which they could have been in a position to translate the Hebrew words according to their true meaning, and even less to pronounce judgment upon such matters.[30]

Better received among Christians was the Yiddish Bible of Joseph ben Alexander Witzenhausen, published by Joseph Athias in Amsterdam in 1679 (with a second edition in 1687), the same year as the translation of Jekuthiel Blitz. Although Witzenhausen's translation, too, came under Christian attack for allegedly incorporating Jewish apologetics into the text and deviating from the meaning of the words in places that bear witness to the coming of Christ,[31] it was usually taken by Christian scholars to be much more agreeable than the one by Blitz in that it contained, in their eyes, much fewer instances of blasphemy and anti-Christian polemics. After vehemently condemning Blitz's Bible, Johann Schudt noted that "a much more honest [*redlicher*] and better Jewish-German translation of the Old Testament is that of *R. Joseph Josel* Witzenhuisen [*sic*], . . . in which neither such sinister glosses nor such distortion of the text are to be found." In a marked contrast to his condemnations of the version of Blitz, the anonymous author of the literary journal *Nachrichten von einer Hallischen Bibliothek* (1749) also provides a fairly neutral description of Witzenhausen's translation, recommending it "to understand the Bible's literal meaning [*Wortverstand*]."[32] Other authors noted the relative similarity of Witzenhausen's translation to Luther's German version as an indication of its good quality.[33]

All these considerations led theologians to view Witzenhausen's translation as a reliable aid for students of theology. This view was clearly expressed in 1711, when Witzenhausen's Yiddish Bible was transcribed with Latin characters and republished in the *Biblia Pentapla*, a collection of five Germanic translations of Scripture: Catholic, Lutheran, Reformed, Jewish (Yiddish), and Dutch. Published in the outskirts of Hamburg by the radical Pietists Johann Otto Glüsing and Hermann Heinrich Holle, this work gained popularity in eighteenth-century Pietistic and enlight-

Schöpfung der Welt samt allem was drinnen ist. (1)

Das erste Buch Mosis / genant GENESIS.

Catholische Ubersetzung.

Das 1. Capitel.

IM Anfang hat GOtt den Himmel und die Erden erschaffen. Act. 14/15. 17/4. Ps. 32/6. 135. 5. Eccl. 18/ 1. Hebr. 11/3.

2. Aber die Erde war ungestalt und öde/ und Finsterniß war über dem Abgrund/ und der Geist Gottes schwebet über den Wassern.
3. Und GOtt sprach: Es werde das Licht/ und das Licht ist worden.
4. Und GOtt sahe das Licht/ daß es gut war/ und scheidet das Licht von der Finsterniß.
5. Und nennet das Licht Tag/ und die Finsterniß/ Nacht; und es war Abend und Morgen/ ein Tag.

6. Und GOtt sprach: Es werde ein Firmament zwischen den Wassern/ und scheide die Wasser von den Wassern.

7. Und GOtt machet das Firmament/ und scheidet die Wasser/ so unter dem Firmament waren/ von denen/ die über dem Firmament waren. Und das geschah also. Ps. 135/ 2. 5.

Lutherische Ubersetzung.

Das 1. Capitel.

AM Anfang* schuff GOtt † Himmel und Erden ‡. * Johan. 1/1. † Psal. 33/6. Psal. 102/26. ‡ Col. 1/16. Ebr. 1/10. c. 11/3

2. Und die Erde war wüste und leer/ und es war finster auf der Tieffe / und der Geist Gottes schwebete auf dem Wasser.

3. Und GOtt sprach: Es werde licht. Und es ward licht *. * 2 Cor. 4/ 6.
4. Und GOtt sahe/ daß das Licht gut war. Da scheidete GOtt das Licht von der Finsterniß †. * Jesa. 45/ 7.
5. Und nennete das Licht Tag / und die Finsterniß Nacht. Da ward aus Abend und Morgen der erste Tag.

6. Und GOtt sprach: Es werde eine Feste zwischen den Wassern / und die sey ein Unterscheid zwischen den Wassern.

7. Da machte GOtt die Feste * / und scheidete das Wasser unter der Festen/ von dem Wasser über der Festen †. Und es geschach also. * Ps. 104/2. Ps. 136/5. Jer. 10/12. 51/15. † Psal. 148/4.

Reformirte Ubersetzung.

Das 1. Cap.

IM Anfang * schuf GOtt den Himmel und die Erde. * Joh. 1/1. Col. 1/16. Ps. 90/ 2. und 136/5. und 89/ 12. Actor. 14/15. und 17/24. Hebr. 11/3.
2. Die Erde aber war öd und leer; und es war finster oben auff dem Abgrund; und der Geist Gottes schwebete oben über dem Gewässer.
3. Da sprach GOtt: Es werde ein Licht; und es ward ein Licht *. * Psal. 33/6. 9.
4. Und GOtt sahe/ daß dasselbe Licht gut war; Und GOtt machet eine * Scheidung zwischen dem Licht/ und der Finsterniß. * Unterscheid.
5. Da nennet GOtt dasselbe Licht Tag/ die Finsterniß aber nennet er Nacht. Also ward es Abend / darnach ward es auch Morgen/ der erste Tag.
6. Darnach sprach GOtt/ * Es werde eine Ausdehnung zwischen den Wassern/ auf daß sie unterscheide zwischen beyderley Wassern. * Jer. 10/12. u. 81/15.

7. Also machet GOtt die Ausdehnung/ welche unterscheidet zwischē den * Wassern/ die unter der Ausdehnung seynd / und den Wassern/ die über der Ausdehnung seynd; und es geschahe also. * Ps. 148/4. u. 33/9.

A

Jüdische Ubersetzung.

Das 1. Capitul.

IN dem Anfang hat Gott beschaffen · die Himmel und die Erd:
2 Und die Erd is gewesen wüst und lehr/ und Finsternis auf dem Abgrund · und die Nevuah (Aushauchung) von Gott schwebet über dem Wassern:
3 Und Gott sprach/ es sol Licht seyn · und es war Licht:
4 Und Gott sach das Licht/ daß es gut war · und Gott machet ein Unterscheid zwischen dem Licht und zwischen der Finsternis:
5 Und Gott hies (rieff) zu dem Licht / Tag/ und zu der Finsternis hies (rieff) er/ Nacht · und es war Abent/ und es war Morgen / ein Tag:
6 Und Gott sprach/ es sol eine Spreitung seyn zwischen dem Wassern · und es sol ein Unterscheid machen zwischen dem [untersten] Wassern/ und dem [übersten] Wassern:
7 Und Gott machet die Aus-Spreitung / und er machet Unterscheiden zwischen dem Wassern / die da waren von unten zu der Aus-spreitung / und zwischen dem Wassern/ die da waren von oben zu der Aus-Spreitung · und es

Holländische Ubersetzung.

Het eerste Capittel.

IN den Beginne * schiep Godt den Hemel / ende de Aerde. * Job. 38/4. Psal. 33/6. ende 89. 12. ende 136/5. Actor. 14/15. ende 17/24. Heb. 11/3.
2. De Aerde nu was woest ende ledigh/ ende Duysternisse was op den Afgront: ende de Geest Godts sweefde op de Wateren.

3. Ende Godt seyde/ Daer zy Licht: eñ daer wert Licht.
4. Ende Godt sagh het Licht/ dat het goet was: ende Godt maeckte Scheydinge tusschen het Licht/ ende tusschen de Duysternisse.
5. Ende Godt noemde het Licht Dagh / ende de Duysternisse noemde hy Nacht: doe was het Avont geweest/ ende het was Morgen geweest/ de eerste Dagh.
6. Ende Godt seyde / * Daer zy een Uytspansel in 't Midden der Wateren: ende dat make Scheydinge tusschen Wateren ende Wateren. * Psal. 33/6. ende 104/ 2. ende 136/5. Prov. 8/28. Jes. 42/5. Jer. 10/12. ende 51/ 15.
7. Ende Godt maeckte dat Uytspansel: ende maeckte Scheydinge tusschen de Wateren die onder † het Uytspansel zijn / ende tusschen de Wateren die boven ‡ het Uytspansel zijn: ende het was alsoo. † Psal. 33/7. ende 136/6. Prov. 8/28. ‡ Psal. 148/4.

Figure 4.2. First page of the *Biblia Pentapla* (Wandsbeck and Schiffbeck 1710–12). The Jewish translation is from the Yiddish Bible published by Joseph Athias (Amsterdam 2nd ed. 1687).

ened circles and could be found in libraries of noblemen and scholars alike.[34] In the introduction to the work, Glüsing explains that, by arranging the five translations side by side, in five parallel columns, he wishes to offer "the Christian student of the Scriptures" a useful instrument for a closer study of the holy text. The publishers maintain that not all translations are of the same quality, and some are clearly better than the others; yet every one of them is useful, as it can illuminate and clarify the others through the method of comparison.[35]

Despite the relatively ecumenical spirit of these words, Glüsing is very well aware how problematic the inclusion of a Jewish translation in a Christian Bible in fact is. As a *Jewish* version, he asserts, it is "still covered with Moses' veil" (*noch mit der Decke Mosis beleget*)—it is directed by rabbinical precepts and incorporates Jewish theological interpretations. However, as far as the *literal understanding* of the text is concerned, the "Jewish-German" translation proves very useful. Indeed, Glüsing admits, this translation "often deviates from the true literal understanding when it comes to the Messiah or Christ," but in most other places it "perfectly well illuminates the Hebrew text" and can therefore render important service to the "investigation of the actual sense of the obscure passages in the Hebrew fundamental text." After all, the author concludes, "most of our scholarship and speculations in the Hebrew language originally derives from the Jews, whose mother tongue it once was; hence many celebrated Doctors of the Church [*Kirchen-Lehrer*] in old and new times were not ashamed either, to be in this respect disciples of the Jews."[36]

Probably expecting objection even in the face of such well founded arguments, Glüsing further justifies the republication of the Yiddish Bible by appeal to authority, assuring his readers that the Yiddish Bible is appreciated and used among scholars of the first rank. As an example he refers to Johann Wagenseil, "who is for many [people] a distinguished man in the Hebrew tongue," citing from the latter's *Belehrung* the part where Wagenseil introduces his own methods for overcoming difficult passages in the Hebrew Bible.[37] In addition to consulting Yiddish biblical lexicons, Wagenseil explains that he also examines biblical translations and interpretations in Yiddish and other languages, such as Aramaic, Greek, and Latin, so as to achieve an accurate literal understanding of the text. But, he notes, it is usually the case "that the

Jewish-German translation of the words and interpretation of a saying is more beneficial for me than all remaining aids, and that I remain with this [translation]: how it then gives word for word, as clear as it can only be, regardless whether it sounds well or foul in the German language."[38] In another instance, Wagenseil notes this point as a reason for his translation of the Yiddish Psalms into German, explaining that this Yiddish work "would serve some as a good instruction to better understand the obscure passages and to come closer to the literal understanding of the text."[39]

While Glüsing concentrated on the biblical text itself, Wagenseil, the experienced Hebraist, was well aware of the benefit one could gain from consulting Jewish commentaries on the holy text, in addition to its various translations. But Wagenseil was also aware how difficult these commentaries could be for anyone not highly proficient in Hebrew and in rabbinic textual tradition. Therefore, for Christian students desiring to get to know the great Jewish commentators, Wagenseil warmly recommended starting from the Yiddish translations and adaptations of such commentaries found in the Yiddish Bible, and especially in the genre of Yiddish homiletic prose.[40] One example mentioned by Wagenseil is *Seyfer ha-magid* (Lublin 1623, with many later editions), a translation of the Prophets and the Hagiography with a paraphrase of Rashi's commentary. Another is the *Tsene-rene*, an adaptation of the Pentateuch, the five scrolls, and the haftarot, supplemented and expounded by numerous interpretations from a broad range of Jewish sources, such as midrashic legends and medieval commentaries, which had themselves been extensively adapted to the taste and common level of Yiddish readership. Given their intended audience of simple Jewish men and women, who did not have sufficient knowledge of the Hebrew language and textual tradition, these works clarified the complexities of the biblical text in a lucid, simplified manner and offered an easy access to the work of primary Jewish commentators. These characteristics of popular homiletic literature in Yiddish made it an easy target for Christian scholars, who denounced it as foolish and risible. At the same time, Christian Hebraists could not deny that it was precisely these characteristics that made this literature a useful pedagogical tool for the study of the Hebrew Bible, not only for a Jewish audience but for a Christian one as well.

Conclusion

The Study of Yiddish and Christian-Jewish Relations in Early Modern Germany

The foregoing chapter attempts to analyze the place of Yiddish studies in the theological work of Christian, especially Protestant, scholars—theologians, Hebraists, and Orientalists—in early modern Germany. Subordinated to the theological needs and aims of these scholars, Yiddish studies were seen first and foremost as complementary to Hebrew and Aramaic studies, normally required for Protestant theologians in their attempt to scrutinize Jewish literature without Jewish assistance, and utilize it for Christian ends. In the case of Yiddish, however, non-scholarly purposes played a more important role. As demonstrated in the first three chapters, Protestant theologians could use their expertise in the Jewish language and its literature in order to fulfill their obligations in a confessional society, in which Jews constituted both a religious and a linguistic minority. Although theological in nature, these obligations also corresponded to a number of social and political needs in the Protestant German lands, such as the conducting of mission among the Jews, exposing and censoring presumed Jewish blasphemies, and strengthening the faith among ordinary Christians.

These two reasons for the involvement of Protestant scholars with Yiddish, namely to use Yiddish for conducting active mission among the Jews, and to obtain information about Jews and Judaism and expose Jewish blasphemies, mirror the two major tendencies in the early modern Protestant approach to Jews and Judaism in the German lands: the hope of converting the Jews, and the need to act against the dangers believed to be posed by them, especially through their blasphemies and anti-Christian propaganda. Both these tendencies were highlighted in the writings of Martin Luther on Jews and Judaism, and they remained decisive factors in Protestant thought and practice concerning the Jews throughout the early modern period.[1] Despite the inevitable tension between these two tendencies, they both express the same ambition: to control the Jews in the German lands, either in a defensive way, by supervising and censoring their publications, or in an active, if not an aggressive way, by trying to convert them. The fact that knowledge of Yiddish and acquaintance with its literature among Christians proved indispensable for both forms of control was acknowledged by early modern Protestant theologians and Hebraists, and played a crucial role in their efforts to promote interest in that language among their coreligionists.

Christian preoccupation with Yiddish, discussed in the previous chapters, reveals both the continuities and the changes in the early modern theological and cultural discourse on Jews and Judaism. On the one hand, proficiency in Yiddish provided Protestant scholars with new possibilities for the pursuit of older purposes, and their writings on this language served them as a new medium for promoting older ideas. On the other hand, the attention given to Yiddish attests to the broadening of Christian interest in Jews and Judaism in early modern Germany. While traditional interest was confined mainly to Jewish scholarly literature and to disputations with the Jewish rabbinical elite, the engagement with the Yiddish language and literature opened for Christian eyes the hitherto unexplored world of the wider circles of contemporary Jewish society. Together with the new genre of Christian ethnographies on Jewish customs and way of life, the interest in the Jews' everyday language shifted the focus of anti-Jewish polemic from disputes over canonical texts to the domestic and private sphere of contemporary Jewish life.[2] The Christian study of Yiddish thus significantly contributed to the domestication of the polemic against the Jews, and lent the discourse on Jews and Judaism a new dimension of actuality.

Seen from a Jewish perspective, the Christian discovery of Yiddish culture in early modern Germany functioned as a double-edged sword. By providing Christians with an important avenue for gaining better knowledge of and more intimate acquaintance with contemporary Jewish culture and society, Christian study of Yiddish played a considerable role in what historian R. Po-chia Hsia has called "the process of disenchantment" of Jews and Judaism, which took place in the German lands starting with the Reformation.[3] It served to diminish the frightening mystery hovering around the closed Jewish world, and allowed Christians to see Jews as mere human beings rather than diabolical magicians with demonic powers. Yet Christian proficiency in Yiddish also rendered more layers of Ashkenazi Jewish culture as subjects of the scrutiny and criticism of Christian scholars, who used their newly gained knowledge as further ammunition in their attack on Jewish culture and religion, drawing on Yiddish sources for presenting a distorted and disparaging picture of contemporary Judaism. In this sense, the knowledge Christians derived from Yiddish literary and oral culture did not lead to more toleration of the Jews but rather to a shift of focus in an ongoing anti-Jewish polemic: as far as the Christian scholars were concerned, contemporary Jewish culture was perhaps not demonic, but it was nonetheless superstitious, blasphemous, and saturated with hatred toward the Christian religion and its adherents.

Part II *Yiddish in the Service of Jewish Deception*

Introduction
Yiddish in the Socioeconomic Sphere

The new forms of intolerance of Jews that gradually replaced the late medieval obsession with ritual murder and desecration of the host went beyond the accusations of blasphemy and theological inferiority to include the more secular spheres of the Christian-Jewish encounter in early modern Germany. The danger posed by the Jews, it was argued, was not only theological but social and political as well.

In the socioeconomic discourse of early modern Germany, stereotypes of the Jew as a defrauder and a thief were common currency. To a large extent, these stereotypes drew on a generalized belief, rooted in Christian theology, that the Jew is innately and unalterably depraved. But they also resulted from the social reality of that time, in which considerable parts of the Jewish population operated in the margins of the economic order, belonged to the large underclass of vagrants and outcasts, and in some cases were actively involved in illegal activities. The socioeconomic discourse on the Jews thus reveals an interesting intersection between religious animosity and economic and social concerns. This was manifested, in particular, in the widespread notion that the alleged Jewish inclination towards fraud, deception, and other forms of criminal activity resulted not only from the Jews' will to gain economic profit but also from their wish to hurt Christians and Christian institutions, and to undermine the existing religious and socioeconomic orders.

As we shall see in the following chapters, discussions about Yiddish were not absent from the discourses on the economic and social place of the Jews in Christian society but played an important role in shaping Jewish stereotypes and perceptions in these areas, too. Specifically, Yiddish was associated with Jewish social and economic behavior on two interrelated levels: as the language of the Jewish merchant or businessman, often presented as conniving and fraudulent, and as the language of the Jewish criminal. Despite the differences between these two aspects of the socioeconomic discourse on Yiddish, they share two important characteristics. First, in both cases, Yiddish was ascribed an active role in the alleged deviant and antisocial behavior of the Jews, serving not only to conceal their illegal behavior but, even more so, as an indispensable means of executing their evil intentions. Second, despite its more secular character, the discourse on Yiddish as the language of Jewish commerce on the one hand and Jewish criminality on the other had strong theological underpinnings. This owes mainly to the stigmatization of Yiddish as a language of blasphemy and anti-Christian sentiments (discussed in Chapter 3), which was also prevalent in the discussions on the role of the Jewish language in the socioeconomic sphere. The discourse on Yiddish thus supported and reinforced the conjunction between social grievances and theological accusations that characterized the broader discourse on the place of the Jew in the socioeconomic sphere.

Alongside the theological and missionary writings on the Jewish language, the rich corpus on the place of Yiddish in the social and economic order presents an integral and substantial part of the discourse on Yiddish in early modern Germany. This literature encompassed a variety of genres and works—from "business Yiddish" manuals, to the presence of Yiddish in trickster narratives, and to outright criminological writings on the Jewish language. The image of Yiddish and its speakers that this literature constructed and propagated continued to inform the discussions on the Jewish language, as well as on the place of the Jew in German society, well into the twentieth century.

Five The Merchants' Tongue
Yiddish and Jewish Commerce

In addition to theologians and missionaries, Christians who had business interactions with Jews were also called to learn Yiddish. As Johann Wagenseil asserted in his *Belehrung der Jüdisch-Teutschen Red- und Schreibart* (1699), "Knowledge of the Jews' Hebrew-German [Yiddish] can be of great use also for merchants and businessmen, as well as for tradespeople, or otherwise for anyone who has dealings with Jews." Since the Jews "conduct their correspondence, write their promissory notes, [and] produce their receipts in no other [language] but this dialect, with Hebrew characters," Wagenseil argued, "it would be wise to know at least what the Jews write, and how to read their letters."[1] Half a century later, Wilhelm Chrysander repeated this idea in his *Unterricht vom Nutzen des Juden-Teutschen* (1750), where he stressed the importance of understanding spoken Yiddish, too, so that "one would understand the conversations of the Jews in trade and commerce, and in other dealings with Jews."[2]

From the beginning of the eighteenth century, the popular demand for a working knowledge of Yiddish gave rise to a new genre of self-study manuals of the Jewish language, intended primarily for merchants and businessmen. Written in German for a broad audience, these works aimed to teach basic Yiddish necessary for conducting business affairs. They offered their readers rudimentary grammatical instructions and elaborated lexicons, which focused on Hebraisms frequently used by Yiddish-speaking merchants. These included monetary terms, weights and measures, as well as other practical information useful for businessmen, such as the numeric system of the Hebrew alphabet and the Jewish way of counting the years. Most works also provided exercises in both the spoken and written language. These comprised samples of Jewish promissory notes written in Yiddish (or at least in German with Hebrew characters), including both printed and handwritten examples,[3] as well as model conversations in Yiddish with facing German translation. The conversations, between two Jewish businessmen or between a Jewish merchant and his Christian client, were written in Latin characters and demonstrated the Ashkenazi pronunciation of those Hebraisms incorporated in Yiddish.[4]

The earliest book of this type known to us is the *Elemental oder lesebuechlein* (Primer, or small reader; 1543), published by the convert Paul Helicz (also: Helic) in Hundesfeld near Breslau.[5] All other known business-oriented Yiddish manuals appeared only in the eighteenth century.[6] In 1731 Eberhard Carl Friedrich Oppenheimer published his *Hodegus ebraeo-rabbinicus*, a manual of commercial Yiddish very similar to Helicz's *Lesebuechlein*, but with more explicit anti-Jewish overtones and polemics. Three decades later, a *Kurze und gründliche Anleitung zu einer leichten Erlernung der Jüdischdeutschen Sprache* (A brief and thorough introduction to an easy learning of the Jewish-German language; 1767) was published by another convert, Gottfried Selig. This booklet quickly ran out of stock, and Selig published a second, revised and enlarged edition entitled *Lehrbuch zur gründlichen Erlernung der jüdischdeutschen Sprache* (Textbook to a thorough learning of the Jewish-German language; 1792). Perhaps unsurprisingly, both Oppenheimer's and Selig's works appeared in the city of Leipzig, an important center of commerce in eighteenth-century Germany. Together with Frankfurt am Main, Leipzig hosted international fairs and was visited by many Jewish merchants. Selig, lecturer for Hebrew at the city's university,[7] dedicated his *Anleitung* to the "highly esteemed businessmen of the city of Leipzig," the driving force behind the publication of the work, as he noted.

Among other popular works of "teach yourself Yiddish," most probably used by Christian businessmen though not only by them, one should note the convert Johann Adam Gottfried's *Anweisung zum Jüdischdeutschen* (Tübingen 1753); *Nützliches Handlexikon der jüdischen Sprache* (Prague 1773, with numerous following editions; first edition probably appeared before 1773), attributed to the Jesuit Leopold Thirsch, a Hebrew teacher and censor of Hebrew books; and Carl Wilhelm Friedrich's *Unterricht in der Judensprache und Schrift. Zum Gebrauch für Gelehrte und Ungelehrte* (Prentzlow 1784). This last work, again written by a convert, offers the first classification of Yiddish dialects and is considered "the finest practical manual of Yiddish."[8]

Some works of the "business Yiddish" genre addressed a more specialized audience, such as Wolf Ehrenfried von Reizenstein's *Der vollkommene Pferde-Kenner* (The complete horse expert; 1764). This manual for horse dealers includes a thirty-six-page appendix on the special variety of Yiddish spoken by Jewish practitioners of the trade. Also known as *Loshen Hakoudesh*, this occupational jargon differed from ordinary Yiddish in that it contained many technical terms of the profession, as well as a much higher proportion of Hebraisms. By deliberately using words of Hebrew origin instead of the German words usually employed in Yiddish, the Jewish horse traders created for themselves a kind of "secret language," unintelligible not only for non-Jews but also for most Jews outside the profession.[9] In his "Appendix, from which those expressions may be learned which the Jews make use of in their dealings with each other and especially at horse markets,"[10] von Reizenstein provided the Hebrew letters with their numerical value, an extensive Yiddish vocabulary in alphabetical order, and several dialogues relating to horse trading, with facing German translation.

One final group of writings that needs to be mentioned here is what came to be known as "anti-Semitic works on the Yiddish language," which aimed to "expose" Jewish blasphemies and anti-Christian abusive words, and in general ridiculed and denigrated the language.[11] Many of these works, including those of "J.W." (circa 1714), "PhilogLottus" (1733), and "Bibliophilus" (1742),[12] explicitly advertised themselves as manuals of "business Yiddish." They specifically addressed merchants and businessmen and included much of the usual apparatus characteristic of the genre.

That the genre of commercial Yiddish guides emerged only in the eighteenth century might be explained by the fact that in general, popular literature on Yiddish was essentially an eighteenth-century phenomenon. Together with the Yiddish missionary grammars and the anti-Semitic writings on the language, the business literature was indicative of a growing *popular* interest in Yiddish, as opposed to the more scholarly one of academic theologians and Hebraists. Already in 1689 the Christian Hebraist and pastor Heinrich Ammersbach explained in his tutorial chapter on Yiddish that similar instructions to the Jewish language already existed, such as those of Johann Buxtorf, Andreas

Sennert, and August Pfeiffer. But, he asserted, since such books serve only the needs of scholars and are not in everyone's possession, he decided to prepare this abridged instruction, which he designated for the broad public.[13] Similar indication of the popularization of knowledge of Yiddish among Christians is found in Johann Callenberg's Yiddish-German dictionary from 1736, where the author designated the work not only for theology students but for anyone who wished to read Yiddish books. The desire to read such books, Callenberg added, "can be found these days also among the uneducated."[14]

In the case of popular Yiddish guides for merchants, the emergence of the genre in the eighteenth century might also be related to the fact that trade vocabularies of other languages, too, were mainly published from this time onwards.[15] But the main motivation for the production of this literature undoubtedly came from the growing prominence of Jews in commerce in early modern Germany, a process that began in the late sixteenth century and intensified during the seventeenth and eighteenth centuries.

In the late sixteenth century, the focal point of Jewish economic activity in the German lands shifted from money lending, their main source of income during the late Middle Ages, to commerce. Excluded from the merchant guilds, as well as most crafts or the right to own land, Jews tended to concentrate in low-status forms of trade, on the margins of corporately protected commerce. These included peddling, pawnbroking, and dealing in sundries and second-hand goods. In addition, Jews traded in goods that were not subject to guild monopolies or that required connections abroad. Many Jews became horse and cattle dealers, while others specialized in luxury items, such as jewelry and precious fabrics. Money lending did not disappear altogether but became a secondary occupation and usually took the form of providing credit for commercial transactions.[16]

The increasing involvement of Jews in commerce, especially during the seventeenth and eighteenth centuries, brought them into more direct contact with their Christian neighbors. Instead of being primarily money borrowers, Christians had now also become customers and suppliers of the Jewish merchants. In the villages, the markets, and the annual fairs, Jews and Christians traded extensively with each other, turning commerce into the main scene of Christian-Jewish interaction.[17]

The prominent role of Jews in commerce, and with it the intensifying business relations between Jews and Christians, were duly noted by Christian contemporaries, including the authors of Yiddish manuals. In the opening to his *Kurze und gründliche Anleitung* (1767), convert Gottfried Selig explained the importance of having a working knowledge of Yiddish for businessmen in that "the Jewish-German language is particular to a nation that, as in the ancient times, so still today, plays an important part in business and commerce, and with whom those who practice commerce have the most dealings."[18] In the same vein, the pseudonymous author PhilogLottus recommended his Yiddish lexicon (1733) to businessmen and tradespeople, noting that any tradesman who extended his business even a bit would not be able to avoid dealing with Jews, at least from time to time.[19]

To be sure, Yiddish business manuals did not merely aim to facilitate commercial transactions between Jews and Christians. Another aim was explicitly promoted by the authors: to help Christians defend themselves in the face of Jewish deception. As Wilhelm Chrysander argued in 1750, "for merchants who do business with Jews and for all those who have dealings with Jews in society, the experience with Jewish-German [Yiddish] can be beneficial or even prevent damage . . . ; from their conversations which it is their practice to exchange openly with one another in their dialect, one can detect their thoughts, their malicious intentions, their true way of thinking . . . and so forth."[20] In pointing out the need for non-Jews to learn Yiddish, so that "one would not be deceived and taken in" (*man nicht betrogen und übervortheilet werde*),[21] the Christian authors were in fact reiterating the same notion that dominated the literature on Jewish blasphemies and anti-Christian expressions, namely the function of Yiddish as the Jews' "secret language."[22] According to this notion, the Jewish merchants' adherence to Yiddish exceeded practical convenience or even the legitimate desire to protect commercial information and keep business matters in confidence. Instead, it became a means for the intentional—and illegitimate—concealment of dishonest economic activities. The image of Yiddish as a secret language is thus extended from the religious domain into the more secular sphere of economic relations, presumably serving the Jews as a tool for hiding yet another aspect of their antisocial, pernicious behavior.

Exposing Jewish Deception: Yiddish in Trickster Narratives

The belief in an alleged Jewish inclination to fraud and deception was a prominent feature of the economic image of the Jew in early modern Europe. And as was usually the case with Jewish stereotypes, it had strong theological underpinnings. As Johann Schudt wrote in 1714, expressing a highly prevalent notion in contemporary discourse on Jews and Judaism:

> The artful deceptions of the Jews are manifold and countless, for there is no deception one can conceive, ever invented and used . . . that the Jews did not resort to, and still do on an everyday basis, as much as they possibly can. . . . For the Jews stand in the foolish persuasion, that the goods of other people, and especially of Christians, belong to them as the lawful masters of the world . . . most Jews believe, therefore, they are allowed to take for themselves such goods with cunning, defrauding and deceit, since the goods of all the heathens are *Hefker* [forfeit].[23]

Throughout its long history, the negative image of Jewish economic behavior was to a large extent the product of a generalized belief, rooted in Christian theology, in the innate, unalterable depravity of the Jews. Starting with the Gospels, this belief was nourished by the representation of Jews in Christian texts as the embodiment of materialism, shrewdness, and avarice. But economic anti-Semitism, to use Derek Penslar's term,[24] was also the product of social reality, reflecting broader anxieties and grievances about Jewish economic activity. During the early modern period, the concentration of Jews in the fields of pawnbroking and trade in second-hand goods, which often involved handling in forfeited pledges and stolen goods, contributed to the linkage between Jews and dishonest dealings. Moreover, the fact that Jews suffered from occupational confinements and were excluded from corporations and guilds led them to find different ways to practice trade, often seen as dishonorable and even fraudulent by Christian competitors. The prohibition on owning stores, for example, drove many Jews into peddling, which involved going directly to the customer and offering him the goods on his doorstep. This practice was very much resented by Christian shopkeepers, who viewed it as unfair and hence dishonest competition. The same was true with regard to the low prices offered by the Jews, who were not bound by guild regulations. Another prevalent complaint, demonstrating the way religious animosity coincided with economic grievances, related to the Jews' trading on Sundays and Christian holidays, which was perceived as devious as well as ungodly.[25]

As with other aspects of Jewish subversive behavior, such as blasphemous or otherwise anti-Christian practices, Jewish economic deception, and the role Yiddish played in it, had to be exposed, documented, and controlled. And in this case, too, converts from Judaism played a prominent role. Eager to prove their loyalty to Christian society by attacking their former coreligionists and at the same time position themselves as "experts" for both theological and social aspects of contemporary discourse on Judaism, converts significantly contributed to the image of Yiddish as the language of Jewish deception. While some converts published their own business manuals of Yiddish, others collected stories illustrating how Jews used Yiddish for business fraud. These stories, like the ones included in the works of seventeenth-century converts Dietrich Schwab and Samuel Friedrich Brenz,[26] served later authors as "proof" for their claims of Jewish deception and the necessity to learn Yiddish in order to fight it.

A prominent example in this respect is the *Jüdischer Sprach-Meister* (circa 1714), a bilingual Yiddish-German dialogue intended to teach Christians the spoken language of the Jews.[27] In the introduction, the convert J.W. reemphasizes the utility of knowing Yiddish for Christians who have commercial and other dealings with Jews. To illustrate this claim he tells a "true anecdote" (*ein wahrhafftiges Exempel*) about a Christian who inherits a collection of counterfeit jewels. After unsuccessful attempts to sell the jewels for a good price, he decides to try and sell them to a couple of Jews. Recognizing a precious stone among the false jewels, the Jews plot in Yiddish to steal it from the Christian. Convinced their conversation is unintelligible to the Christian, one Jew says to his friend (recounted by J.W. in Yiddish with a simultaneous German translation): "*M'lochen, daß du den zu dir lekeiechst*; that is: make so, that you take it [the precious stone] to yourself without being noticed," and later: "*M'lochen, daß ich den in der Jad bekum, eni will den ganffen*; that is: make so, that I get it in my hand, I want to bring it already without being noticed [that is, to steal it]."[28] Luckily enough, the Christian understands Yiddish from previous interactions with Jews and thus manages to take the precious stone before the Jews can carry out their deceitful intentions.

Another convert who substantially contributed to the discourse on Yiddish as the language of Jewish deception was Dietrich Schwab from Paderborn, the author of the influential work *Jüdischer Deckmantel* (1619). In the third part of his work, "About the Jews' finances and usury, which they apply when they come from the synagogue, in order to ruin the Christians," Schwab relates numerous stories of Jewish fraud in business dealings with Christians. In these stories, Yiddish stars as the language of Jewish conspiracy, as it constitutes one of the important tools the Jews use to deceive their non-Jewish neighbors. In one of the stories, repeated in many of the later works on this subject, a couple of Jews are engaged in a money transaction with a Christian. Planning their fraud in advance, one Jew says to the other: "*Er ist Lou Iodaea das Mees*, that is, he [the Christian] does not know the money, *man kan ihm wol Scheker ausse sein*, [that is] one can easily defraud him." After the Christian arrives and the Jews start calculating the amount to be paid, one of the Jews instructs his friend in Yiddish, in the presence of the Christian: "*sey ihm meiat messapper*, count too little [money] for him, or *sey ihm scheker ausse* [that is], defraud him."[29]

The genre discussing Yiddish with regard to Jewish economic behavior undoubtedly had a more secular character than the theological and missionary works on the language. But nonetheless, the intersection between religious and social accusations that dominated early modern discourse on Jewish economic behavior found expression in the works on Yiddish as well. In the trickster narratives, for instance, the anti-Christian character of Jewish deceit is emphasized by the derogatory remarks incorporated into the Jews' Yiddish conversations. Thus, for example, we hear that "*der Orl* [in another case: *der edom* (the Edomite)] *is tippisch*" (the uncircumcised is a fool); that "*Goi naeman is chasir kaschar*" (the most trustable Christian is a kosher pig); and that "*Ayn orl is mutt'r zu beganfen*" (it is allowed to steal from a non-Jew).[30] In his *Unterricht vom Nutzen des Juden-Teutschen* Wilhelm Chrysander warns his readers against the abusive words and slander the Jews allegedly use when their schemes fail to succeed. In this case, according to Chrysander, it is not unusual for a Jew to "wish" the Christian "*daß*

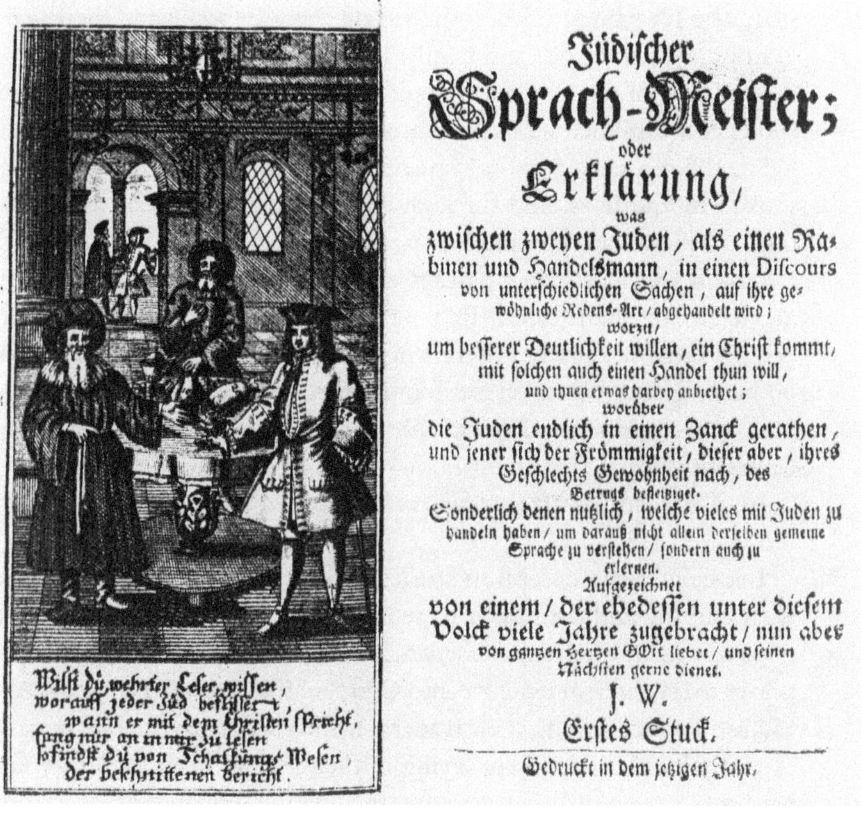

Wilst du, wehrter Leser, wissen,
worauff jeder Jüd beflissen,
wann er mit dem Christen spricht,
fang nur an in mir zu lesen
so findst du von Schachrungs Wesen,
der beschnittenen bericht.

Jüdischer
Sprach-Meister;
oder
Erklärung,
was
zwischen zweyen Juden, als einen Rabinen und Handelsmann, in einen Discours von unterschiedlichen Sachen, auf ihre gewöhnliche Redens-Art / abgehandelt wird;
worzu/
um besserer Deutlichkeit willen, ein Christ kommt, mit solchen auch einen Handel thun will, und ihnen etwas darbey anbiethet;
worüber
die Juden endlich in einen Zanck gerathen, und jener sich der Frömmigkeit, dieser aber, ihres Geschlechts Gewohnheit nach, des Betrugs befleissiget.
Sonderlich denen nützlich, welche vieles mit Juden zu handeln haben/ um darauß nicht allein derselben gemeine Sprache zu verstehen/ sondern auch zu erlernen.
Aufgezeichnet
von einem/ der ehedessen unter diesem Volck viele Jahre zugebracht/ nun aber von gantzen Hertzen GOtt liebet/ und seinen Nächsten gerne dienet.
J. W.
Erstes Stuck.

Gedruckt in dem jetzigen Jahr.

Figure 5.1. Title page of J.W.'s *Jüdischer Sprach-Meister* (ca. 1714)

dich die kinnim aufachlen" (that the lice will devour you), or to say to his Jewish friend, referring to the Christian, "*Die pegeira wäre gar jopha an ihm*" (the pestilence will suit him well).[31] The standard attacks on Jewish deception, in other words, are coupled in these stories with the charge that the Jews possess a "hidden transcript," through which they express their resentment of their fellow Christians.[32] Yiddish, the secret language of the Jews, is presented in these stories as the means both for deception and for expressing anti-Christian sentiments, thus contributing to the notion that Jewish deception is motivated not only by the Jews' will to gain economic profit but also by their hatred for non-Jews.

In some of these trickster tales the role of Yiddish is not confined to the act of deception. After successfully cheating a Christian, so runs the story, the Jews boast of their success on the way home and then again in front of their friends and family. Like the deception acts themselves, the boasting of the Jews and the supportive reactions of their admiring audience are imbued with anti-Christian overtones, which are transmitted to the reader in a twofold manner: via the medium of Yiddish, as spoken by the Jews, and through an accompanying German translation. An illuminating example is to be found in Johann Eisenmenger's *Entdecktes Judenthum* in a passage entitled "How the Jews boast their deceit among themselves." Relying on information from the convert Samuel Friedrich Brenz, Eisenmenger relates how the Jewish listeners, on hearing about a successful fraud, express their approval: "*man soll den Gojim das lef aus der nephesch lokeach seyn*, that is, one should take the Christians' hearts from their bodies [*sic*]." By cheating a Christian, we learn, the fraudulent Jew "*habe ein Korban, das ist ein Opffer gebracht*" (he offered a sacrifice).[33]

Looking at the deception stories, one cannot help but wonder to what end the authors saw fit to render the Jews' conspiring conversations in the original Yiddish. As made clear by the immediate translation of every Yiddish sentence into German, the authors did not assume Yiddish fluency among their readers. If their sole purpose had been to expose what the Jews were saying in their "secret language," it would have surely been sufficient to bring the text in German only. We therefore have to consider the possibility that by using Yiddish in their texts, the authors were not merely communicating information. Rather, they were *performing* some further actions, beyond what was being said. In other words, the Christian authors were assigning Yiddish additional, extralinguistic functions, which transcended the language's primary utility as a carrier of content.[34]

On a very basic level, one could argue that by rendering the Jews' conversation in the original Yiddish the authors were conveying the impression they were delivering "first-hand" information, and thus according their work an aura of authenticity and reliability. At the same time, the authors were also demonstrating their own proficiency in the Jewish language, thus strengthening their authority and credibility as experts in the exposure of Jewish secrets. Another, perhaps more complex level of linguistic performance implicit in the stories relates to the function of Yiddish as a signifier of affect. By the very use of Yiddish the authors in fact did more than simply *tell* a deception story. Rather, they *reenacted* it for their readers, positioning them in the place of the victim. Since the Yiddish words were phonetically transliterated with Latin characters, the Christian readers had no difficulty reading them, albeit without understanding their full meaning. By this they could relive the experience of the deceived Christians, in whose earshot the Jews' conversation took place: they could "hear" the conversation, but were unable to decode it. Thus, the semantic value of the Yiddish text, revealed to the readers via the German translation, became secondary to its form. In its distinctive sound and cadences, Yiddish came to serve as an emotionally charged metaphor within the story, invoking a sense of anxiety and helplessness in the face of Jewish threat. If the German translation could disclose to the readers the content of the Jews' conversation, it was only by "hearing" the Yiddish idiom that readers could fully experience their own disadvantage when dealing with Jews, and the consequences of failing to master the Jewish language. The medium had thus become part of the message, complementary to what was being said.

The way in which the foreign, ominous sound of Yiddish serves to reinforce the threatening content it communicates becomes even more evident in the stories about Jews who tell their friends about their successful fraud. Beyond the content of these "heroic tales," the mere use of Yiddish is itself performing the Jews' esprit de corps, their belonging to a closed group from which the reader is excluded. Sharing the trickster tales with their rejoicing coreligionists extends the anti-Christian implications of the deceitful acts to the entire Jewish population. As the medium that carried this effect, Yiddish became indicative of Jewish animosity toward the rest of society.

The German language, too, was more than simply a means of linguistic expression in these texts. By translating the Jews' conversations, the authors were also performing certain actions intended to regain control over the Jews and their hidden discourse. If the Jews used Yiddish to create a closed world of their own, in which they could plan and execute their evil schemes, it was with the aid of German that this world could be made accessible to non-Jews, and the danger it posed mitigated. On a practical level, this took the form of training Christians in Yiddish by providing them bilingual, Yiddish-German texts.

In other words, the stories both exemplified the importance of learning Yiddish and at the same time helped the readers to do just that, serving them as Yiddish-German manuals. On a symbolic level, the German translations functioned to strip Yiddish of its secretive qualities and hence deprive the Jews of their privileged position as speakers of a secret language. Translating from Yiddish into German became a demonstration of dominance, asserting power over the Jews and their hidden language: if the Jews were using their language to subvert the existing power relations, rendering everything in German could reverse this process and restore the readers' sense of domination over the Jews.

By providing the subversive conversations of the Jews in both Yiddish and German, the authors were enhancing the sense of anxiety and threat in their readers, only to restore—through the act of translation—their sense of control and superiority over the Jews. In the process, the authors were also asserting their own privileged position as those who commanded both languages, positioning themselves as translators in the service of Christian society. This last point gains a particularly clear expression in J.W.'s anecdote about the two Jewish jewelers and the precious stone, presented in the introduction to his *Sprach-Meister*. In the anecdote, one of the Jews is engaged in two parallel conversations: with his Jewish friend, instructing him in Yiddish how to deceive their Christian business partner; and with the very same business partner, deliberately mistranslating for him in German the content of the Yiddish conversation. The Jew's practice of switching between Yiddish and German demonstrates his bilingual competence, but also the danger inherent in it. As a former Jew, J.W. possesses the very same bilingual competence; and like the Jew in the story, he demonstrates this competence by switching between the two languages. However, while the Jew in the story switches between Yiddish and German as a means to conceal his true intentions from the Christian, J.W. uses this same practice in order to bridge the language gap and expose the Jew's deception. While the Jew in the story exploits his command of both Yiddish and German for mistranslation and deception, J.W., along with the other authors, utilizes the same competence in order to reverse and mitigate the destructive effects of Jewish bilingualism.

Ix per fix, or What Do You Do with a Yiddish Bill?

The problem of Jews conversing in Yiddish in order to deceive Christians was only one aspect of the relation between Yiddish and Jewish deception. Another aspect that dominated Christian literature on this subject concerned the writing of commercial documents, such as bills of exchange, receipts, and promissory notes. As Johann Schudt reported, "the Jews possess various deceitful tricks . . . , by means of which they outwit the poor Christians. . . . One of the finest among these is when they write their prescriptions and bills of exchange in Hebrew, or rather in Jewish-German with Hebrew letters, which the Christians are unable to read."[35]

The idea that Jews used to deceive Christians by writing their commercial documents in Yiddish and with Hebrew script was promoted by many of the authors under discussion. To illustrate this claim, and hence the importance of learning the Hebrew script in order to avoid the traps of Yiddish-writing Jews, the authors provided what has become the "standard anecdote" for this subject. Going back to the work of the convert Dietrich Schwab, the anecdote tells of a Jew from Prague who in the year 1610 bought at the Frankfurt fair fox skins from a Christian merchant for 400 fl. In return he gave the Christian a promissory note in Hebrew handwriting, to be paid at the next fair. The merchant took the note in good faith and brought it with him to the next fair, confident that he would receive his 400 fl. After the Jew failed to appear, the merchant gave the bill to another Jew to read it for him. In the note was written: "*Ix per fix, Hasen sind keine Füchß, ich gestehe dir mein Lebtag nichts*" (*Ix per fix*, hares are not foxes, I grant you nothing as long as I live). And so, Schwab concludes, the merchant found out how he was deceived.[36]

As made clear by Schudt's words, cited above, writing in Yiddish and with Hebrew letters was only one of the ways Jews allegedly cheated with their business documents. Other methods, such as changing the sum indicated in a document or conveniently "losing" the receipt for a paid debt, were also discussed by Schudt and other authors with the same purpose of warning readers to guard themselves against Jewish deceit. Rather than a legitimate linguistic practice of a certain group of people, Yiddish was reduced to being no more than a deliberate method of de-

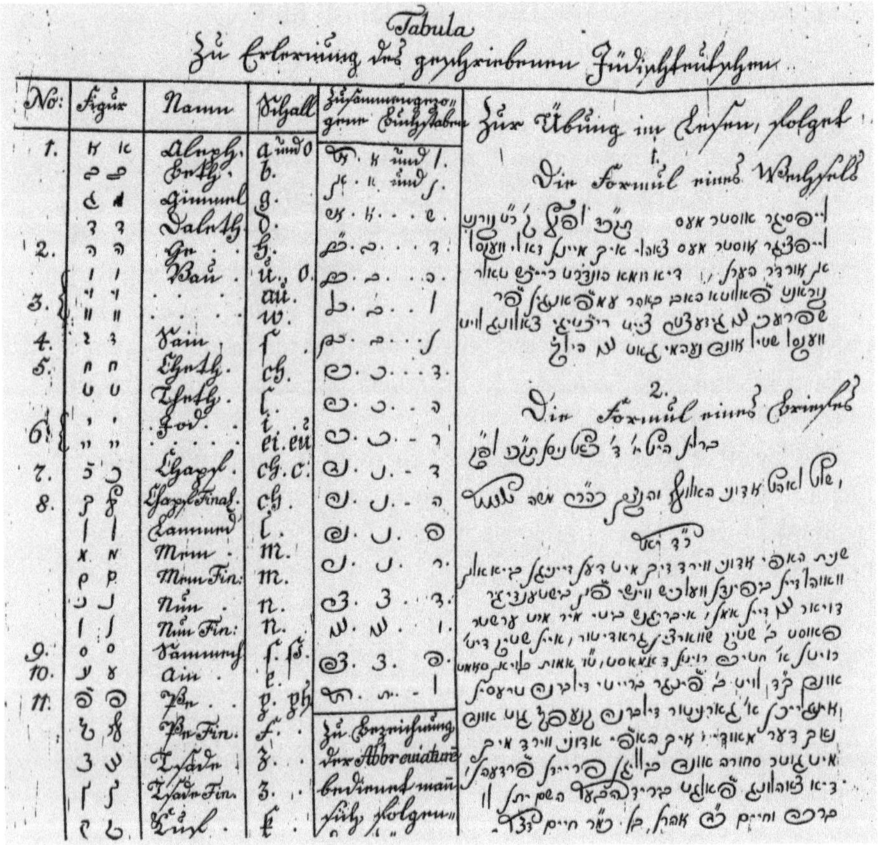

Figure 5.2. Samples of Yiddish handwritten promissory notes: Gottfried Selig, *Kurze und gründliche Anleitung zu einer leichten Erlernung der Jüdischdeutschen Sprache* (Leipzig 1767)

ception, one among many others used by the Jews in their business transactions. In this sense, the claims against the way the Jews allegedly used their language—both spoken and written—for business fraud were not different from the general anti-Jewish claims made by Christian businessmen. Just as the Jews were accused of taking advantage of their marginal position in society to practice unfair and dubious business methods, so were they also accused of taking advantage of their marginal language to undermine the Christian economic order.

Christian authors often went on to discuss possible solutions to the problem of commercial documents in Yiddish. Judging from the proliferation of Yiddish manuals for merchants, learning the Jewish language as a means to guard against Jewish deception was considered by many to be a useful solution. Naturally, prominent in the promotion of this solution were the authors of the manuals themselves. Unfortunately for them, not everyone agreed with this solution. After warning his readers of fraudulent Yiddish documents, Johann Schudt mentions Wagenseil's suggestion that "It is recommendable to the businessmen and tradespeople, that they learn to read and understand the Jewish-German [language], written in Hebrew [characters] [*das Hebräisch-geschriebene Juden-Teutsch*]."[37] Discontent with this option, Schudt asks, "And why should the Christians take upon themselves the effort of learning how to read and write the Hebrew-German [language], instead of the Jews taking upon themselves the effort of learning how to read and write our German [*unser Hochdeutsch*]?" Schudt rejects Wagenseil's assertion that one cannot expect Jews to learn German since they are not able to send their children to German schools or take Christian tutors for them. He notes cases of Jews, especially in seventeenth-century Worms and Frankfurt, who sent their children to German schools. As for finding Christian tutors who would be willing to teach Jewish children, Schudt does not see where the problem is. Money, he asserts, can buy anything, even literacy in German. According to Schudt, there are indeed plenty of Christians who teach Jewish children reading and writing in German, so that there are in fact many Jews who are perfectly literate in *Hochdeutsch*.[38]

The demand that Jewish businessmen conduct commercial transactions in German rather than Yiddish was raised by other authors as well, such as Dietrich Schwab and Johann Eisenmenger.[39] It also appeared in governmental edicts from as early as the sixteenth century. Schudt mentioned these edicts as a legal support for his argument, quoting, for example, from an edict issued on November 9, 1577, regarding Jewish usury and money transactions. In this edict the Jews were required to compose all relevant documents "not in the Jewish, but in the German language," in order to prevent cheating.[40]

Schudt's assertion regarding the existence of German literacy among contemporary Jews finds support in both Christian and Jewish sources from the seventeenth and eighteenth centuries. As these sources suggest, the tendency of Jewish parents to have their children educated in

German and other European languages was especially evident among the wealthier strata in the cities, and became ever more prevalent with time.[41] However, the linguistic shift from Yiddish to German was not always perceived as an adequate solution to the deceitful nature of the Jews. The Christian notary Nicolaus de Bonn, for example, suggested in the 1670s that the Jews were learning to read and write German in order to sign secret loan agreements with their debtors without having to turn to notaries and other legal authorities. In 1689 the Christian booksellers in Frankfurt denounced two Jewish practitioners of the trade, complaining among other things that the Jews taught their children German and other languages "only in order to ruin the Christians with their competition."[42] For many Christians, so it seems, Jewish deception was a multilingual phenomenon.

Six The Thieves' Jargon
Yiddish and Jewish Criminality

The image of Yiddish as the Jews' "secret language," serving them as a means to conceal their dishonest dealings and deceitful intentions, was significantly reinforced by the fact that Yiddish was not only the language of the Jewish merchants but also the language of the large Jewish underclass of paupers, vagrants, beggars, and criminals. The linguistic affinity between Yiddish and *Rotwelsch*, the secret language of the German underworld, further contributed to the association of Yiddish with criminality. This gave rise to "criminological" research on the Jewish language, usually, but not always as a by-product of the interest in *Rotwelsch*.

Poverty was a grave social problem in early modern Germany, and the Jews, as historian Derek Penslar notes, "were among the poorest of the poor":

> As a result of the expulsions from the empire in the 15th and 16th centuries, the percentage of the poor among German Jewry increased dramatically, and there emerged a class of impoverished vagrants known as *Schalantjuden*, or, in Hebrew, *archei-u-farchei* (flotsam and jetsam). In the 1500s, this group was relatively small, but by the end of the next century, Jewish vagrancy had become a serious social problem for the Jewish communities of Germany, Austria, Bohemia, and Moravia. High taxes, restricted settlement rights and occupational choices, natural increase, and waves of refugees fleeing persecution in Poland created a mass of what came to be known from the late 1600s onward as *Betteljuden* [beggar Jews]. In the mid-1700s, as many as two-thirds of the sixty thousand Jews in Germany lived in poverty.[1]

The desperate economic situation induced growing numbers of Jews to engage in criminal activity focusing on crimes against property: pocket-picking, burglary, theft, and disposing of stolen goods. The fact that many Jews did not possess residential rights increased their numbers on the roads and hence their chances of becoming criminals. Furthermore, some of the trades open to Jews were almost by definition criminality-prone, forcing Jews to operate in the economy's risky marginal zone. Pawnbroking, petty trade, and dealings in second-hand goods encouraged theft and burglary, as they created convenient opportunities for fencing and marketing of stolen goods.[2]

Life on the road and involvement in criminal activity brought the lower strata of the Jewish population into closer contact with other parts of the German underworld: vagrants and itinerants, who often relied on begging for their living; outcasts and "the dishonorable" (*unehrliche Leute*), excluded from the guilds and settled society; demobilized soldiers; Gypsies; and professional criminals. This preindustrial underworld constituted to a large extent a world of its own, united by common customs, institutions, and the use of a secret language, called *Rotwelsch*, "which marked off their existence as taking place outside proper society and indicated at least a limited contempt for dominant social norms."[3]

Dating back to the thirteenth century, *Rotwelsch* (also known as *Kochemer-Loschen*, "the language of the clever ones")[4] served the various groups of the German underworld as a secret code for concealing their affairs from outsiders, especially potential victims and the police. The function of secrecy, necessary for the survival of this socially marginalized and often persecuted underclass, has been emphasized in descriptions of the language from as early as the beginning of the sixteenth century. But beyond its importance for maintaining secrecy, either as a mechanism of defense or as a means for deception, *Rotwelsch* also carried semiological significance. As historian Robert Jütte points out, the thieves' jargon was more than just a special vocabulary of a highly specialized profession; it was "a kind of a watchword which signaled that somebody was part of a vagrant community with its own codes of honour and its various, often illegal, strategies of survival." As "a kind of protective mental buffer between the beggars on the road and the outside world," *Rotwelsch* had an important symbolic function, both encouraging and expressing the sense of solidarity among the members of the underworld vis-à-vis the rest of society. Indeed, *Rotwelsch* is taken by historians as best evidence for the existence of a broader subculture of the underworld in the period under discussion.[5]

The linguistic characteristics of *Rotwelsch* were determined to a large extent by its function as a secret language. Using the German syntactic structure, speakers of *Rotwelsch* made their language opaque for outsiders by a massive lexicon replacement ("relexification") of the "usual" German vocabulary. One way of doing this was by forming new words from the German ones through the application of different linguistic devices: either change of meaning (for example, metaphors) or formal techniques such as substitution, affixing, or reversal of consonants, vowels, and syllables. Another way was by replacing German words with foreign ones, incomprehensible for German-speakers. Aside from its German vocabulary, *Rotwelsch* contained many words derived from outside sources, especially Hebrew, Yiddish, Dutch, Latin, and Romany, the Indic language spoken by the Gypsies.[6]

Hebrew and Yiddish words—predominantly words from the Hebraic component of the latter—found their way into the *Rotwelsch* vocabulary through the encounters between Jewish and Christian vagrants, beggars, and criminals. Thanks to their foreignness, these words served ideally as a "secret code" within the thieves' language. Thus we find in *Rotwelsch* words like *lehem* for "bread," *johan* for "wine," and *sone* for "prostitute," as well as *acheln* for "eating," *schöchern* for "drinking," and *genffen* for "stealing."[7] With the growing interest in documenting the language of the underclass from the late fifteenth century onwards, these words and others derived from Hebrew and Yiddish received attention in some of the most popular works of the genre. Writers like Sebastian Brant in his *Narrenschiff* (1494), or Wencel Scherffer and Hanß-Michael Moscherosch in their depictions of soldiers' life in the mid-seventeenth century, incorporated *Rotwelsch* words into their works—including many of Jewish origin.[8]

The presence of Jewish words in literary documentations of *Rotwelsch* undoubtedly contributed to the association of the Jews' language with the language of the thieves. But an explicit and unequivocal connection between the two languages was also made in a very early stage. In 1528 Martin Luther published a new edition of the *Liber Vagatorum* (Book of vagabonds), the most influential study on the German underworld and its language in the early modern period. This anonymous booklet appeared for the first time around the year 1510 and went through numerous editions. It describes the various types of thieves and false beggars that roamed the German countryside at the time, and concludes with a thorough compilation of *Rotwelsch* vocabulary. In his famous introduction to the work, Luther specifically pointed out the Jewish component of *Rotwelsch*, asserting that "this Rotwelsch has certainly come from the Jews, for it contains many Hebrew words."[9]

Many of the Jewish words Luther referred to were Yiddish rather than Hebrew, but this of course did not change the implications of his statement. The notion that the thieves' language emanated from the Jews became common knowledge in the following centuries, and was reiterated in later depictions of the underworld's language. In a detailed study on secret languages and scripts from the early seventeenth century, the Orientalist and mathematician Daniel Schwenter from Altdorf discusses the secret language of the underworld, "which is very much in use among the soldiers these days." Noting that after German, Hebrew serves as the major lexical source of *Rotwelsch*, Schwenter creates a clear analogy between this language and the language of the German Jews, who also mix Hebrew in their German. Schwenter notes, for example, that the Jews say "*er achelt in der Schul*, that is he eats in the school/synagogue: For next to the German [words] the word . . . *achelt* is Hebrew. From this the soldiers say . . . *wir wollen acheln*, that is to eat; *Adone* means in Rotwelsch God, [which] comes from *Adonai*, that also means God for the Hebrews," and so on.[10] A somewhat more scholarly, and certainly more pretentious, analysis of the Hebraic component in *Rotwelsch* was presented in 1679 in Samuel Reyher's *Mathesis Mosaica*. The author, professor of law and mathematics at the University of Kiel, dedicates the lion's share of his short discussion on the thieves' language to this issue. According to Reyher, the *Rotwelsch* vocabulary included in the work of Moscherosch (1650; see above) clearly shows that many of the words were taken from Hebrew. He then attempts to prove this point by presenting some of the words with their etymological roots traced back to their Hebrew origin, thus providing a clear, visual illustration of the relation between the languages. For example:

Essen *Acheln* אכל [*akhal*] Edidit [*sic*], devoravit
Gott *Adone* אדן [*adon*] Dominus
Gehen *Alchen* הלך [*halakh*] Ambulavit

For this reason, Reyher concludes, the first origins of this language are justly ascribed to the Jews.[11]

In some cases, the recognition that *Rotwelsch* contained words derived from Hebrew and Yiddish gave rise to rather unique notions regarding the German Jews, their language, and their relation to other marginal groups in early modern Germany. In the introduction to a work from 1697, the famous Hebraist and Yiddishist Johann Christoph Wagenseil discusses the mystery of the Gypsies' origin in the German lands. Asserting that the Gypsies, who "live in great freedom, . . . plunder, rob, and steal . . . and commit many other misdeeds," appeared in Germany for the first time around the year 1417, Wagenseil suggests a very interesting theory concerning their origin. The very first Gypsies, according to Wagenseil, originated from no others but the German Jews. Wagenseil explains that following the Black Death in 1348 and the subsequent persecutions of the Jews, the remaining Jews took cover in holes they had dug in the ground. There they secretly lived and multiplied for some decades, until they finally came out at the beginning of the fifteenth century. Afraid to reveal their true Jewish identity, they made up a story about coming from Egypt after rejecting Christianity. Thus they came to be known as Gypsies.[12]

As main proof for this somewhat unusual theory, Wagenseil presents some insights concerning the language of these primordial German-Jewish Gypsies. In order to maintain their disguise as Egyptian immigrants, so runs the argument, the Jews needed a foreign and unfamiliar language. Pure Hebrew, it was clear, would not suit the task. After all, only a very small part of these Jews was fluent in the language, which was in any case inadequate for idle talk. Moreover, speaking Hebrew could obviously betray their Jewish origin. Therefore, a new language was created, "according to what such people were capable of creating, that is, [a language] which is a mixture [*Mischmasch*] of Hebrew and German thrown together, whereas the German words are completely transformed and accommodated to the manner of the Hebrew [tongue]."[13]

As one might have suspected, Wagenseil did not have much evidence to support his theory. Indeed, the famous Hebraist admits that he could not find any documentation of this language, aside from a small vocabulary included in the work of Moscherosch, in the part depicting soldiers' life. Although this vocabulary was taken from soldiers'

Rotwelsch and not from the Gypsies' language,[14] this would not sway a determined linguist such as Wagenseil from his deep conviction. Having diligently isolated the words derived from Hebrew and Yiddish, almost fifty in number, he presents them in a new list with their original Hebrew root, in quite the same manner as Reyher had done almost twenty years before.

Content with the results of his linguistic investigation, Wagenseil reasserts his theory that the first Gypsies in Germany were in fact Jews; otherwise, he claims, "where could so many Hebrew words among so few German ones come from, if not from the Jews, especially at a time when the Gypsies excelled, since almost no one [at that time] was proficient in Hebrew, except for the Jews." Finally, in case someone would find this explanation lacking, Wagenseil supports his historical analysis by pointing out the linguistic situation in his own time, asserting that this so-called "Gypsies' *Rotwelsch*," this "mixture of Hebrew and German thrown together," displays an unmitigated affinity (*eine vollkommene Verwantschafft*) with the idiom spoken by the Jews everywhere in Germany.[15] For Wagenseil, in other words, it is not only the existence of Hebraic roots in the alleged "Gypsies' language" that proves its Jewish origin but also its close affinity with Yiddish, the language of the German Jews in his own time.

Yiddish-Speaking Bandits

The association between Yiddish and the language of the criminals gained new impetus in the first half of the eighteenth century. As in previous centuries, Yiddish found its way into general presentations of the thieves' language due to its linguistic affinity with *Rotwelsch*. From the beginning of the eighteenth century, however, it was mainly the rising interest in *Jewish* criminals and criminality that brought attention to Yiddish in literature on the thieves' language, rather than its relation to the non-Jewish jargon. Yiddish was seen as a conspicuous characteristic of the Jewish criminal, serving him as a ready-made secret language for illegal purposes.

By the end of the seventeenth century, the equation between Jews and thieves, implicit already in Luther's introduction to the *Liber Vagatorum*, evolved into a powerful and all-embracing stereotype—"that of the Jews as a people of thieves and robbers extraordinaire."[16] In the words of historian Otto Ulbricht: "By 1700, Jews were viewed as thieves and robbers, an image that survived well into the nineteenth century. Writers no longer distinguished between *Gauner* and *Spitzbuben* (crooks and scoundrels) and Jews . . . the stereotype became even more widely accepted during the following decades."[17]

This development was closely linked to the rise of Jewish banditry from the late seventeenth century, with Jews participating in Christian robber-bands or establishing exclusively Jewish ones.[18] The robber-bands in eighteenth-century Germany were composed of highly professional bandits, and aroused the fear—and fascination—of the German public. Popular curiosity led to the publication of criminal reports describing the investigations and trials of bandits that had been arrested. Considerable attention was given to the language of the bandits, and the criminal reports often included word-lists of the thieves' jargon.[19] These vocabularies were much more extensive than the ones of previous centuries, and as many of the new words were of Hebrew and Yiddish origin, the Hebraic component of the thieves' language became even more dominant than before.[20] Moreover, while seventeenth-century poets like Scherffer and Moscherosch used the thieves' language as a literary device and incorporated glossaries of *Rotwelsch* into their fictional works, the eighteenth-century vocabularies produced by legal authorities—investigators and police officials—had a much more realistic character. They documented the language of real-life criminals and enjoyed an aura of professionalism and objectivity. Presented in a realistic, authoritative manner, the danger embodied in the criminals and their special language was more tangible than ever before. Indeed, the authors of the reports emphasized that the *Rotwelsch* glossaries were meant to provide the decent reader with a means to recognize a criminal and beware of him. Acquiring proficiency in the thieves' jargon, in other words, became a tool of survival, not only for the criminals but also for the decent readers.

Among the criminological literature of the period one can find works that concentrated on specifically *Jewish* robber-bands. Although the largest part of Jewish criminals at the time consisted of purse-cutters or individual burglars, it was the work of robber-bands that stereotyped

Jewish criminality in the eyes of contemporaries and attracted their fascination. One of the best-known bandit gangs in eighteenth-century Germany was exposed in the mid-1730s in Coburg, the capital of the Duchy of Saxe-Coburg (in present-day Bavaria). Investigations of a large robbery that took place in December 1733 led to the arrest of the Court Jew Mendel Garbe (also: Carben) from Hildburghausen, who confessed to having been the *Baldober*, or ringleader, who had commissioned the robbery. In the meantime more Jews were arrested. Soon a picture of a large band of robbers emerged, almost entirely Jewish, which had been responsible for numerous robberies in different parts of the land.[21]

The trial of the Jewish *Baldober* and his associates was among the most celebrated bandit trials of the time, and aroused great public interest. The chief investigator, state official Paul Nicol Einert, anonymously published painstaking documentations of the investigations and trials against the members of the Jewish gang. The first publication, *Actenmäßige Designation Derer von einer Diebischen Juden-Bande verübten Kirchen-Raubereyen und gewaltsamen mörderischen Einbrüche* (Documentary description of church robberies and violent murderous burglaries, committed by a thievish band of Jews), appeared in Coburg in 1735 and quickly went through several editions and reprints in different German territories.[22]

A second publication, the voluminous *Entdeckter Jüdischer Baldober* (Jewish ringleader detected), appeared in Coburg in 1737 (second edition in 1758), encompassing more than six hundred pages. With the outright aim of exposing "many, and until now unknown evil doings and acts of theft of the Jewish people," Einert stressed the importance of his work for both ordinary people and professional investigators. The descriptions of the robbers, together with their deeds and tactics, would help honest Christians recognize Jewish criminals and beware them, whereas the authorities would be able to draw on these descriptions in their investigations.[23] With the same purpose of providing his readers with tools to handle the problem of Jewish criminals, Einert appended to the second edition of his work (1758) a glossary of words from the "*Spitzbuben-Sprache*" (scoundrels' language; thieves' jargon). As in similar glossaries from the period, Einert differentiates between the words common among the "*Juden-Spitzbuben*," derived mainly from Hebrew and Yiddish, and the ones more common among the "other," that is non-Jewish, criminals.

Two main ideas run throughout Einert's presentation of Jewish banditry. The first idea is that of Jewish solidarity. Einert emphasizes over and over again that the Jewish criminals are much admired by their coreligionists and that the entire Jewish population supports the criminals and helps them abscond from justice. This solidarity between the "straight" and criminal Jews makes, according to Einert, all Jews accomplices to their brethren's crimes. The second idea relates to the specific anti-Christian character of Jewish criminality. In Einert's descriptions the Jewish bandits are motivated not merely by greed and the wish to achieve economic gain. It is, more fundamentally, the hatred against Christians and Christianity and the will to harm Christian institutions and social fabric in any way possible that underlie their actions. The practice of robbing churches and monasteries, for example, is explained by Einert not as resulting from the precious goods they contained or the fact that they were relatively easy to break into,[24] but as motivated primarily by the will to desecrate these places and their

Mendelius foedi sceleris director et auctor
detectus laqueo, jure jubente, perit.

Entdeckter
Jüdischer
Baldober,
Oder
Sachsen-Coburgische
ACTA CRIMINALIA
wider eine
Jüdische Diebs- und Rauber-Bande,
Worinnen
zu jedermänniglicher Wahrnehmung, vor die Jüdische
Nachstellungen sich hüten zu lernen,
Besonders aber
zum nützlichen Gebrauch
Derer Criminal-Gerichte,
viele bisher noch nicht bekannt gewesene Bosheiten und Diebs-Streiche
des Jüdischen Volcks deutlich geoffenbahret,
Und zum Behuf künftiger Inquisitions-Processe,
mit practischen Anmerckungen
erläutert werden.

Zweyte Auflage.

Coburg, bey Georg Otto, 1758.

Figure 6.1. Title page of Paul Einert's *Entdeckter Jüdischer Baldober* (Coburg 1758)

holy objects. Jewish crimes, in other words, were both sacrilegious as well as illegal.

These two ideas, which dominate other works as well on Jewish bandits, are highly interesting. They suggest that at least for these authors, Jewish robbers were a kind of "social bandits," to use Eric Hobsbawm's term, visiting the revenge of their fellow Jews on the world that oppressed them and that they ideologically opposed.[25] The question whether early modern Jewish robbers can indeed be seen as social bandits is much debated in modern historiography.[26] Our concern here will be the possible implications this image of Jewish banditry had for the interest of Christian "criminologists" in the language of Jewish robbers, and for the way they presented it in their works.

The purpose of the Jewish glossary appended to Einert's book, so it seems, was not confined to helping Christians recognize and understand the language of the Jewish criminals in order to better defend themselves. It was also meant to substantiate Einert's claims regarding the support Jewish criminals enjoyed among their brethren and the anti-Christian character of Jewish banditry. In the definition of the word "*Chochum*," for example, which indicates "an artful, crafty, intelligent man," Einert explains that by this term the Jewish thieves refer to themselves, "and also among *the entire Jewish population* they are not scolded as thieves, but rather called *Chochumen*, [that is] clever, crafty people." "*Moser*," on the other hand, is "a traitor, or godless man" that handed over a *Benn-Israels* (fellow Jew) to a *Mischpot Gojim* (the Christian court), and is therefore banned and persecuted by the Jews.[27] As far as the anti-Christian character of Jewish criminality is concerned, Einert explains that the Jews use particularly derogatory and blasphemous words when indicating Christian terms, especially from the religious domain. This claim is well illustrated in his glossary of the Jewish *Spitzbuben-Sprache*, where he includes words such as *Goi* or *Thola-Achler* ("an eater of the hanged-one," that is, Jesus) for a Christian, *Kelef* (dog) for *Kelch* (chalice), and *Tifle* (from the Hebrew word for tastelessness) for a church.[28]

The issue of Jewish anti-Christian expressions, we might recall, was a ubiquitous concern in early modern discourse on Jews and Judaism. Discussed in the context of Jewish criminality, these expressions come to signify the twofold threat the Jewish language posed to Christian society. In an indirect manner, these expressions posed a threat to Christian order since they served Jewish criminals as secret code-words, a tool for executing their crimes against honest people. In that, the Jewish expressions listed above were no different from other terms in *Rotwelsch*, used by Jewish and non-Jewish criminals alike to conceal their deeds. They did differ from other expressions in that they were no neutral code simply taken from a foreign language in order to keep conversations opaque to outsiders. Rather, it was the very utterance of these words that was considered a direct threat to Christian religion and society. *Rotwelsch*, according to Robert Jütte, was indeed the language of the criminals, but its content was not in itself ethically negative. It was only the use of the language in a certain social milieu and for certain illegitimate activities that gave it its negative implications.[29] But for Einert and other authors of the time, the language of the *Jewish* thieves was not a neutral language that derived its negative value from the social context in which it was used; rather, the language itself was seen as ideologically dangerous, the language of Jewish resistance to dominant Christian order.

By the mid-eighteenth century, the close connection between Jews and criminality, and between the Jewish language and the language of the criminals, was well established in contemporary literature. When a certain Christoph Friedrich Krackherr decided to append to his 1766 lexicon of foreign words that were used in German a separate dictionary of Yiddish and *Rotwelsch*,[30] it was not only the linguistic affinity between the two languages that led to their being included together in the same appendix. Another reason was the similar purpose for including both languages in his work. As Krackherr himself noted on the title page to the second edition, he appended a dictionary "of Yiddish and *Rotwelsch*, or the so-called thieves' jargon [*Spitzbuben Sprache*], for the use of those who deal with Jews, or have to conduct judicial investigations about them."[31] Both Yiddish and *Rotwelsch*, in Krackherr's opinion, were important to anyone dealing with *Jews*, either in the commercial or legal sphere.

Language of the Merchants, Language of the Thieves

The linkage between Yiddish and the thieves' jargon, promoted in early modern criminological literature, found clear expression in the Christian literature on Yiddish as well. In this case, too, the association between the Yiddish language and the underworld was constructed by pointing out the linguistic affinity between Yiddish and *Rotwelsch* on the one hand, and the misuse of Yiddish by Jewish criminals as a ready-made secret language on the other hand. Wilhelm Chrysander, for example, noted the fact that "the so-called *Ziegeunerische-Rottwelsch* [Gypsies' *Rotwelsch*], as the actual language of the thieves, has certain similarity with the Jewish-German [language]" as one of the reasons to learn Yiddish. After all, according to Chrysander, "anyone who understands Jewish-German conversations will also have easier access to *Rotwelsch*, which is used among the vagrant Jews, the beggars in the countryside, and other riffraff. For it is patched up from German and other, most notably Hebrew, words."[32] In a special addendum to his discussion on Yiddish, Chrysander elaborates on the connection between the Jewish language and the thieves' jargon, relying in his analysis on the list of *Rotwelsch* vocabulary provided by Moscherosch a century before.[33] A similar assertion regarding the advantage of knowing Yiddish as a key to unlock the language of the underworld appears in the Yiddish-German dictionary *Jüdischer Sprach-Meister* (1742) by the pseudonymous author Bibliophilus. In the introduction to his work, Bibliophilus emphasizes the notion that proficiency in Yiddish could help one understand the conspiring conversations of the Jewish thieves—known in *Rotwelsch* as *Bal-dobers*, *Cochumen*, and *Achproschen*—and thus defend oneself against their evil deeds.[34]

In both works on the Yiddish language, that of Chrysander and that of Bibliophilus, one cannot but notice the close proximity between the authors' recommendation to master the Jewish language for anyone who has business interactions with the Jews, and for anyone who wishes to defend himself against Jewish thieves and other criminals. The image of Yiddish as the language of the merchants is thus conflated with its image as the language of the thieves, blurring any clear distinction between the two groups. Further than that, the representations of Yiddish as the language of Jewish deception and criminality created a feedback loop of negative images, in which the image of the Jew as a crook and a thief projects these qualities onto his language, and the association of the Yiddish with the thieves' jargon projects back onto the image of the Jew. In this vicious circle, every Yiddish-speaking merchant, or indeed every Yiddish-speaking Jew, becomes suspect of being a potential thief, not only for being a Jew but also for speaking the Jewish language.

The intertwined motifs of the deceitful Jewish merchant, operating from *inside* the socioeconomic order, and the dangerous Jewish criminal, operating from *outside* it, continued to dominate the Christian discourse on Yiddish well into the late eighteenth and nineteenth centuries. The Christian attempt to fight Jewish deception by depriving the Jews of their secret language resulted, as we have seen, in the publication of Yiddish business manuals, designed to equip Christians with sufficient knowledge of the language. Another solution that gained popularity during the eighteenth and nineteenth centuries was to forbid the use of Yiddish and the Hebrew alphabet in commercial records and economic transactions. The demand that Jews conduct business and keep their books in German and with Latin characters was explicitly stipulated in many of the Jews' laws in different places in the German territories.[35] This demand was raised, for example, in the Trier *Judenordnung* from 1723; in Prussia in 1730, as part of the renewal of the *Priviliegium* from 1714, and again in 1752; and in 1739 in the principality of Hessen-Kassel. Later on, it was also introduced into tolerance patents and emancipation edicts in Austria and the various German states. Article 15 of the *Toleranzpatent* promulgated in Austria by Joseph II (January 2, 1782) explicitly stated that "Considering the numerous openings in trades and the manifold contacts with Christians resulting thereof, the care for maintaining common confidence requires that the Hebrew and the Hebrew intermixed with German, the so-called Jewish language and script, shall be abolished." In Prussia, the so-called Edict of Emancipation (March 11, 1812) conditioned the continuance of Jews' qualification as natives and state citizens in that "they shall use the German or another living language not only in keeping their commercial books but also upon drawing their contracts and declaratory acts, and that they should use no other than German or Latin characters for their signatures."[36]

During the nineteenth century, the genre of Yiddish manuals for merchants and others who had dealings with Jews became less significant in the German lands. Although works of this kind were still published in Germany as late as the 1880s,[37] the demand that the Jewish language be abolished from commerce, as well as the growing tendency among "respectable" Jews to use German colloquially and in writing, seem to have reduced the necessity of this type of instruction of Yiddish for non-Jews. But the shift of "respectable" Jews from Yiddish to German also meant that Yiddish had now become—perhaps even more than before—stigmatized as the language of the underworld.[38] From this perspective, it is probably not surprising that despite the drastic decline in Jewish banditry in the first half of the nineteenth century, criminological literature on Yiddish continued to flourish in Germany well into the era of emancipation.[39]

Yiddish and the Authorities

The idea that one had to master the Jews' secret language in order to exert control on this minority led Christian authors to stress the importance of proficiency in Yiddish for legal and administrative purposes, and to call upon civic authorities, especially bureaucrats and jurists, to master the Jewish language. Himself a professor of law, Johann Christoph Wagenseil argued in 1699 that

> Experience with the Jewish-German dialect will stand in good stead both higher and lower authorities, as also counselors and advisors, among whom court assessors, attorneys and magistrates are also to be reckoned, when Jewish wills, rental and sales contracts, indemnities, debenture bonds and other financial instruments and documents, written according to common practice in the German language with Hebrew letters, are brought before them, so that they can themselves have insight into the contents and meaning and thus make their judgments, decisions, objections, suits and countersuits.[40]

Wagenseil illustrates this point by recounting an incident from the year before in which a couple of Jews had a business quarrel and wished to settle the matter in a Christian court. However, since the documents the Jews provided were written in Yiddish, the court magistrates could not read them. They therefore had to advise the Jews to seek the help of rabbis, thus undermining the authority of the Christian court and compromising its ability to exert legal and administrative control over the Jewish minority. In another instance, a certain Jew was arrested on suspicion of having conducted "a harmful exchange of letters." After the authorities took possession of the correspondence, they sent it to theologians for German translation. Wagenseil asserts that if the letters had been written in pure Hebrew, the theologians would have surely been able to translate them. However, since none of them were fluent in Yiddish, the suspicious letters had to be sent to the university to be deciphered by a certain professor of Hebrew.[41]

But what exactly were these suspicious letters, this "harmful correspondence" the Jew was suspected of? Wagenseil mentions the need to be able to read Yiddish in case "their suspicious letters would be intercepted,"[42] but he does not explain what these letters might be. One could assume these were simply business letters, being inspected for the fear of Jewish fraud. Another possibility is that the Jews were suspected of using their secret language for acts of treachery against the country, illegally corresponding with hostile parties in times of war. After all, accusations against Jews of betraying their country, spying, and assisting the enemy in different ways were common currency in early modern Germany[43]: if Jewish deception and criminality resulted not only from the prospect of economic gain but also from the sheer desire to harm Christians in any possible way, why should they not try to harm the latter in the military and political spheres as well?

That such suspicions indeed existed can be concluded from different cases in times of war, when the Jews' special language was regarded as a threat to the security of their homelands. In 1689, at the height of the war against Louis XIV, the city council of Frankfurt demanded that all Jewish correspondence, especially outgoing and arriving letters from abroad, be written in German. When the Jews objected, claiming that only very few of them were literate in this language, they were allowed to use Hebrew characters, but only when exchanging letters with Jews from countries that were not in alliance with France, and only under the condition that the language, though written with Hebrew characters, would be as similar to German as possible. A convert named Bleibtreu was appointed as censor for the Jews' letters to make sure they did not contain any dangerous content, such as anti-Christian expressions or words of treason.[44] A century later, convert Gottfried Selig recalls that he was asked on different occasions to translate letters and notes of Jewish criminals, including those of spies.[45] Converts were of course perfect candidates for supervising and censoring "suspicious" Jewish correspondence. Another group considered qualified for this sensitive work consisted of missionaries, who used Yiddish in their attempts to convert the Jews. In 1760, during the Seven Years' War, Johann Callenberg and other missionaries at the Institutum Judaicum in Halle were asked by the secular authorities to use their skills as readers and translators of Yiddish, skills originally obtained for missionary purposes, in the service of their government. Bundles of Jewish letters, confiscated from the Royal Prussian Post Office in Dessau, were brought to the institute to be scrutinized for evidence of Jewish betrayal.[46]

Yiddish and the Jewish Oath

Back in the courtroom, the Jews' special language presented Christian authorities with yet another challenge: the Jewish oath. Known as *Judeneid* or *oath more judaico*, the Jewish oath was required of Jews testifying in Christian courts from the Middle Ages to the late eighteenth century. In some places, this practice persisted even later.[47] Both the oath and the symbolic rituals involved in taking it were meant to ensure that the Jew spoke truthfully; they were also meant to frighten the Jew and emphasize his inferior status. Taking the oath in a synagogue while wearing a prayer shawl and holding a Torah scroll, or sitting on a coffin in a shroud and holding a butcher knife, are only some of the (more progressive) measures taken in an attempt to prevail upon the Jew's deceitful nature and force him to tell the truth.[48]

The oath itself, in Joshua Trachtenberg's words, "was essentially a magically coercive formula, binding upon the maker and *upon God and His agents*, in the European view, and the *more judaico* was therefore designed by Christians to incorporate what they conceived to be magically binding Jewish components. Thus the Jew was required quite generally to swear by the Hebrew name of God, *Adonay*."[49] Other Hebrew key words, too, were sometimes incorporated in the oath-formula, demonstrating the perception of Hebrew as "a magical language with performative powers beyond its communicative capacities."[50]

The issue of the Jewish oath gained immortality in the history of Yiddish when, in 1782, Moses Mendelssohn vehemently opposed the use of the "*jüdischdeutsche Mundart*" (Jewish-German idiom) in court, advocating instead "either pure German or pure Hebrew . . . only, no mixing of the languages!"[51] The suggestion to insert more Hebrew words into the basically German text of the oath and thus make it more Yiddish than German, which aroused the ire of Mendelssohn, was made by a Jew of Mendelssohn's generation, Rabbi Fränkel of Breslau. Earlier Christian authors like Wagenseil or Chrysander, on the other hand, who relate to the issue of the oath in their writings on Yiddish, do not advocate the use of the Jewish language for this purpose.[52] Wagenseil, in fact, explicitly supports the German formulations of the oath that existed at the time, merely calling to keep them as short as possible. Further than that, Wagenseil calls to remove the few Hebrew words incorporated in them, due to what he considers the corrupt and incomprehensible way in which these words were written.[53] Yiddish, on the other hand, is accorded only a minor role in Wagenseil's plans for reforming the Jewish oath, where it is aimed to function more as a surrogate for German than as a language in its own right.

Discussing the procedure of Jewish oath-taking, Wagenseil is especially disturbed by one stage of the process. Before the Jew was to utter the oath itself, the court magistrate presented him with a Hebrew Pentateuch. The Jew had to confirm that he acknowledged it as God's Word, and the magistrate would then administer the oath by quoting in Hebrew Exodus 20:7: "*Lo tissa et shem adonai elohekha lashav, ki lo yenakkeh adonai et asher yissa et shemo lashav*" (You shall not misuse the name of the LORD your God, for the LORD will not hold anyone guiltless who misuses his name).

Wagenseil expresses his deep concern that the magistrate might mispronounce the Hebrew words or simply read them not in accordance with the pronunciation common among the German Jews. In such cases, Wagenseil warns his readers, the Jew would secretly laugh at the oath and would not feel himself obliged in any way.[54] This point was further developed in Wilhelm Chrysander's *Unterricht vom Nutzen des Juden-Teutschen* from 1750. The author explains that the Hebrew pronunciation common among Christians is the one used by Sephardi Jews, whereas the German Jews use a different one (the so-called Ashkenazi pronunciation). This seemingly minor difference, according to Chrysander, has grave consequences for the Jewish oath, "because the Jews believe they are not bound by the oath if it is read [to them] in a different pronunciation, than the one that is customary among them."

All the rituals accompanying the taking of the oath are therefore useless "without observing the pronunciation common among the German Jews. . . . The Jew laughs in the face of the gravest oath when this does not sound the way his people endorses."[55]

Both Wagenseil and Chrysander, we might recall, were ardent supporters of the idea of linguistic adaptation for missionary undertakings among the Jews. Like the missionaries and the question of true religion, the court magistrates could not force the Jew to *believe* his oath was binding; all they could do was try to convince him this was the case. For that they needed to adjust to Jewish "peculiarities," among which was the language agreeable to the Jew taking the oath. In order to overcome this linguistic complication, Chrysander suggests that magistrates learn how to read the verse from Exodus "according to the Hebrew idiom common among the Jews."[56] Wagenseil, however, has a different suggestion. In order to entirely avoid the problem, he argues, one could simply take "a German Pentateuch [*Teutsches Chumasch*], that is their [the Jews'] German translation of the five books of Moses" instead of the Hebrew original. By "*Teutsches Chumasch*" Wagenseil means the Yiddish translations of the Pentateuch (known in Ashkenazi Jewish tradition as *taytsh-khumesh*) that were in use among German Jews at the time. Wagenseil suggests that the magistrate ask the Jew to read the required verse in front of the court; and since the words in the *taytsh-khumesh* are basically German, the issue of the correct Hebrew pronunciation would be completely removed. In Wagenseil's words: "in this way one would not prostitute oneself by pronouncing the Hebrew words in a false and odd manner; in this way the Jews will not secretly laugh up their sleeve, and the opportunity to use their quibbling and hair-splitting tricks [*cavillationibus und Sophisticationibus*] would be reduced to the minimum."[57]

But if Wagenseil prefers the words of the oath to be German rather than Hebrew, why not use a German translation of the Bible rather than a Yiddish one? In that case the magistrate could read the verse correctly and the Jew would repeat the words after him. The problem with this solution was the authority—or indeed lack of authority—of the German translation in the Jew's eyes. Unless the Jew acknowledged the text as God's Word, he would not consider his oath binding; and if Jews regarded the Hebrew Bibles published by Christians as not kosher, and hence unbinding in case of an oath,[58] they would most probably not consider a German, Christian translation kosher either. But a *Yiddish* Bible, Wagenseil assures his readers, would surely be recognized by the Jews as "one of their own"; after all, "such translation originates from the Jews; their uneducated, as well as the women and children use it at home and in the synagogues." No Jew, therefore, would be able to deny its authority as containing God's Word.

Wagenseil's solution reveals an interesting shift of emphasis with regard to the Jewish oath: it is no longer the magical attributes of Hebrew that guarantee truth-telling, but rather the Jew's understanding—and accepting—the validity and authority of the biblical verse. In order for this solution to work, however, one more condition needs to be fulfilled: "the authorities and judges will make the effort and learn how to read the German, which is written and printed with Hebrew characters."[59] In his *Unterricht* Chrysander elaborates on this point, noting the necessity "that one, by demand of the authorities, will be able to tell if a Jew who is taking the oath is reading the translation of Exodus 20:7 from the Yiddish Bible in a correct manner, without additions, omissions, or altering the pronunciation" as one of the reasons why Christians should learn the Yiddish language.[60] The idea that Jews deceive even when under oath, and the fear that they would misuse their secret language to manipulate the legal process and undermine Christian authority in the court of law, rendered the need to supervise the procedure of the Jewish oath, including its linguistic aspects, all the more urgent.

Conclusion
Yiddish as Antilanguage

In his article "Evidence for the Appearance of the 'Criminal' Type in the Jewish Stereotype in Germany at the End of the Middle Ages and the Beginning of the Modern Period," historian Ben-Zion Degani writes:

> In the early modern period, too, religion was the dominant reason for anti-Judaism. However, the growing complexity of social, economic, and cultural life between Luther's death and the beginning of the era of tolerance has also influenced the different expressions of the negative Jewish stereotype. . . . Among the components that "enriched" the negative stereotype was the one of the "criminal Jew." In Germany one can find the greatest contribution to the creating of this source of hatred and to its dissemination.[1]

In the article, Degani discusses the various manifestations of the criminal stereotype of the Jew, including the denunciation of Jews as swindlers and deceivers, thieves, traitors, and spies—a list of charges to which blasphemy and perjury can also be added. The alleged Jewish inclination to crime was frequently presented as resulting from the wish to hurt Christians and Christian institutions, thus illustrating the interdependence of theological and social discourses about the Jews in early modern Germany and the perception of Jews as presenting a threat to both the religious and the social orders.

As was demonstrated in the foregoing chapters, the Yiddish language has been linked to each and all of these accusations against the Jews. Furthermore, it was ascribed an active role in these alleged crimes, equipping the Jews with a potent "weapon of the weak": a hidden tongue to conceal their deviant behavior and in many cases an indispensable means to execute their evil intentions. The different ways in which the association between Yiddish and Jewish subversiveness was depicted in Christian literature suggest that the Christian authors perceived Yiddish not merely as a secret language but rather as what was defined by the sociolinguist Michael Halliday as an "antilanguage," the language of an antisociety.[2]

An antisociety, according to Halliday, is "a society that is set up within another society as a conscious alternative to it," with its own systems of values and beliefs that create an alternative identity for its members. The relationship between the society and antisociety is one of tension and conflict, or in Halliday's words, "the alternative reality [of the antisociety] is a *counter*-reality, set up *in opposition to* some established norm." An antisociety, moreover, "is a mode of resistance, resistance which may take the form either of passive symbiosis or of active hostility and even destruction."[3]

The two conflicting groups, the society and the antisociety contained within it, are generated and sustained by a matching linguistic order: two mutually opposed linguistic varieties, a language and an antilanguage.[4] An antilanguage is thus a classic case of "sociolinguistic pathology," to use Halliday's term: it is an extreme version of a nonstandard social dialect, intentionally created by subordinate and marginalized groups antagonistic to the dominant society. Antilanguages are created through a process of *relexicalization* (also *relexification*), the introduction of new or alternative words not found in the mainstream language. The grammar of the parent language may be preserved, but a distinctive vocabulary develops, particularly—but not solely—in certain areas, "typically those that are central to the activities of the subculture and that set it off most sharply from the established society." Such central areas are also prone to *overlexicalization*—when several words are available to refer to the same or similar concepts.[5]

The linguistic processes of relexicalization and overlexicalization contribute to an important feature of the antilanguage—its secrecy, with the straightforward intent to make it incomprehensible to outsiders and to exclude them. At the same time, it serves to consolidate and maintain the sense of solidarity between the members of the group, and to keep their frequently illicit dealings hidden, even when conducted in public. But the main feature of an antilanguage, which distinguishes it from other forms of social dialects and secret languages, is that "the subjective reality that is realized by it is a *conscious counter-reality*, not just a subcultural variant of, or angle on, a reality that is accepted by all."[6] An antilanguage, in other words, expresses—as well as helps create and defend—a distinct worldview and value system that entirely reject and even invert those of the dominant society. The view of the world constructed in and by the antilanguage thus serves as an ideological, oppositional alternative to the existing social order, and not simply as a device for outlawed groups to conceal their deeds.

The image of Yiddish that emerges from the Christian sources has distinctive antilanguage features, both in its ideological function and in its sociolinguistic status. Yiddish is depicted as a language of social conflict, consciously used by the marginalized Jewish minority both in the form of passive resistance, in order to maintain and defend their particular social reality (for example, the claim that the Jews adhere consciously and deliberately to Yiddish in order to prevent Christian influences from entering the Jewish realm), or in the form of an active or even offensive opposition to dominant society (as in the claim that the Jews use Yiddish to blaspheme, deceive, or otherwise harm non-Jews). Rejecting the language of established society, and the Christian values it stands for, as "*loshn tome*" (an impure language), the Jews, so runs the argument, deliberately and comprehensively relexicalize the German language.[7] They introduce Hebrew words in addition or as a substitute to the normative German ones, especially in areas that are seen as central to the activities of the Jewish minority, such as dubious economic behavior and other criminal practices, or in areas that set it off most clearly from the established society, most notably the religious domain. Christian sources tend to emphasize the special vocabulary of the Jews in this latter domain (a vocabulary that we have termed, following Weinreich, *lehavdl loshn*), as well as its function in demarcating the lines between Jews and non-Jews. The proliferation of terms (overlexicalization) intended to serve this function is also thoroughly discussed in Christian literature, as in the enumerating of over thirty, mostly derogatory, designations for Christians in Eisenmeger's work.[8]

A commonly accepted assertion among the Christian authors was that the lexical items inserted by the Jews into the German language were meant to safeguard Jewish secrets and disguise their unlawful activities—from allowing them to resort to their hidden transcript in the presence of Christians to serving as secretive codes in the language of the underworld. But in addition to its function as a secret language, the image of Yiddish fostered in Christian sources was that of a language which represented an alternative ideology: by the means of linguistic transformations the Jews adapted the German language to a distinct Jewish worldview and a set of values that were opposed to the dominant social and linguistic orders. Yiddish was seen as the bearer of an alternative social reality in which Judaism gained supremacy and Christianity was under attack. It was the language of a world turned upside down, the antilanguage of an antisociety.

Part III *The Discourse on Yiddish in Early Modern Germany*

Introduction

Between Hebrew and German: The Depictions of Yiddish in Christian Writings

Without ruling out sincere thirst for knowledge as a possible incentive for Christian scholars' engagement with Yiddish culture, the evidence we have examined suggests that the Christian study of Yiddish was hardly an exercise in cross-cultural understanding. Rather, the body of philological knowledge created by the Christian scholars on the Yiddish language and literature was directly linked to the exercise of power: it was conceived as an effective tool for exerting control over the Jews living in their midst, for missionizing them, and for utilizing their sources in the service of Christian theology. But the authors' interest in Yiddish transcended the practical uses of the Jewish language for a "profitable dialectic of information and control."[1] By mediating Yiddish culture to their readers, they were also participating in a broader discourse on Jews and Judaism that was taking place in the German world at the time. Shaped by contemporary attitudes toward the Jewish minority on the one hand, and by intra-Christian concerns on the other, this discourse expressed—and supported—the asymmetrical power relations between Jews and Christians, and the status of the Jew as the marginal Other in German culture and society.

The following chapters discuss two central motifs in the early modern Christian literature on Yiddish: one concerns the relation between Yiddish and German, and the other, between Yiddish and Hebrew. The first chapter in this part focuses on how the authors defined and described the Jewish language via its relation to German. Although the authors formulated their criticism on Yiddish in linguistic categories, their stance toward the Jewish language should be seen against the backdrop of the broader cultural and social concerns of the time, most notably the attempts of German scholars to cultivate and purify the

German language, attempts that were motivated to a large extent by the role of language as a constituent of German nationhood. Another aspect of the Christian concern with the relation between Yiddish and German, discussed in Chapter 8, was the attempts of missionaries to "Germanize" Yiddish in order to "improve" the Jewish language and make it more adequate for the missionary cause.

The relation between Yiddish and its other parent language, Hebrew, is the topic of the final chapter. In particular, the chapter explores the discussions of Christian scholars concerning the state of Hebrew among Yiddish-speaking Jews, as part of their attempt to assert Christian supremacy over the Jewish minority. Despite its focus on theological polemics, this discourse also involved notions of culture and ethnicity, and showed strong resemblance to what we would term today an Orientalist discourse.[2] In addition to the fact that Christian literature on Yiddish supports the conjunction between knowledge and power, a close reading of these texts reveals how Christian authors used their writing on the Yiddish language and literature to construct a denigrating image of contemporary Jewish culture and religion. It is against this image that they could then assert and confirm their own religious superiority and cultural hegemony.

Seven German of the Jews
Linguistic Affinity and the Politics of Differentiation

In their attempt to define and explain the Yiddish language to their readers, the Christian authors usually discussed the Jewish language vis-à-vis its relation to German. This is of course not surprising, considering the close linguistic affinity between the two languages and the fact that Yiddish contains a major Germanic component. Further, the Christian literature on Yiddish was mainly a *German* phenomenon: the works were written first and foremost by German-speaking scholars and were published, either in Latin or in German, in the German-speaking lands. The question that will concern us here is *how* the Christian authors depicted the relation between Yiddish and German: both in the structural, or linguistic, dimension, which is descriptive of the language itself (its phonology, grammar, and vocabulary), and in the functional dimension, which relates to the social uses of Yiddish as a means of communication within German society.[1] We shall also consider the social and cultural factors that shaped the Christian depictions of Yiddish and its relation to German, and examine the notions these depictions helped promote, regarding the place of the Jews and their language in German society, and in the consolidating German *Sprachnation*.

The Structural Dimension: Yiddish as a German Variant

The close linguistic affinity between Yiddish and German is a recurrent and much emphasized theme in the Christian literature, as can be seen already from the names given to this language. Whereas the term *Jiddisch* (Yiddish) was brought into wide use in German only at the beginning of the twentieth century, expressing the notion of Yiddish as an independent language, the names for Yiddish in the early modern literature suggest that it was perceived as some kind of German dialect, as the Christian authors sometimes call it, or sociolect (social dialect), as we would call it today. Yiddish is referred to as *Juden-deutsch*, *jüdisch-deutsch*, *Rabbinisch-Teutsch*, *hebräisch-deutsch* (or in Latin, *Hebraeo-Germanica*, *Judaeo-Germanica*, *Germanica Judaeorum*), and sometimes simply as "German" (*Teutsch*, *lingua Germanica*).[2] That some authors considered the Yiddish of their time as no more than German written with Hebrew characters can be seen from their choice of terms like *deutsch mit ebräischen o. Jüdischen buchstaben*, *Germanica literis Ebraicis*, and *hebreas litteras teutonice*, which were also commonly used. In some cases these terms were indeed chosen to designate texts that were basically German transliterated with Hebrew or Yiddish letters. But in many instances they function as names for Yiddish and appear interchangeably, and even in the same text, with the other designations such as *Juden-deutsch* or *jüdisch-deutsch*.

In 1711 a Yiddish translation of the entire Bible, published in Amsterdam in 1687, was transcribed with Latin characters and republished in the *Biblia Pentapla*, a collection of five Germanic translations of Scripture: Catholic, Lutheran, Reformed, Jewish (Yiddish), and Dutch.[3] The title of the first volume informs the readers that the volume includes "The Old Testament . . . according to the finest four *High German translations* together with the Dutch."[4] The editor of the work, Johann Otto Glüsing, explains in the introduction that the Jew Joseph Athias originally prepared the translation for publication "very meticulously, but with rabbinic letters, in the German language." In this edition, Glüsing assures his readers, the rabbinic letters have been replaced with Latin ones; Athias's Bible could be now considered "officially German."

The notion of Yiddish as basically a German variant is also reflected in the way the authors attempt to define and depict the language. Many of the Christian writers emphasize that Yiddish "consists mostly of German words and phrases," or even assert that it is "*eigentlich Teutsch*" (in fact German).[5] As Yiddish scholar Jerold C. Frakes has argued, these linguistic depictions of Yiddish were mostly German-oriented: "conceiving of the language as German that is merely 'disguised' by the Hebrew alphabet," the authors usually did not seek to present a systematic codification of Yiddish phonology, syntax, morphology, and semantics but mainly to demonstrate how one can transcribe German with Hebrew letters. Moreover, the general tendency to view Yiddish simply as a slightly modified German resulted in gross inadequacies and Germanizing distortions in the presentations: in different cases authors described German usages rather than Yiddish ones, provided examples inconceivable in authentic Yiddish, and in general failed to recognize the differences between the German and Yiddish languages of their time. The reading exercises provided by the Christian authors, too, were often not actual Yiddish texts but German texts transcribed into the Hebrew alphabet by the authors, according to "distinctly non-Yiddish orthography" and "vocabulary inconceivable in Yiddish of any period."[6]

Another result of this Germanocentric approach to Yiddish was the practice of some of the authors to emphasize how easy it is for a German-speaker to learn Yiddish. Already in the sixteenth century, the convert Paul Helicz, a publisher of Hebrew books from Hundesfeld (near Breslau), asserted at the beginning of his Yiddish tutorial that "anyone who can already read our German script can also easily read this Jewish-German script, if he only learns the alphabet and knows what their vowels are. Thus he has already learned most of it."[7] Half a century later, Christian Hebraist Johann Buxtorf noted at the end of his appendix on Yiddish that "someone who is knowledgeable in the German language can easily observe for himself other things that relate to the reading and writing [of Hebrew-German]."[8] Eighteenth-century authors continued to promote this idea, asserting that for anyone proficient in German, learning Yiddish should not take more than a few days, or indeed, a few hours.[9] After all, as the Frankfurter theologian Johann Jacob Schudt assured his readers, Yiddish "is for anyone, who understands only little Hebrew, very easy to understand; since it's German, and the words are familiar, one can easily guess most of it."[10]

Nevertheless, the Christian authors did not completely ignore the many ways in which the Yiddish of their time differed from German. In addition to providing rules for transcribing German with Hebrew letters, they also explained that the Jews' language contained many Hebrew and Aramaic words as well as Germanized words based on Hebrew roots. They also mentioned that many of the German words were pronounced differently in Yiddish, and that the Jews used also "peculiar words" (*sonderliche Wörter*), that is words from other (mainly Romance) languages as well as older German words, which were no longer in use among the general population. However, the Christian authors usually presented these characteristics of Yiddish as mere deviations from—or indeed, corruption of—their own German language. Thus, for instance, we read that "[the] German [language] among them is never pure," that "they have, in German, some peculiar and improper [in another place: "peculiar and almost barbaric"] turns of speech," and that in general they have created a corrupt, mutilated (*verstümmelt*), and even barbaric language (*Character barbarus*).[11]

One of the recurrent criticisms refers to the way the Jews pronounce (or rather *mis*pronounce) the German words in Yiddish, in a manner

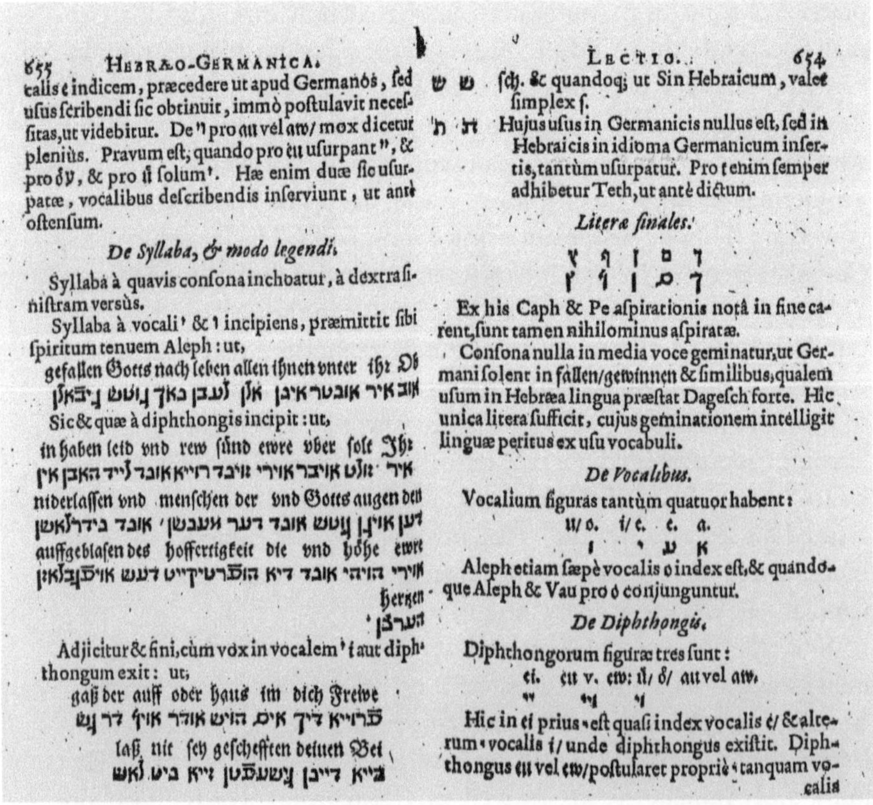

655 HEBRÆO-GERMANICA.

calis e indicem, præcedere ut apud Germanos, sed usus scribendi sic obtinuit, immò postulavit necessitas, ut videbitur. De pro au vel aw/ mox dicetur pleniùs. Pravum est, quando pro eu usurpant, & pro dy, & pro ü solum. Hæ enim duæ sic usurpatæ, vocalibus describendis inserviunt, ut antè ostensum.

De Syllaba, & modo legendi.

Syllaba à quavis consona inchoatur, à dextra sinistram versùs.

Syllaba à vocali & incipiens, præmittit sibi spiritum tenuem Aleph: ut,

gefallen Gotts nach leben allen jhnen vnter jhr Ob

Sic & quæ à diphthongis incipit: ut,

in haben leid vnd rew sünd ewre vber solt Jhr

niderlassen vnd menschen der vnd Gotts augen den

auffgeblasen des hoffertigkeit die vnd höhe ewre

hertzen

Adjicitur & fini, cùm vox in vocalem i aut diphthongum exit: ut;

gaß der auff oder haus im dich Frewe

laß nit sey geschefften deinen Bei

LECTIO. 654

sch. & quandoq; ut Sin Hebraicum, valet simplex s.

Hujus usus in Germanicis nullus est, sed in Hebraicis in idioma Germanicum insertis, tantùm usurpatur. Pro t enim semper adhibetur Teth, ut antè dictum.

Literæ finales.

Ex his Caph & Pe aspirationis notâ in fine carent, sunt tamen nihilominus aspiratæ.

Consona nulla in media voce geminatur, ut Germani solent in fallen/gewinnen & similibus, qualem usum in Hebræa lingua præstat Dagesch forte. Hîc unica litera sufficit, cujus geminationem intelligit linguæ peritus ex usu vocabuli.

De Vocalibus.

Vocalium figuras tantùm quatuor habent:

u/o. i/e. e. a.

Aleph etiam sæpè vocalis o index est, & quandoque Aleph & Vau pro o conjunguntur.

De Diphthongis.

Diphthongorum figuræ tres sunt:

ei. eu v. ew: ü/ ö/ au vel aw.

Hic in ei prius est quasi index vocalis e/ & alterum vocalis i/ unde diphthongus existit. Diphthongus eu vel ew/ postularet propriè tanquam vocalis

Figure 7.1. Page from Johann Buxtorf's tutorial chapter on Yiddish in his *Thesaurus grammaticus linguae sanctae hebraeae* (Basel 1609)

"unpleasant for German ears."[12] Johann Schudt, for example, asserted in his ethnographic work *Jüdische Merckwürdigkeiten* from 1714 that "the German Jews have a peculiar, ridiculous pronunciation, a corrupted German and eccentric accent"; and in another passage, that "they pronounce the German words coarsely and foully, such as *mei liben* for *mein Leben*, . . . *nicks* for *nichts*, *asso* for *also*," and so forth.[13] Eighteenth-century convert Gottfried Selig, Hebrew lecturer at the University of Leipzig and author of a comprehensive Yiddish textbook, also emphasized this point repeatedly, explaining that "the German language sounds in the Jews' mouth so corrupt because they eagerly switch the vowels. For they use the *a* as *ei*, *au* for *a*, *ei* for *e*, *o* for *a* and *au*, and *u* for *o*, as in: . . . *aach* for *auch*, *geit* for *geht*, *hot* for *hat*, . . . *Sunne* for *Sonne* etc."[14] Some authors pointed out that due to the unique Jewish pronunciation it is very difficult for German Christians to understand even the German words in Yiddish. The author of a popular Yiddish-German lexicon, most probably the Jesuit and Hebrew censor from Prague Leopold Thirsch, claimed in the introduction to his work that "they pronounce even the genuine German words [in Yiddish] in such a coarse, such a confused manner, that one has to be very attentive in order to understand them."[15] Moreover, as convert Johann Gottfried maintained in his Yiddish textbook from 1753, since the Jews write the German words "according to their corrupt pronunciation," it is no wonder that "one finds in the Jewish writings words with wrong vowels."[16] Gottfried further asserted that "most Jews write in a very erroneous [*fehlerhaft*] manner," and he adds in a footnote: "The Jews who write in the most accurate manner are those that exercise diligently in the reading and writing of German, for they find out that many words sound completely different than the way the Jews pronounce them."[17]

The notion of Yiddish as no more than a slightly modified German, resulting in linguistic presentations that hardly went beyond a description of the alphabet, basic information about the vowels and consonants, and some additional details concerning "deviations" from German usage,[18] was typical first and foremost of the earlier works on Yiddish, from the sixteenth and seventeenth centuries. In the eighteenth century, on the other hand, one can observe a certain shift in the Christian works on Yiddish. Although during this period, too, the authors were preoccupied not with establishing grammatical rules of correct usage but merely with presenting Yiddish as "corrupted" German, the depictions of the Jewish language presented by most of them nonetheless show greater complexity and a deeper understanding of the nature of Yiddish than in the previous centuries. Most noticeable is the greater attention given to the Hebraic component of Yiddish. Side by side with the assertions of how easy it is for German-speakers to learn Yiddish, we also find the opposite opinion, emphasizing the necessity of at least a certain proficiency in Hebrew in order to learn Yiddish, or even claiming that Yiddish is quite difficult to learn due to its considerable Hebrew component.[19] Indicative of this new trend are the many dictionaries and lexicons dedicated almost entirely to the Hebrew vocabulary in Yiddish, which appeared during the eighteenth century.[20] Moreover, with the greater attention given to the Hebraic component came a greater appreciation of the nature of Yiddish as a mixed language, or *fusion language*, as we refer to it today.[21]

The recognition of Yiddish as a mixed language evoked equally mixed and even contradictory evaluations of the Jewish language. On the one hand, it led to a growing appreciation of Yiddish as a language in its own right. The Pietist missionary and professor of philosophy and Oriental languages in Halle, Johann Heinrich Callenberg, made a place of honor for himself in the history of Yiddish studies when he decided to open his *Kurtze Anleitunng zur Jüdischteutschen Sprache* (A brief introduction to the Jewish-German language; 1733) with the following assertion: "The Jewish-German language is a mixed language [*eine vermischte Sprache*], composed to a large extent from German, but also from Hebrew words. One speaks here about a noticeable mixture. A minor mixture does not make an independent language."[22] Wilhelm Christian Justus Chrysander, the most important Yiddish grammarian of his time, took up the same argument almost twenty years later, explaining that "because of this noticeable mixture and composition of two types of languages [German and Hebrew], one may also call it a hybrid language [*hibridam linguam*]." This assertion made Chrysander wonder if there were other Jewish languages in addition to the Jewish-German one, such as a Jewish-Spanish or a Jewish-French, or even a Jewish-English. After conducting a small "test," in which he tried to apply the fusion principles of Yiddish to other European languages (would an English Jew say, "With a[n] *Amhorez* i have not *koved* to be *mefalp'l*"? would a French Jew say, "se faire *schmadd*er" [from the Hebrew word *shmad*], like the German Jews say "*sich schmadden lassen*" [to convert]?), Chrysander came to the conclusion that such forms do not possibly exist. It was only with the German language, he asserted, that the Jews made "such a mixture" (*eine solche Vermischung*).[23]

On the other hand, not only did the perception of Yiddish as a German dialect continue in the works published after Callenberg's dramatic assertion (and for that matter in other places of Callenberg's own work); it was precisely this fusion nature of the Jewish language that induced other eighteenth-century authors to deny Yiddish the status of a full-blown language. Only twenty years after Callenberg's pathbreaking recognition of the existence of a Yiddish *language*, Johann Gottfried made it very explicit that "the language of the Jews is not a proper language, but is only composed of a corrupt and mutilated German, next to an excessive interspersion of Hebrew words and entire phrases"[24]; whereas Gottfried Selig claimed, "The Jews' language, or the so-called Jewish-German, is not an independent language, orderly arranged according to defined rules, but is much more a mixture [*Gemengsel*], composed of corrupt, foul-sounding and badly pronounced German, Polish, French, Latin, self invented and Hebrew words."[25]

Like the notion of Yiddish as a corrupt German, the recognition of its mixed character also drew fire to the Jewish language, leading it to be branded as a "confused mongrel language," "gibberish," "an impure language," and "a pitiful mishmash." The confused nature of Yiddish was further emphasized by the idea that Yiddish did not have a clear set of rules. The authors complained that Yiddish suffered from grave orthographic inconsistencies; that the vowels could be interpreted in various ways; that there was no sufficient distinction of the grammatical categories of number, gender, and tenses; and that practically any Jew spoke and wrote Yiddish as he liked. Together with the insertion of foreign loanwords deriving from various linguistic sources, the absence of clear and binding rules rendered Yiddish, according to the authors, hardly comprehensible and not easy to acquire—an assertion that stood in contradiction to the idea that Yiddish, due to its affinity with German, was very easy to learn.[26]

The developments in the linguistic presentations of Yiddish in the works of eighteenth-century Christian authors were closely related to other developments in the genre as a whole: while the Christian works on Yiddish from the sixteenth and seventeenth centuries were mainly scholarly, written almost exclusively in Latin, the ones produced in the late seventeenth century and during the eighteenth century were of a more popular character. Written mainly in German, they were directed at broader Christian audiences, such as missionaries, businessmen, or "anyone else who had dealings with Jews,"[27] and paid more attention to the *spoken* language in addition to the written one. Eighteenth-century works on Yiddish were also more extensive, as elaborated discussions on the nature of Yiddish, its literature, and its Jewish speakers replaced the laconic, more strictly linguistic presentations of the earlier period.[28]

But at least from a sociolinguistic perspective, the most interesting development that took place in the Christian literature on Yiddish from the late seventeenth century onwards was the incorporation of highly negative evaluations of the Jewish language, especially its relation to German. As seen from the examples presented above, the harsh criticism of the linguistic characteristics of Yiddish comes almost exclusively, and in the most explicit manner, in works from the later period. Not content with merely providing a linguistic description of the Jewish language—distorted and unauthentic as it may have been—eighteenth-century authors defined Yiddish and its relation to German in highly moralistic terms, presenting its speakers, the Jews, as damaging, perverting, and even desecrating the "real," "pure" German tongue.

An illuminating example in this respect is found in the words of Johann Christoph Wagenseil, one of the most famous Christian Hebraists and a prominent Yiddish scholar in the early modern period. In the introduction to his influential Yiddish textbook *Belehrung der Jüdisch-Deutschen Red- und Schreibart* (1699), Wagenseil writes:

> The Jews have never dealt with any language . . . so sinfully [*lästerlich*] as with our German, for they have given it a totally foreign intonation and pronunciation, mutilated the good German words, tortured and distorted them, invented new words unknown to us, and also mixed countless Hebrew words and phrases into German, so that whoever hears them speak German [Yiddish] cannot but believe that they are speaking nothing but pure Hebrew, since hardly a single comprehensible word comes out.[29]

In these words we encounter a very serious, though not uncommon, accusation against the Jews, as if they were trying, deliberately and maliciously, to corrupt and abuse the German language; as if there were some kind of Jewish conspiracy to take over the German and turn it into a Jewish language. The key word here is "*lästerlich*," which may be translated as "calumniously," thus suggesting an insulting and disparaging treatment of German at the hands of the Jews; but it can also mean "sinfully" or "blasphemously," with clear religious connotations. According to this interpretation, Yiddish was considered a sin against the German language, reflecting the popular view that anything the Jews did was an attack on Christianity and the Christian order.[30] Interestingly enough, Wagenseil himself was known as a fierce opponent of the traditional accusations raised against the Jews, such as the blood libels or desecration of the host, and for this he is usually regarded in Jewish historiography as a friend of the Jews. But here we can see that despite his renunciation of traditional anti-Jewish accusations as unfounded superstitions, Wagenseil in fact preserved the notion that the Jews posed a threat to Christian society, while shifting the discussion from the medieval, religious domain into the more "enlightened" and even "scientific" one of linguistics.

Similar accusations against the way Jews handle, or rather mishandle, the German language can be found in Wilhelm Chrysander's *Jüdisch-Teutsche Grammatick* from the year 1750. In a passage entitled "About [the] German words [in Yiddish], and how these are being mishandled," Chrysander explains:

> Since the Jews consider German a pagan language [*Heydensprache*], they do not think it worth learning in an accurate manner. They write without grammar. They do not always distinguish number and gender, and substantives from adjectives, etc. Since they care little for accuracy in our language, they are even less concerned with its purity. . . . There is an element of dominance involved, when the Jewish nation everywhere, even beyond Germany, diverges from the language of the country and uses words which they have misshapen, distorted, and torn to bits.[31]

In other works, too, we read that "In speaking and writing German, contemporary Jews are guilty of absolute barbarisms and solecisms [*Barbarismos et Soloecismos*]"; that through their "Jewish manner of writing" the Jews have produced an "incorrect, corrupted, unreadable, and incomprehensible German"; and that by incorporating Hebrew words in German, "and this completely against its grammar," the Jews "thus offend the beautiful language so greatly, that one is left astonished."[32]

That the Christian authors incorporated negative evaluations into their linguistic depictions of Yiddish should not surprise us. In every speech community, the awareness of linguistic variants is inevitably accompanied by value judgment and by establishing a hierarchy of languages and dialects.[33] Although such judgment is often rationalized in terms of aesthetic appeal or by preference to certain notions of alleged linguistic propriety, there are in fact no purely linguistic grounds for preferring one form of speech habits to another. Rather, it is a matter of social attitude: the speech patterns of the dominant social group assume a prestige value as "correct" or "pleasant," whereas those of subordinate groups come to be stigmatized as "incorrect" or "ugly."

As the British linguist Michael Halliday claims, social dialects (including religious and ethnic ones) are particularly subject to hostile attitudes from other members of the speech community. While regional dialects can be explained away as geographically determined, a social dialect is the embodiment of a different worldview—"one which is therefore potentially threatening, if it does not coincide with one's own." According to Halliday, "This is undoubtedly the explanation of the violent attitudes that under certain social conditions come to be held by one group towards the speech of others. A different set of *vowels* is perceived as the symbol of a different set of *values*, and hence takes on the character of a threat."[34] With the working assumption that the differences between Yiddish and German, as between any two languages or language variants, are linguistically arbitrary (that is, that there was nothing inherently "wrong" or "corrupt" in early modern Yiddish), we shall now explore the "certain social conditions" under which these differences became subject to linguistic prejudice and negative evaluation in early modern Christian writings.

German and the Jewish Threat

The fact that Yiddish is a *Jewish* language may certainly serve as one explanation for the fervor with which it was condemned by the German authors. Because attitudes toward a certain language are necessarily colored by the attitudes toward the people who use it, we may assume that the derogatory remarks made by early modern Christian authors against Yiddish resulted largely from the generally negative stance toward the Jewish minority, which was common among the Christian authors as well as among the general population in early modern Germany. As a "language of Jewishness," or *yidishkayt*, to use Max Weinreich's term, Yiddish was shaped and defined by the Jewish religion and the experience of Ashkenazi Jewry as a religious minority group, and was permeated with what Weinreich has called "a Jewish spirit."[35] The Hebrew alphabet, the *loshn-koydesh* vocabulary, the Jewish intonation and way of speech, and the Jewish content of its literature—all these features made Yiddish a conspicuous and powerful manifestation of *yidishkayt*, and a distinctive marker of Jewish identity. In this sense, the negative evaluation of Yiddish should be seen as an expression of the Christian rejection of Jewish religion and culture as a whole, in which the conscious motif of "I don't like their *vowels*" symbolizes an underlying motif of "I don't like their *values*."[36] In the early modern period in particular, when languages were taken as signs of the psychic and moral characteristics of their speakers, the evaluation of languages was characterized by the tendency "to equate the characteristics of language with the characteristics of the people who speak it, and thus to move within an overlapping area of linguistics and cultural psychology."[37] The association of Yiddish with the prevalent Jewish stereotypes of the time, most notably that of the Jew as deceitful and degenerate, must have contributed to the pejorative attitudes of Christians toward the Jews' language. Another possibility we should consider is that the negative stance toward the Jews' language was closely related to the way the Christian authors perceived and understood the place of the Jews in German society. Since in every society the *social* hierarchy is reflected and sustained by the *linguistic* hierarchy,[38] the attempt of Christian authors to marginalize the Yiddish language and stigmatize it as an inferior German variant can be seen as a means to sustain and reinforce the existing social order, in which the Jewish minority was subordinate to the Christian, German-speaking majority. Any attempt, in other words, to recognize Yiddish as a legitimate German variant had to be avoided, for it could lead to an unwelcome modification of the existing social order.

Yet it seems that Yiddish aroused hostile reactions among German, Christian authors, not only for being a *Jewish* language but also for being a *German* language; that is, because of the close linguistic relation between Yiddish and German. In the seventeenth and eighteenth centuries, intense discussions took place among German academics, writers, and intellectuals regarding the "question of the German language."[39] In their writings and statements on the subject, often accompanied by strong patriotic and even nationalistic overtones, the German scholars emphasized the virtue and excellence of the German language and its superiority over other languages, most notably French and Latin. Unlike the Romance languages, which were mixed and therefore "polluted," the authors maintained, German had remained pure and unpolluted over many thousands of years. With the assertion that "nature speaks German," some authors even identified this language as the original language spoken by Adam in paradise, thus promoting it to the status of the holiest, most ancient, and most natural of all languages in the world. In addition to purity and old age, the authors ascribed to German other linguistic values, such as euphony, or a superb pronunciation, richness of vocabulary, and semantic precision. German was considered lovely (*lieblich*) because of the poetry written in it, and ingenious and salutary (*geist- und lehrreich*) because of Luther's translation of the Bible. In accordance with the idea of the "genius of language" (*Geist der Sprache*), which asserted that languages indicate the characteristics of their respective speech communities, German was often described in moralistic terms as "language of the heroes" (*Heldensprache*), "masculine" (*männlich*), and "honest" (*ehrlich*, *redlich*).

However, as historian Peter Burke notes with regard to eulogies (*Lobschriften*) of this kind, "the way in which these treatises should be read remains a problem, less simple than it may appear. . . . They may be expressions of confidence, but they may also be signs of an inferiority complex relative to Latin, Italian, or . . . French."[40] Indeed, the very same authors who praised and complimented their German mother tongue also expressed considerable dissatisfaction with the state of the language in their own day. German was divided into numerous dialects, and the differences between them were sometimes so great as to prevent mutual understanding. In the absence of a standard variant, German men of letters struggled with the question of what was "good German," and the debates regarding the desired standard continued into the second half of the eighteenth century. An even graver concern of the German intellectuals was what they considered to be the neglect of the mother tongue among their fellow Germans. The authors repeatedly complained that although the German language had many clear advantages over French and Latin, it was not used for serious writings. Latin and later on French were the languages of academic discourse, of official correspondence, and of the German nobility. For many Germans with social or cultural aspirations, too, writing in foreign languages was a sign of prestige, which German obviously lacked. Moreover, even when Germans did use their language, either in speaking or in writing, they would incorporate foreign words and phrases into their German. This common practice of inserting French, Latin, Italian, or Spanish words into German was condemned with special vehemence by the advocates of the German language. They considered it a corruption of the language, a practice that "obscures the majestic glamour of our *Heldensprache*."[41]

The great love and appreciation of the German language on the one hand, and the grave concern about its state as a means of literary and intellectual expression on the other, led German scholars and men of letters to take practical measures for the cultivation and improvement of the language. They aimed to establish and propagate a German standard that would serve as an effective means of communication, suitable for all literary activities and intelligible to Germans from all regions, and also to increase the prestige of the German language by putting it on a level with other national languages in Europe. This process of language cultivation (*Sprachkultivierung*), perceived by its adherents as a moral and patriotic duty of highest importance, entailed the consolidation of the language through codification of its orthography and grammatical rules in order to ensure its unity and stability. Considerable attention was also given to the purification of the German language (*Sprachpurismus*) from foreign elements, as well as from archaisms and dialectal forms that were considered a corruption of the standard language. The cultivation project that began with the establishment of language societies (*Sprachgesellschaften*) in the seventeenth century developed into a fully fledged process of language standardization in the eighteenth century and was completed—at least as far as the written language was concerned—towards the year 1800.

Throughout the process of cultivation and standardization, the German language continued to be the focus of ardent discussions concerning its status, its functions, and the dangers lurking for it. As is usually the case in standardizations of vernaculars,[42] the discussions that accompanied the standardization process of German were characterized by linguistic chauvinism and unmistakable intolerance. The need to distinguish the rising standard both from other languages and from other variants of the language entailed a determined rejection of every linguistic instance that did not conform to the newly founded norms, or otherwise seemed to threaten the still uncertain position of the emerging standard. Seen in this context, the pejorative statements against Yiddish should be interpreted as a defense mechanism applied by the German authors to protect the status and integrity of the emerging German language. Due to its unique linguistic structure, Yiddish was resented both as a German dialect, deviating from the desired standard, and as a mixed language, contaminating the "purity" of German by the insertion of foreign words and phrases. Lacking a fixed and clearly defined set of rules, Yiddish presented a chaotic version of German, an antithesis to the meticulously regulated language the German scholars were striving to create. As a mixed, confused, and impure kind of German, Yiddish represented all the language qualities the German scholars tried to avoid. It thus aroused their abhorrence and was perceived to interfere with the German process of standardization, to compromise it, and to threaten to undermine it from within. The vulnerable state of German at the time did not leave much room for linguistic cousins, let alone for the German of the Jews.

Yiddish and German: The National Perspective

An important aspect of the discourse on German in the early modern period was that of "linguistic nationalism," namely the prominent role the German language had played in defining and shaping German national consciousness from the late Middle Ages onwards. Although the close connection between language and nationhood is not a unique German phenomenon, the notion that *gentum lingua facit* (the language makes the people) seems to be especially true for the German case, where other unifying national characteristics, such as a well defined territory and a central government, were lacking for many centuries.[43]

Despite the fact that the political realization of German national aspirations did not occur before the nineteenth century, the roots of German national consciousness can be traced back to the late Middle Ages and the beginning of the early modern period.[44] As historian Wolfgang Hardtwig argues, nationalism, and even essential elements of a specifically "modern" nationalism, existed in Germany already since the end of the fifteenth and the beginning of the sixteenth centuries at the latest, even if those were common only among the thin layers of the newly rising elite at the time—writers, intellectuals, and officials[45]—most of whom advocated the cultivation of German and its use in new domains as part of their national agenda.

In his book *Mother-Tongue and Fatherland*, historian Michael Townson relates the role of language as a major constituent of German nationhood to the fact that the Germans (*die Deutschen*) as a nation were defined originally by their language—those who spoke German (*deutsch*). By the late fifteenth century, the close relationship between the Germans and their language had become sufficiently strong for the name of the empire to be expanded to "Das Heilige Römische Reich Deutscher Nation." This phrase testifies to a decline in the sense of belonging to an international empire, and the rise of a sense of belonging to a specifically German linguistic and cultural entity. The perception and role of the German language as a symbol of national identity, promoted in the writings of late fifteenth-century and early sixteenth-century German Humanists, reached a first climax with Martin Luther and the German Reformation. Luther's German translation of the Bible and his many other German writings significantly contributed to the establishment of a model for a German literary language and to the increasing popularity of works in the vernacular. Most important, Luther's Bible considerably enhanced the prestige of the German language, promoting German to the status of a "holy language," a language in which the Word of God is transmitted.[46] As was the case in other early modern European nations, the transition from Latin to the vernacular as the language of praying and of reading Scripture considerably contributed to the rise of national consciousness in German Protestant circles. The translation of the Old Testament into the European vernaculars was especially influential in the growing claims of the different nations, including the Germans, to be the holy, elected nation.[47]

The long tradition of the Germans as a nation defined primarily by its language (*Sprachnation*) continued into the seventeenth and eighteenth centuries as an essential component of German national identity in general, and of the German Protestant one in particular. As the Thirty Years' War put an end to any chance of political or religious unification in the foreseeable future, language assumed an even greater role than before as a sole unifying German characteristic. Indeed, the efforts of German scholars in the seventeenth and eighteenth centuries, described above, to standardize the German language and purify it from foreign influences were not merely expressions of apolitical aesthetics. What came to be known as the baroque *Sprachpatriotismus* was driven by the desire to protect the fragile German nationhood from the invasion of foreign elements, and from a further decline in its political strength as a result of the weakening of lingual-cultural unity. The vehemence with which contemporary authors condemned the linguistic practices of their fellow Germans (namely the neglect of the German language and the incorporation of foreign words and phrases into it) resulted, at least in part, from the association made by the authors between the state of the language and the state of the German nation as a whole. Gottfried Wilhelm Leibniz, for example, linked the pitiful state of the German language to the disastrous effects inflicted on the German people by the Thirty Years' War. In two treatises from the late seventeenth century Leibniz warned his readers that the failure to cultivate their native language and the adoption of foreign tongues led to national subjugation and loss of liberty. Asserting that the German language was as much in a state of vassalage as were other aspects of national life, Leibniz argued that this state of servitude and inferiority to other nations (most notably France) would continue unless Germans turned to their own language with the respect it deserved.[48]

The unique status of the German language as a constitutive element of German national consciousness might shed further light on the attitudes toward Yiddish at the time. As Adrian Hastings explains in his book *The Construction of Nationhood*, a nation that is defined by its language "is blissfully open to newcomers in a way that a bristly national spirit, a little unsure of its precise identity, is unlikely to tolerate." After all, anyone can acquire a language and thus claim his belonging to the nation. "A principle of national unity which is so inclusivist," Hastings maintains, "may be all very well if you have the matrix of a strong state[;] but the very vagueness of the German nation in hard fact, disunited politically and spread across huge tracts of central and eastern Europe," made the language criterion highly problematic for the Germans, especially in the German-Jewish context. If Yiddish was considered a variant of German, then a nationalism grounded explicitly on language must, at least theoretically, include the Yiddish-speaking Jews within the German nation. According to Hastings, the Germans resolved this problem by adopting "a mythical principle of unity which laid down a hard frontier of separation"—an ethnic criterion of common origin.[49]

In the writings on Yiddish, it seems that the authors preferred to deal with the problem in the linguistic domain, by resorting to the social quality of language as a potent means of maintaining boundaries. As Peter Burke aptly notes, "One of the most important of the signs of collective identity is language. Speaking the same language, or variety of language, as someone else is a simple and effective way of indicating solidarity; speaking a different language or variety of language is an equally effective way of distinguishing oneself from other individuals or groups."[50] It is therefore not surprising that alongside their acknowledgment of the close relation between Yiddish and German, the German authors also endeavored to accentuate the distance between the two languages as a means of distinguishing themselves from the Jews. Thus, for example, many authors constructed a clear opposition between their own German (*unser Teutsch*, *nostra germanica*) and the German of the Jews (*ihr Teutsch*, *Teutsch ihrer Art nach*), indicating how certain linguistic instances were written or pronounced by the Jews, and conversely, how it was written or pronounced "by us Germans." The "ours" versus "theirs" scheme was further emphasized by another claim presented in many of the works: that it was in fact very difficult for German Christians to understand the Jewish-German language of their neighbors. Leopold Thirsch, for instance, claimed in the introduction to his Yiddish-German lexicon that Yiddish "cannot be easily understood by anyone else but them [the Jews]"; whereas seventeenth-century convert Christian Gerson asserted that the Jews "can speak with one another so that hardly any Christian can understand [them]."[51]

Some authors also promoted the idea that due to the Jews' peculiar language, "one can easily distinguish them from German Christians."[52] Therefore, one would always be able to recognize a Jew. Even if the latter tried to disguise his Jewish identity and pretend to be a Christian, his language would betray him.

A very early example of Christians identifying a Jew by his language comes to us from fifteenth-century Magdeburg, where a Christian plaintiff believed a certain thief to be Jewish since "he had a long face with a long nose and he talked like a Jew."[53] While it is hard to judge from this example if the plaintiff indeed meant that the Jew spoke a different language variant, or whether he simply wished to indicate that the Jew had a particular accent or intonation, later examples refer more explicitly to the Jews' *language* as an overt marker of Jewish identity. In the 1730s, a supporter of Callenberg's missionary institute in Halle reports from Wittenberg that while he was selling copies of the missionary tract *Or le'eys erev*, one of the buyers presented himself as a Christian. Identifying the buyer to be a Jew, the supporter asked him why he pretended to be a Christian; after all, "he cannot deny his religion since his language, too, betrayed him."[54] A similar notion appears in eighteenth-century Yiddish manuals as well. A popular reading exercise in Yiddish and German, which presents a dialogue between a Christian and a Jew, opens with the following lines:

> Christian: Are you a Jew?
> Jew: That is correct. How can you tell that I am Jewish?
> Christian: Your beard [*Sokon/Bart*] and your language [*Loschon/Sprache*] sell you out, so that I believe it to be so.[55]

But were there no Jews at all who could speak "proper" German? According to the Christian authors, such Jews indeed existed. These were the Jewish criminals, who by speaking German attempted to hide their Jewish identity. In his *Jüdische Merckwürdigkeiten* from 1714, Johann Schudt claims that

> such a language [Yiddish] have all the German Jews, wherever they may live, and therefore [they] cannot easily salvage themselves, but rather their language . . . betrays them. . . . The swindlers among them might seek to change the language, like the thievish Jew "Jonas Meyer, who spoke the High-German language entirely purely and neatly, without

the usual accent that the Jews use, and by which one can immediately recognize them."[56]

This notion is further promoted in the criminal literature of the time, where we sometimes read of police officials who were surprised to find a Jew who could speak *Hochdeutsch* and was therefore considered "*bald Jude, bald Christ* [sometimes a Jew, sometimes a Christian]."[57] But in general the good German of the Jewish thieves is presented in this literature as simply another method they apply in order to disguise themselves as Christians, like the shaving of the beard or greeting other people in the name of Jesus.[58] And just as changing one's appearance or greeting in Jesus' name do not turn the Jewish criminals into Christians, so their speaking German does not make them Germans, but simply impostors.

If demarcating distinct lines between Yiddish and German could serve the authors as an effective mechanism of excluding the Jews from the German national community, the close linguistic affinity between the two languages certainly did not make that easy. Like the Jews themselves, Yiddish was both foreign and very close at one and the same time—an awkward situation that most probably contributed to the vehemence with which this language was condemned in the works of German authors. As a classic case of what Sigmund Freud would later term "the narcissism of minor differences," it seems that Yiddish evoked hostile and dismissive reactions among the German authors precisely because the differences between Yiddish and German were relatively subtle. Freud came to the recognition that it is precisely the minor differences that form the basis of estrangement and hostility between people, and that the intolerance of groups toward the "outsider" is expressed more vigorously against small differences than against fundamental ones.[59]

In the decades since Freud's work, the fundamental psychological phenomenon of the "proximate other" has continued to preoccupy scholars from the humanities and the social sciences. In an article entitled "What a Difference a Difference Makes" from 1985, historian of religions Jonathan Z. Smith addresses this issue as part of an attempt toward formulating a "theory of Otherness." Asserting that "difference is seldom a comparison between entities judged to be equivalent, [but rather] entails a hierarchy of prestige and the concomitant political ranking of superordinate and subordinate," Smith emphasizes the idea that "such distinctions are found to be drawn most sharply between 'near neighbors,' with respect to what has been termed the 'proximate other'": "While the 'other' may be perceived as being either LIKE-US or NOT-LIKE-US, he is, in fact, most problematic when he is TOO-MUCH-LIKE-US. . . . This is not a matter of the 'far,' but, preeminently, of the 'near.' The problem is not alterity, but similarity—at times, even identity."[60] This is also true in the case of reactions to language variation, in particular when a language is undergoing a process of standardization. In that case, to use Smith's formulation, "what appears from a linguistic point of view to be 'near,' appears from a political vantage to be exceedingly 'far.'"[61] Discussing the linguistic standard as a national symbol, John E. Joseph argues that "For any unit of loyalty, but particularly the nation, the standard language transcends its practical functions and is ideologized. . . . When a relatively uniform linguistic community is split politically [or in the case of Christian-Jewish relations, socially and ethnically], those responsible for standardization often ideologize whatever minor differences do separate them, so as to create the illusion of a greater *Abstand*."[62]

The constructing of distance and even contrast between "our German" and the "German of the Jews," which enabled the Christian authors to exclude the Jews from the consolidating German nation, also enabled them to define German in opposition to Yiddish, and hence to constitute the German identity in opposition to the Jewish one. In the last decades of the twentieth century there was a growing recognition of the importance of differences—especially minor ones—for the formation and maintenance of group identity.[63] After all, solidarity and conflict, internal cohesion and external distinction, are opposite sides of the same coin. In an influential work from 1969, the anthropologist Fredrik Barth asserted the significance of boundaries in shaping ethnic identity.[64] According to Barth, a group's identity is defined by its interactions with other groups, and not by some permanent or fixed "essence" of ethnic character. In other words, groups tend to define themselves not only by reference to their own characteristics but in opposition to and rejection of the characteristics of their neighbors.

The idea that identity is essentially "reactive" or "oppositional," in that it develops as a reaction to contact with the "other" and in opposition to him, seems especially insightful in the case of early modern

German identity. As already noted, German identity was defined almost exclusively by the criterion of a common language. At the same time, this language suffered from a considerable dialectal diversity and was not clearly delimited from neighboring languages, such as Dutch. This paradoxical situation rendered the questions of "what is German" and therefore "who is German" highly problematic, resulting in the need to define German identity in a largely negative manner, by what it is not. Thus, for example, it has been suggested by historians that the sense of a common German identity arose and consolidated in the Middle Ages from the contrast between the language of the Germanic-speakers on the one hand, and the Latin of the Church and the Romance vernaculars of the neighboring groups in France and Italy on the other.[65] In their writings on Yiddish, so it seems, the German authors were pursuing a similar goal: instead of defining what "true" German is, they used the language of the Jews, the classic "other" in European history,[66] as a border stone demarcating the boundaries of their own language. This allowed them to define the German language and identity negatively—German is *not* Yiddish, and its speakers are Christians, *not* Jews. It also allowed them to create a comparison between Yiddish and German, which presented the latter in a favorable light. When compared with the mixed and irregular character of Yiddish, all the flaws of German at the time, such as the inconsistent orthography or the dialectal forms and many foreign elements that infiltrated it, became insignificant in these depictions. It is against the German of the Jews that the Christian authors could thus conveniently construct "our German," the pure, true, intact *Hochdeutsch*, common among "us Christians"[67]—as if such a pure and homogenous German language indeed existed.

The Functional Dimension: Yiddish in German Society

Besides their treatment of the *structural* or *linguistic* dimension of the relationship between Yiddish and German, many Christian authors also discussed the *functional* dimension of Yiddish as a means of communication within German society. Of particular importance in this point was the attempt of the Christian authors to ascertain the reasons for the Jewish "corruption" of the German language, and by implication to explain the mere existence of a distinct Jewish language inside German-speaking society. The resemblance between German and Yiddish on the one hand, and the differences between them on the other, led the authors to the question, Why do the German Jews speak and write differently from the general population? Why do they use a dialect of their own? These questions seem to have bothered the Christian authors, especially because they recognized that possessing a unique language was not a pan-Judaic phenomenon but a specifically German-Jewish, or rather, Ashkenazi-Jewish, one. This point was made very explicit in Chrysander's attempt, described above, to apply the fusion principles of Yiddish to other European languages, after which he concluded that it was only with the *German* language that the Jews had made "such a mixture." The Jews in other lands, Chrysander asserted, who do not speak Yiddish, speak the tongues of their respective lands in a correct manner. They also write in the non-Jewish languages, albeit with Hebrew characters or entirely in rabbinical Hebrew.[68] Johann Wagenseil, too, referred to the practice of Jews from different lands to write the languages of their non-Jewish surroundings with Hebrew characters, but he immediately asserted that it was only "with our German" that the Jews had ever dealt "so sinfully."[69] In the second half of the eighteenth century, the Pietist missionary and professor of Oriental languages at the University of Bützow in Mecklenburg, Oluf Gerhard Tychsen, also discussed this problem. Himself an ardent Yiddishist, Tychsen nonetheless criticized the fact that the Ashkenazi Jews of his time spoke and read a language "that was customary a thousand years ago." Claiming that "neither Oriental, Portuguese, English nor French Jews write their mother tongue that badly," Tychsen then wondered why the German and Polish Jews still held on to Yiddish, "when no [Jewish religious] law obliges them to do so."[70]

Some of the answers to this problem, suggested by the authors, related the unique language of the German Jews to the external or objective circumstances of the Jewish experience in early modern Germany. Johann Wagenseil, for instance, advocated the idea that the Jews did not speak or write correct German simply because they were not educated in German schools and could not take a German tutor for their children—for who would want to work for the Jews? In Wagenseil's words,

> The reason [why the Jews are not proficient in German] is mainly, that the Jews cannot send their children to any Christian school, for one

> would hardly accept them, the Christian children would not tolerate them and would cause them all kinds of hardship. . . . With Christian private tutors it would not work either; no one would be found that would let himself be so employed since one would consider it a disgrace to take upon oneself the teaching of the Jewish children, and to have to be prepared because of that for mockery and being laughed at. . . . Besides, the simple Jews, who do not have many possessions, would not be able to pay the necessary costs of a private tutor.

And so, Wagenseil concludes, there are hardly any means left by which the Jews could achieve proficiency in the German language.[71]

Other authors pointed out the dispersion of the Jews in different German regions, as well as in different parts of Europe, as a major cause for what they considered to be the Jews' peculiar vocabulary and turns of speech in German, especially their inconsistencies and various "corruptions" in the pronunciation and spelling of German words. Although a full-blown dialectal analysis of Yiddish did not appear until 1784,[72] awareness of the existence of Yiddish dialects and their relation to the German ones appeared in the Christian literature at a much earlier stage. After a few brief references in the seventeenth century to the fact that the Jews' language differed from one locality to the other, we encounter more direct and elaborated statements on this subject. In 1699 Wagenseil explained that "the Jews also have German words of their own, which are, at least in our places, not used, but they are derived from the dialects of several German peoples"; whereas Callenberg asserted that "the German words that the Jews use derive from different dialects of the German language: e.g. from the High German, Low German, Dutch."[73] In the introduction to his *Gloria Christi* from 1710, Calvör noted the fact that "the Jews have no certain and commonly agreed manner of writing, but one [Jew] writes German in this way, the other in another way, following the dialects of the German peoples among which they live" as a prominent reason for what he described as the "confusions and hardships" (*Verwirrungen und Schwierigkeiten*) of the Yiddish language.[74] Gottfried Selig took up a similar argument in his Yiddish textbook from 1767, where he claimed that "the Jews pronounce the German language itself very corruptly, and this cannot be any other way since they assemble from all the lands, and almost in every land they adopt another dialect."[75]

Special attention was given to the differences between the Yiddish of the German Jews (Western Yiddish) and that of the east-European Jews (Eastern Yiddish). Because Eastern Yiddish was less similar to German, it was viewed by the authors as a more "corrupted" German than the Yiddish of the German Jews. Already in 1609 Johann Buxtorf noted that the Jews born and educated in the German lands used to translate Hebrew works into Yiddish in a much better way—that is, closer to German—than the Jews in Moravia, Bohemia, and Poland.[76] Later authors criticized other characteristics of the language of the Eastern Jews, especially those from Poland, such as the latter's "long-sounding accent and singing tone . . . which is very difficult to understand."[77] In an even more condemning manner, Selig noted in the late eighteenth century that "most of the Jews, but especially those from Bohemia and Poland, pronounce and write the German words so incomprehensibly, so that anyone, who is not well acquainted with their utterly corrupted, sluggish, and ill-sounding idiom, would find it very difficult to understand."[78] The large-scale Jewish immigration from Poland to the German lands, which supplied most rabbis and *melamdim* (teachers) to the German-Jewish youth at the time, was seen by eighteenth-century authors like Calvör and Chrysander as a major cause of the corrupt and confused nature of Yiddish among the German Jews.[79]

Despite such acknowledgments of the external or objective reasons for the unique German of the German Jews, most authors promoted the idea that the Jews *chose* consciously and deliberately to deviate from German and to cultivate a distinct language (or language variant) of their own. A popular argument in this respect ascribed the Jewish practice of "corrupting" the German language to the fact that the Jews disregarded and even despised German as a non-Jewish language. This suggestion was raised, for example, by the Lutheran theologian Caspar Calvör. In the introduction to his missionary tractate from 1710, Calvör stated that "the Jews pay only little attention to German, as a non-Jewish and pagan language [*eine Goim und Heyden Sprache*], and therefore do not have any certain German grammar."[80] This claim was repeated in Wilhelm Chrysander's *Jüdisch-Teutsche Grammatick* (1750), where he argued that "since the Jews consider German a pagan language, they do not think it worth learning in an accurate manner" and are even less concerned with its purity.[81] In another work, Chrysander added that they also called

German "*loschon tome*," an impure language.[82] Closely linked with this notion was the idea that the Jews preferred to deviate from German due to their "tendency to cultivate distinctive modes of life" (*aus Neigung zum sonderlichen Wesen*), as Chrysander termed it,[83] namely as a means to distance themselves from their non-Jewish surroundings. According to this notion, the Jews were reluctant to learn German because they wished to maintain their existence as a distinct minority, and not expose themselves to Christian influence.[84] Advocating the use of Yiddish for missionary purposes, Johann Wagenseil connected the Jews' unwillingness to learn German to their disinclination to learn Christian tenets. In order to missionize among the Jews, Wagenseil explained, one had to approach them in Yiddish, "since one does not encounter any desire among them to learn about our religious precepts, or to learn how to read, write, and speak good German."[85] Wagenseil also mentioned the Jewish fear of Christian influence as one of the reasons why Jews did not send their children to German schools, in addition to his claim that they would be rejected by such institutions.[86]

That Yiddish, like many other Jewish practices, served the separatistic tendencies of the Jews was also suggested in some of the Christian ethnographies of the time. In their respective chapters on the upbringing of Jewish children, Johann Buxtorf and Johann Christoph Bodenschatz created a clear association between the claim that Jewish parents taught their children to incorporate Hebrew elements into their German, rendering it incomprehensible for non-Jews, and the assertion that Jewish parents forbade their children to play with non-Jewish children, neither eat nor drink with them, "and in this way the wicked Jews implant in their children indelible hatred against the Christians."[87]

Yet the most popular argument was the one that related the Jews' reluctance to speak and write proper German to their wish to conceal their illicit affairs from Christian eyes. This suggestion coincides with the image of Yiddish as the Jews' secret language, serving them as a means to deceive and harm their Christian neighbors. As demonstrated in previous chapters, this image of Yiddish was common currency in early modern Germany. It was often maintained that the Jews used their special language in order to deceive their Christian business partners, to blaspheme and curse Christians to their faces, or otherwise to plot and execute various kinds of crimes against Christian society.

But secrecy, as suggested by many of the authors, was not a mere feature of Yiddish. Rather, it was the raison d'être of the language, the major cause of its existence. According to this notion, it was precisely the need to hide their unlawful activities that led the Jews to manipulate and to corrupt the German language in the first place, either by phonological distortions or by introducing words from Hebrew and other non-Germanic languages.

Franz Haselbauer, a Jesuit and professor of Hebrew from Prague, made this idea explicit in his Yiddish tutorial from 1742. After discussing the various ways in which Yiddish deviates from the German language, Haselbauer explains that "The purpose of this corruption is so that Christians who are present may not understand what they are saying, which results in their being more easily castigated and deceived, as we have experienced." And later he adds, "So that in speaking German, Jews can better hide their secrets and guard unknown things from us, not only do they intermingle Hebrew words (both pure and corrupt), as indicated above . . . , but they also have certain Germanisms that are peculiar to them alone."[88]

Three decades later, we encounter similar accusations in the work attributed to the Jesuit Leopold Thirsch. In the introduction to his *Nützliches Handlexikon der jüdischen Sprache* (1773), a Yiddish-German lexicon which went through several editions within a decade, the author asserts:

> The Jews residing in Bohemia, Moravia, and all the other lands in which the German language dominates make use, it is true, of the same [language]; but only in order that they may more suitably deceive [and] take advantage of the Christians, can unabashedly curse and confound them; thus they borrow many words, partly from the pure Hebrew partly from the rabbinic language, and mix them with the German language to such an extent, that through this emerges such a confused and incomprehensible mixture, which cannot be easily understood by anyone except for them.[89]

By presenting the features that distinguished Yiddish from German as no more than linguistic camouflage, aimed to render the language opaque to non-Jews, the Christian authors reduced the Jewish language to the status of a criminal jargon. As in the case of *Rotwelsch*, the language of the German underworld at the time, it was the function of Yiddish as a means to hide the unlawful purposes and dealings of its Jewish speakers that determined its linguistic structure. In the eyes of the Christian authors, the Jews did not simply take advantage of the fact that their language was incomprehensible to the rest of society, and hence *used* it to maintain secrecy; rather, they had *created* their special language in the first place exactly for this purpose.

The idea that the Jews created their own language was further sustained by other elements in the Christian depictions of Yiddish; most notably, by the authors' claim that the Jews simply *invented* large portions of the Yiddish vocabulary. Some authors chose to designate the Yiddish words that they could relate neither to German nor to Hebrew origin as "self-invented" (*selbst erdachten*, *gantz von ihnen erfunden*), whereas others suggested that one could arbitrarily combine Hebrew roots with German prefixes and suffixes to create Yiddish verbs at will.[90] The perception of Yiddish as a "*lingua fictitia*," an artificial, invented language, supported the association of the Jews' language with the criminal jargon; it also coincided with the ancient motif in Christian anti-Jewish polemics that denounced post-biblical Judaism as a man-made, invented religion, in contrast to the divine origin of Christianity.

We may certainly assume that the image of Yiddish as the Jews' secret language significantly contributed to the negative attitudes toward this language among the German authors. As sociolinguist Joshua A. Fishman maintains, "Language varieties rise and fall in symbolic value as the status of their most characteristic or marked functions rises and falls."[91] Therefore, even if the condemnations of Yiddish referred to its linguistic features (its mixed character, its incomprehensibility, its unpleasant pronunciation, and so on), the possible *extra*linguistic reasons for these condemnations should not be overlooked. The double function of Yiddish as the language of *yidishkayt* on the one hand, and from a Christian perspective as a language of criminality and deviant behavior on the other, goes a long way toward explaining the pejorative representations of the Jewish language in early modern Christian works.

In discussing the Yiddish language and its relation to German in both the structural and the functional dimensions, the authors created an interesting analogy between the threat Yiddish posed to the German language and the threat its speakers—via their Jewish-German language—posed to German society and Christian religious order. This analogy is particularly important for our understanding of the attitudes toward Yiddish since it further supports the claim that Yiddish was perceived by the non-Jewish authors as what we would term today an "antilanguage" (see earlier). With the underlying assumption that language and the relation between languages stand as a metaphor for society and the relation between different groups within it, an antilanguage is characterized by its opposition to the norms of the established language, just as the antisociety is self-consciously opposed to the norms of established society. In the Christian writings on Yiddish, the Jews are accused of defying and subverting the norms and values of the society in which they live, in the same manner that their language defies and subverts the norms and values of the non-Jewish dominant language. Like other antilanguages, Yiddish is parasitic on German, taking its basic system of rules from the non-Jewish language; at the same time, Yiddish expresses its resistance to the normative German language through a set of inversions and transformations, which symbolize Jewish resistance to the dominant society. These transformations also turn Yiddish into a secret language, a means in the hands of the Jews to translate their passive hostility into an active and even offensive opposition to the existing social and religious order.

Eight Yiddish and German in the *Judenmission*
The Limits of Linguistic Adaptation

As becomes clear from our discussion so far, early modern Christian preoccupation with Yiddish was characterized by two dominant tendencies: the attempt of Christians to utilize the Jewish language for their own purposes, and their practice of severely criticizing Yiddish—its linguistic qualities, the literature written in it, and its functions within German society. Most of the time, these two tendencies in early modern Christian Yiddishism did not contradict one another. In some cases, however, this situation confronted Christian Yiddishists with challenging dilemmas. This was especially the case with the endeavors of Christians to use Yiddish for the composition of missionary literature, as we shall now turn to see.

Although the importance of linguistic adaptation for the missionary cause was constantly emphasized in the works on missionizing in Yiddish,[1] we are faced with the interesting phenomenon that some of the most important "Yiddish" missionary writings were not in fact written in Yiddish but rather in *German* with Hebrew or Yiddish letters,[2] or at least in a very "Germanized" version of Yiddish, not necessarily suitable for Jewish readers. This was the case, for example, with the translations of the New Testament prepared for Jewish readership by Paul Helic (Cracow 1540), Elias Schadeus (Strasbourg 1592), and to a large extent Christian Moller (Frankfurt/Oder 1700), which were simply Yiddish transcriptions of Martin Luther's version. Similarly, a substantial part of the missionary works published by Callenberg in Halle consisted in fact of German texts written with Yiddish letters. Another prominent example is Caspar Calvör's *Gloria Christi* (Leipzig 1710), a bilingual text in Yiddish and German, where in the "Yiddish" part of the work the German text was merely transcribed into the Hebrew alphabet.

The missionaries' practice of writing in a Germanized Yiddish is quite puzzling, since by this they would seem to have undermined their own assertions regarding the need to adapt to the *Jewish* manner of speaking and writing. One could of course argue that the missionaries were simply not proficient enough in the Jewish language and mistakenly assumed that by transcribing German texts into the Hebrew alphabet they were indeed writing in Yiddish.[3] One could also attribute this practice to the state of the Yiddish language at the time. In the period under consideration Yiddish was far from being standardized, so that it is quite difficult to say what exactly was this "proper" Yiddish the missionaries should have been using. In fact, many contemporary Jewish works, which we consider as "Yiddish literature," were not written in proper Yiddish either: at that time, Yiddish still lacked a literary standard, and Jewish authors and translators used to adjust their language in varying degrees to Hebrew or to German according to their specific needs and goals. In some cases, German texts were indeed simply transcribed into the Hebrew alphabet.[4]

The Christian scholars, as we have seen, were aware of the inconsistency in the use of literary Yiddish. No wonder, therefore, that they saw fit to do the same in their missionary writings. For them, as for many Jewish writers, the decisive factor which differentiated a non-Jewish work from a Jewish one was the alphabet: as long as a certain work was written in Hebrew or Yiddish characters, it was considered suitable for a Jewish readership. Thus, for example, Schadeus could designate his Yiddish New Testament, which he published, as he himself notes, "although in our German [language] but with Hebrew letters and Jewish cursive [Yiddish type-font]," as intended specifically for a Jewish audience. A century later, Wagenseil stressed the idea that the obstacle preventing Jews from reading German works was not so much the German language, which the Jews more or less understood, but the Latin alphabet in which these works were printed, and he constantly reminded his readers to use the Hebrew alphabet when writing for the Jews.[5]

Although these two arguments are plausible enough, they seem insufficient. First, it would be mistaken to claim that none of the Christian authors knew Yiddish well enough or properly understood the differences between Yiddish and German. Paul Helic, for example, was a convert, who had learned Yiddish at home and not from Christian textbooks; while Callenberg employed converts as translators, editors, and compositors with the explicit aim of adjusting the missionary texts to the "Jewish manner of writing." Second, despite its inconsistent literary style, there is enough evidence to suggest that already in the sixteenth century Yiddish was distinct from German and not merely German written in Yiddish letters.[6] The Christian authors under discussion, familiar with contemporary Jewish literature, must have known that many of these works were indeed written in Yiddish (the so-called Old Literary Yiddish), and not in a transcribed German.

Most important, however, the missionaries themselves were very much aware of the importance of writing for the Jews in a Jewish manner, at least from the late seventeenth century onwards, as discussed above.[7] Thus, even if one could argue that a concern for a far-reaching adaptation to the Jewish language did not play a significant role in the earlier works from the sixteenth century,[8] it was certainly an issue in the later ones. Therefore, we have to consider the possibility that at least in some cases the missionaries consciously and deliberately limited their adaptation to the Jewish language. This brings us to the question why the missionaries would choose to restrict themselves and not tap into the full potential of linguistic adaptation.

One possible explanation might be that by writing in a Germanized Yiddish the missionaries had an additional aim: to accustom the Jews to the German language in order to assist their conversion. The underlying assumption was that teaching German to the German Jews would help dissolve the cultural and social barriers between the Jewish minority and their non-Jewish environment. Thus, the protective function of the Jews' special language would be lost, making them less attached to the Jewish community and more exposed to Christian influence. Referring to the bilingual texts in Yiddish and German published as reading exercises in his *Belehrung der Jüdisch-Teutschen Red- und Schreibart*, Wagenseil expressed his hope that these texts, which were meant to serve Christians who wished to learn the Jewish language, would serve the German *Jews* too, as an aid to learn the German language. Wagenseil hoped that once the Jews had learned to read German, they would become curious to read German books, and thus eventually come across the New Testament.[9] In a later work, he also interpreted the fact that Jews had started to employ Christian tutors for their children in order to teach them to read and write in the European vernaculars as an indication that Jews were attempting to draw nearer to their Christian surroundings. And this, to his mind, was a sign of their imminent conversion.[10] A similar notion can be found in the work of Heinrich Ammersbach, a Christian Hebraist and pastor in Halberstadt, who emphasized the urgency of conducting missionary work "in these last days before the end of the world." For this purpose, he both advocated the training of missionaries in Oriental languages, especially in Hebrew, and called for the authorities to enable Jews to learn German so that they would be able to converse with Christians on religious matters.[11]

Until now we have discussed the possibility that missionaries sought to promote the study of German among the Jews due to the perceived *advantages* of this language for the missionary cause. But we should also consider the possibility that they promoted the study of German due to what they considered to be the *disadvantages* of Yiddish as a language of conversion.

Early modern missionary writings in Yiddish often convey an impression of reluctance on the side of the Christian authors to use this language, or at least a certain ambivalence regarding the missionary imperative to adapt oneself to the Jewish language and literary style, even if only for tactical purposes. An early example can be found in Paulus Fagius' German introduction to his Yiddish Bible from 1544. After explaining to his Christian readers that he was publishing his Bible in Yiddish, in accordance with the Jewish way of writing and translating, Fagius notes that it might seem surprising that he chose to publish a "Jewish Bible," for there were already plenty of good Bibles (that is, Christian ones) without "first having to drink the Jewish drivel with which they besmirched the worthy, holy book." Later on, Fagius remarks that he would have preferred to see the Jews read the Bible in other versions, presumably German, Christian ones.[12] Despite his discontent with the "Jewish Bible," the text Fagius eventually published was adapted to the Jewish way of writing and translating, even if only to a limited extent.[13] Schadeus, on the other hand, makes clear that he intentionally chose *not* to translate the books from the New Testament according to the Jewish manner (*auff Jüdische art*), but rather transcribe

Luther's German version with Yiddish letters, although he does not give a specific reason for his decision.[14] A century later, Christian Moller also voices dissatisfaction with the need to adapt his translation of the New Testament to the Jewish manner of speaking and writing, emphasizing that "willing or not" he was compelled to do it because of the intended Jewish readership. In any case, Moller assures his (Christian) readers, he only employed such adaptations provided they did not compromise the content of the text.[15]

The most explicit expression of the dilemma of how far one should go in adapting a text to Jewish language and style can be found in the introduction to the missionary tractate *Gloria Christi*, published in Leipzig in 1710. A bilingual text in Yiddish and German, it is addressed to both Jewish and Christian readers. The author, the Lutheran theologian Caspar Calvör, dedicates a considerable part of his introduction to the different considerations that guided him in composing the Yiddish part of the book.[16]

Calvör emphasizes, on the one hand, the importance of linguistic adaptation for the missionary cause and claims persistently that he did the best he could in order to adjust (he uses the verb *accommodieren*) his writing to the Jewish manner. He even apologizes to his Christian readers, asking them "to accept with Christian love and understanding that I sometimes had to lower myself and force myself to adjust to Jewish weakness, even when it meant that theological accuracy . . . could not always be duly kept." On the other hand, Calvör explains that in many instances he in fact deviated from the common Jewish way of writing Yiddish, attempting to make it less "Jewish" and more in accordance with the German style of writing. Referring to this somewhat peculiar initiative to correct and improve the Yiddish language, the author presents us with the interesting assertion that by correcting their language, he was in fact acting for the benefit of his Jewish readers. Calvör explains that since Yiddish is no more than "incorrect, corrupted, unreadable, and incomprehensible German," without proper grammar or orthography, readers of Yiddish works, even the German Jews themselves, often cannot reach a true understanding of such texts. Of course, Calvör claims, Jews can read Jewish literature in Yiddish, as it repeats ideas and notions they already know. However, when confronted with new and more challenging material, such as Christian truths, their language

ספרי
הברית חדשה
כתובים מן תלמידי ישוע הנצרי :

דאס נייאי טעסטאמענט אין דיא יודישי שריפט פער זעצט · דא מיט אללעס היינטיגס טאגס
אלי ליב האבער דער יודישן שריפט · אונ׳ אלי יודן לעזן קענן : פון

כרישטיאן מילערו

פרעדיגערן צו זאנדויא אין דער נייא מארק :

נדפס פה פרנקפורט דאדרה

ביים הערן מיכל גאטשאלק · אונ׳ דורך מיך פער לעגט : שנת אורות לישוע הנצרי א׳ ת״ש

hoc eſt

NOVUM TESTAMENTUM
Hebræo - Teutonicum operâ
M. CHRISTIANI MOLLERI,
Paſt. Ecclеſ. Sandov. deſcriptum.

Francofurti ad Oderam
Sumptibus Michaelis Gottſchalckii, Anno 1700.

O G Tychsen P.P.O

Figure 8.1. Title page of Christian Moller's Yiddish translation of the New Testament (Frankfurt/Oder 1700). *Source*: Sammlung Tychsen, Harald Fischer Verlag.

prevents them from any true comprehension. After listing the different "flaws" of the Yiddish language (most of which refer to its "deviation" from German), Calvör concludes: "In order to remove these disarrays and inconveniencies I sometimes deviated from the Jews' common way of writing, first and foremost when the writing was ambiguous or otherwise made the issue obscure and incomprehensible."

The notion that Yiddish was no more than a corrupted and unintelligible German, and therefore inadequate for serious theological writings, was already prevalent among Christian scholars in the sixteenth and seventeenth centuries. For these scholars, German was the model for a comprehensible literary language and hence the standard against which they evaluated Yiddish, only to find it wanting. This was especially the case with the Jewish translations of religious texts from Hebrew into Yiddish, in which the Jewish practice of word-for-word translation further contributed to the deviation of the language of translation (the so-called *khumesh-taytsh*) from the syntactic structure of German. Paulus

GLORIA
CHRISTI,
Oder
Herrligkeit
Jesu Christi/
Das ist:
Beweißthum der Warheit Christlicher Religion wider die Ungläubigen/
insonderheit wider die Juden:
In Form eines Dialogi oder Unterredung
durch Frage und Antwort aus der H. Schrifft/ Talmud, Targumim, Rabbinen und gesunden Vernunfft-Gründen verfasset/
Und nebst einem
Juden-Catechißmus/
So wol in gewöhnlichen als Jüdisch-Teutschen heraus gegeben
Durch
CASPAREM CALVÖR,
Communion-Superintendenten auff dem Haartz.
LEIPZIG/
In Verlegung Johann Christoph König/
gedruckt bey Christian Gözens sel. Wittwe.
Im Jahr 1710.

כבוד
ישוע משיח
הערליקייט ישוע
כרישט״א:
בווייזשטום דער ווארהייט דעש
קריסטליכן גלויבנס׳
בג״ח
פון
קאשפאר קאלוויאר׳
סופריכטנדענטן אויף דעם הארץ:
תהל׳ ב׳ י״ב
PATIOR UT POTIAR
שנת מולדת לישוע הנצרי א׳ תש״י:

Figure 8.2. Title pages of Caspar Calvör's missionary tract *Gloria Christi* (Leipzig 1710). *Source*: Sammlung Tychsen, Harald Fischer Verlag.

Fagius, for example, criticized the Jews' translations of biblical texts into Yiddish, claiming, "when one reads or hears it, one might think it is gibberish rather than German."[17] A similar critique can also be found in the words of the prominent Christian Hebraist and Yiddishist Johann Buxtorf. In his highly influential work, *Thesaurus grammaticus linguae sanctae hebraeae* (1609), Buxtorf sharply criticizes Jewish translations from Hebrew into Yiddish, in which "one is left now with nonsense, now obscurity, now an unpalatable sense." Anyone better informed, Buxtorf claims further, "strives toward a clearer and more elegant version and adapts to the properties of the German language."[18]

Such notions regarding Yiddish persisted in the works of Christian scholars in the eighteenth century. In these works, more direct and elaborated critique on the Yiddish language itself joined the older denunciations of the Jewish manner of translation.[19] Reviewing two Yiddish Bibles published in Amsterdam in the late 1670s, the theologian and Hebraist Johann Gottlob Carpzov denounced their language and literary style as "highly unsatisfactory, neither for Christian nor for German ears." According to Carpzov, because of the characteristics of the Yiddish language and the fact that the Jewish translators "regard the character and true essence of the German language as completely unimportant, corrupting and falsifying it, it is sometimes difficult to understand the meaning of the text."[20] A few years later, pastor Philipp H. Willemer complained in the introduction to his translation of a Jewish prayer book from Yiddish into German that because of the language and structure of the Yiddish original "it took a lot of effort to bring out the sense of the text," and that such incomprehensible expressions were more difficult to translate than if everything were written entirely in Hebrew.[21] In other cases of Christian translations from Yiddish into German the translators or editors assured their readers that as part of the act of translation they also "corrected" the Yiddish text, so as to make it more comprehensible for Christians.[22]

In all these examples, however, the Christian authors either made some general statement regarding the unintelligibility of Yiddish as a literary medium, or specifically asserted that Yiddish texts were incomprehensible for *Christian* readers, assuming that if the latter had been proficient enough in this language, they would have understood it despite its "flaws" and inconsistencies. Thus, for example, Buxtorf maintained that despite its inconsistent orthography, Yiddish "can be easily understood by someone who knows the language well."[23] Caspar Calvör's assertion, on the other hand, that Yiddish was not comprehensible enough for Yiddish-speaking *Jews* as well, presented the missionary cause with a grave problem, for it questioned the most basic concept of missionary activity in Yiddish—to address the Jews in an understandable language. If Yiddish was not an adequate vessel for delivering the Christian message, what was the point of missionizing in Yiddish? Furthermore, if the only language the Jews understood was in fact inadequate for missionary purposes, was there any hope at all for Jewish conversion?

The solution of Germanizing Yiddish to make it more comprehensible and hence more adequate for missionary purposes might be seen as an extension of missionary concepts into the realm of language. Like the Jewish religion itself, the Jewish language was seen as an obstacle preventing Jews from understanding and accepting Christian truths. And as the Jews could not save themselves, neither from their erroneous and corrupted religion nor from their equally erroneous and corrupted language, they had to rely on Christians for their salvation. Committed to his missionary calling, Calvör decided to overcome this linguistic obstacle and correct the Jewish language, "in order to offer the Jewish people . . . the difficult and hitherto unknown faith articles in a simple and pleasant manner."[24]

This solution, which might have also been the motivational force behind other cases of missionary works written in Germanized Yiddish, had its own shortcomings. As Calvör himself admits in the same introduction, this deviation from the common Jewish way of writing Yiddish would most probably create a sense of alienation, or estrangement, among the Jewish readers. Another, even weightier problem was of course the possibility that the Jews would not understand the Germanized Yiddish. In other words, both advantages of using Yiddish for conversion, that of comprehension and that of familiarity, would be lost. In an attempt to overcome this problem, Calvör declares that he sometimes adapted his language more to the Jewish manner, sometimes more to the German one, as he saw fit.

Not everyone approved of Calvör's solution of Germanizing the Yiddish language as a means to a more effective mission. Johann Callenberg, who published and distributed many excerpts from Calvör's

Gloria Christi, is a case in point. In an account from 1732, Callenberg reports on his intention to prepare an extract of this work, and

> as far as the manner of writing is concerned, to have it properly adjusted to Jewish convention; for at present, there is hardly anything Yiddish about it, except for the letters. Because of this it would be very difficult for the Jews—even for the local [German] ones, who are more familiar with *Hochdeutsch* than the others, let alone for other European Jews, who use a particular old-German dialect mixed with many Hebrew and rabbinic words—to fully understand the meaning of the text.[25]

Callenberg eventually carried out his plan to correct Calvör's "German" Yiddish back into "Jewish" Yiddish. In 1733 he published the catechism from *Gloria Christi*, noting on the title page that this work was republished "more in accordance with the understanding of this [the Jewish] nation." In the Latin introduction to this edition, addressed to the Christian reader, Callenberg reemphasized this point: "The author of this booklet, the blessed Caspar Calvör, had it published in German with Jewish letters; I, with a young educated translator [the convert Heinrich Christian Immanuel Frommann], have replaced the language with another one, friendlier to the Jews [*iudaeis familiarius*]."[26] A comparison between the two versions of the catechism shows that the language of the text has indeed been modified, and most notably the new version contains many more Hebraisms. In addition, the German part of Calvör's bilingual text was removed in Callenberg's edition.

Three years after the publication of the "Judaized" catechism, Callenberg published a Yiddish translation of the Gospel of Matthew, which was in fact a republication of this Gospel from the aforementioned Yiddish New Testament prepared by Christian Moller in 1700. That Moller's text, like that of Calvör's, was "too German" and hence inadequate for Jewish readers was pointed out already by eighteenth-century critics. In a review published in the literary journal *Nachrichten von einer Hallischen Bibliothek* in 1749, the anonymous reviewer maintains that Moller's translation is "nothing but Luther's translation with Jewish-German letters, except for some small changes, necessary due to the Jews' German pronunciation, such as *mir* instead of *wir*, *is* instead of *ist*, *nit* instead of *nicht*, etc." According to the reviewer, in order for the text to fulfill its purpose and prove useful for the Jews, more changes of phrases and expressions would be necessary, espe-

J.N.J.A.

Einleitung.

בסד"ש

הקדמיה

Die erste Frage.

Ich höre/ daß denen Juden wird beygemessen/ daß sie viel Redens und Rühmens machen von dem güldenen אף Aff, und sprechen/ es sey werth/ daß es mit güldenen Buchstaben geschrieben werde: Kanstu mir wol sagen/ mein Freund/ was sie damit haben wollen?

Antwort.

Sie verstehen dadurch die schöne Verheissung/ welche GOtt der Allmächtige dem Volck Israel hat gethan Levit. 26, 44. ואף גם זארת וגו' Ve Aff gam Zoth &c. Auch wenn sie schon in der Feinde Land sind/ habe ich sie gleichwol nicht verworffen/ und eckelt mich ihrer nicht/ also daß es mit ihnen aus seyn solte/ und mein Bund mit ihnen solt nicht mehr gelten/ dann ich bin der HErr ihr GOtt. Hie stehet das Wort AF fornen auff der Spitze/ drum nennete Käyser Maximilian diesen Spruch/ weiln die Juden so viel Wesens daraus machen/ der Juden güldenen Affen.

שאילה א' אדר ערסטיא פראגי

איך הויר / דש פון דן יהודים געזאגט ווערט / דש זיא פיל רידנס אונ' ריאמנס מאכן פון דם גילדנן אף אונ' ספרעכן עס זייא זוכה / דש עס מיט גילדנן בוכשטבן גשריבן ווערד קאנסטו מיר וואל זאגן / מיין פריינד / וואס זיא דמאיט האבן וואלן:

תשובה אדר ענטפערטי

דיא פרשטין דאדורך דיא שוין פרהייזונג / וועלך הקב"ה דעם פאלק ישראל גטון האט בויקרא בסימן כ"ו ואף גם זארת וגו' דאס איז טייטש אונ' אך דיז / ווען זיא זיין אים לאנד אירער פיינדיא / ניט האב איך זיא פרווארפן אונ' ניט עקעלט איך מיר / זיא אויסצוטרייבן אויפצוהעבן איין בונד מיט אין / דאן איך בין דער העד איר גאט היא שטיט דאס ווארט אף פורן אוף דער ספיץ / דארום נענטע קייסר מאקסימיליאן דיזן פסוק / וויל דיא יודן זא פיל וועזנס דראויס מאכן / דען גילדנן אפן:

הקבה

Zweyte A שאילה

Figure 8.3. First page of Caspar Calvör's *Gloria Christi* (Leipzig 1710). *Source*: Sammlung Tychsen, Harald Fischer Verlag.

cially the insertion of Hebrew words "which constitute an essential part of the Jewish-German idiom."[27]

The need to adapt the Germanized language of Moller's translation to a language more adequate for the Jews was clear enough to Callenberg. Unfortunately, the convert who was employed in the publishing house, Heinrich Frommann, passed away in 1735 before he could start working on the Gospel of Matthew. This work was therefore carried out by Callenberg himself, who admitted in a letter to the Orientalist Gustav G. Zeltner that time pressure and the growing demand for missionary tracts prevented him from a thorough revision of Moller's translation.[28] But apparently Callenberg was reluctant to publish Moller's text completely unrevised, and eventually did manage to carry out some minimal changes, most notably replacing certain words that to his mind "might have appeared too obscure and unpleasant to Jewish eyes."[29]

Callenberg's insistence on a higher degree of linguistic adaptation in the Yiddish missionary writings had to do, undoubtedly, with the audience to which he designated these writings. Whereas Calvör, for example, notes in the introduction to *Gloria Christi* that he composed this work "first and foremost for the Jews who live in the German lands," Callenberg's missionary project directed its efforts largely to the vast terrain of Jewish settlement in Eastern Europe, especially Poland. As was well acknowledged by the Christian missionaries, the Yiddish spoken in these areas was less similar to the German language than the Yiddish spoken by the Jews in the German lands. An excessively Germanized Yiddish, therefore, like the one offered by Calvör and Moller, was hardly appropriate for this public.

Another factor, which probably influenced Callenberg to employ a higher degree of linguistic adaptation in his missionary writings, was his close work with Jewish converts. Callenberg employed converts as translators, compositors, and proofreaders, who were to ensure that the Yiddish in which the missionary tracts were published would be as authentic as possible. Moreover, Callenberg and his missionaries used to receive feedback from converts and even Jews who read the institute's tracts. One of the points repeated in such feedback was a complaint that the Yiddish of these tracts was "too German," and a request to insert more words from Hebrew and bring it closer to the Jewish way of writing. In some cases Jews even offered their help in proofreading the Yiddish translations prepared by the institute, to ensure that the Yiddish was correct and well adapted to Jewish readers.[30]

Despite his statements and actions in favor of a high degree of linguistic adaptation for missionary purposes, Callenberg, too, was in fact very ambivalent and inconsistent regarding the missionary imperative of adaptation to the Yiddish language. In addition to the fact mentioned above, namely that many of the tracts published by the institute were also in German transcribed into the Hebrew alphabet, Callenberg himself expressed his reservations regarding a too far-reaching adaptation to the Jewish language. In 1733, only one year after his explicit disagreement with Calvör's decision to deviate from the Jewish manner of writing Yiddish, Callenberg notes in his Yiddish textbook that the Jews, in speaking this language, "corrupt" many German words. And he immediately adds, "It is however not necessary, that we follow them in this practice, when we converse with them or write something for them to use."[31] A more elaborate statement on this topic can be found in the introduction to his Yiddish-German lexicon from 1736, where Callenberg expresses his hope that the Hebrew and rabbinic words presented in the lexicon "would put one in a position to discuss with the Jews theological issues in a way clear to them. However, as far as the German part of this language is concerned," Callenberg continues, "one should act in accordance with the following remarks of Caspar Calvör."[32] At this point Callenberg quotes at length from the introduction to *Gloria Christi*, in which Calvör explains why he decided to deviate from the Jewish manner of writing Yiddish; Callenberg thus recommends that his students follow Calvör's practice, to which he himself had objected only a few years before.

Callenberg's inconsistency regarding the desired degree of accommodation to the language of the Jews attests to the problem this missionary, like Moller and Calvör before him, had to face: finding the linguistic form that would best serve the missionary cause. It seems, however, that the reluctance to use Yiddish for missionary work had another reason as well, not necessarily related to the adequacy of Yiddish for missionary purposes. Just before concluding his aforementioned introduction, Calvör writes the following passage:

> Therefore, since our beloved ancestors had to endure that one had poured their old German into a purer mould, and even entire *fruchtbringende Gesellschafften*—also of high-ranking personalities—were

> established for this purpose, how could the Jew possibly object to us Germans making the effort to wash and cleanse our beloved mother tongue from the abominable mess and filth in which it is mired among the Jews, so that in this way as well the hidden secret of Christ would shine in front of the eyes of the eclipsed Jewish religion, with a brighter, purer, and lovelier radiance.[33]

Although this passage asserts the missionary cause, it also reveals another motive for Calvör's attempts to correct the Yiddish language: the sense of duty and respect towards the German language and the fear that a far-reaching adaptation to the Jewish-German language might lead to an unwelcome "Judaization" of the German tongue.

The need to protect the German language from outside derogatory influences might also explain Callenberg's reluctance to adapt too much to Yiddish, as was made clear in his writings from 1733 and 1736. While he was well aware of the importance of incorporating Hebrew words and phrases into texts addressed to a Jewish audience, Callenberg was anxious to preserve the German component of Yiddish as intact as possible and protect it from potential Jewish "corruption." Thus, the same Johann Callenberg, who in some cases supported a high degree of linguistic adaptation in the name of the missionary cause, was now putting limits to this adaptation in the name of the German language.

As these examples show, the decision of missionaries as to how far one could go in adapting to the Jewish language was not always influenced exclusively by missionary considerations. Other concerns, most notably cultural patriotism and loyalty to the German mother tongue, and the fear of its Judaization, influenced the way Yiddish was perceived by German Protestant scholars, and played an important role in the discussions on Yiddish as a language of conversion.

Yiddish, German, and Jewish Conversion

The basic assumption underlying the use of linguistic adaptation for missionary purposes is that any language is adequate for communication of the Christian message. Any language, in other words, can be "Christianized" and thereby promoted to the status of a "holy language," a language in which the Gospel is preached and written.[34] And yet it seems that for the Protestant missionaries we have discussed, Yiddish was an exception to this rule. Not content merely with the attempt to *Christianize* this language by using it for the communication of Christian teachings and inserting Christian meaning into Jewish terms, these missionaries sought to *Germanize* it, too. By this, it seems, they wished to avoid what they considered to be a Judaization and hence corruption of the German language. Even more fundamentally from a missionary perspective was the desire both to overcome the alleged shortcomings of Yiddish as a language of conversion, and to accustom the Jews to the German language as a means to support their conversion.

Yet the need to accustom the Jews to the German language might have had an additional aim—to achieve Jewish conversion that was both religious *and* linguistic. True conversion, in other words, consisted in the eyes of the missionaries of a twofold process of transition: from Judaism to Christianity, and from Yiddish to German.

The requirement that converts replace their language together with their religion stemmed from both theological and social considerations. From a social point of view, since conversion was, at least officially, an entrance ticket to German society, a Jew who turned Christian was expected to abandon the language of his old community and adopt the language of general society. Further than that, as the language most associated with the Jews' social and economic image of the time as small traders, pedlars, and beggars, the expectation that converts would give up Yiddish should be seen as part of the larger missionary (especially Pietistic) project of converting the Jews, not only from their religion but also from their traditional occupations as well as the entire socioeconomic state that accompanied these occupations.[35] From a theological point of view, since conversion was seen as an act of rebirth, newborn converts were expected to shed their former Jewish identity as a whole, including their language. The notion that a religious conversion meant also a linguistic one was indeed so deeply rooted that proficiency in German was often perceived as an indicator of true conversion.[36]

It is therefore not surprising that alongside the phenomenon of converts taking advantage of their knowledge of Yiddish (and other aspects of Jewish life) to present themselves as exposers of Jewish "secrets" in the service of their new coreligionists, there are many instances of converts trying to distance themselves from their old language and display proficiency in German as proof of their new identity as both Christians and Germans. In their conversion narratives and other works addressed to Christian audiences, converts proudly announced their achievements in mastering German. They referred interchangeably to themselves as "*wir Christen*" and "*uns Teutschen*," exhibiting their acquaintance with their newly adopted language by frequently citing "common sayings" among "us Germans."[37] In their writings on Yiddish, converts regularly contrasted "our German language" and the language of the Jews, a contrast usually accompanied by debasing remarks directed by the converts towards their own mother tongue. Converts condemned the state of the German language among their former coreligionists while, by writing their own texts in "Christian" German, implicitly distancing themselves from Jewish linguistic practices.[38]

As demonstrated above (Chapter 7), negative evaluations of the Jews' language, as well as the attempt to draw distinct lines between the Jews' Yiddish and the authors' German, were by no means confined to the works of converts. Yet the need of former Jews to establish their new identity as Christians and Germans should certainly be seen as a factor that influenced their attitudes to Yiddish. The popular accusations often directed at converts from Judaism in early modern Germany, as if their conversion were in fact a form of deception motivated by the will to gain some profit rather than by true belief in the Christian religion, resulted in a persistent drive by converts to prove their loyalty to Christians by attacking their former religion and coreligionists.[39] This may certainly be one of the reasons for their attacks on the Jewish language as well. Another reason may be the popular image of Yiddish as a language of deception (see Part II above). Displaying their shift from a language closely associated with dishonesty and fraud (an image constructed, not to a small extent, in the writings of converts), to a language that was associated by its speakers with loyalty and honesty, must have constituted an important element in the efforts of converts to prove that their conversion was indeed sincere.

The expectation that converts from Judaism would give up their mother tongue reveals a certain paradox inherent in the usage of Yiddish as a language of conversion: on the one hand, the wide array of missionary activities conducted in Yiddish served, though perhaps not intentionally, to promote the usage of this language as a legitimate literary medium. These activities contributed to the codification of Yiddish, enriched its literary corpus, and initiated linguistic and philological investigations of the Jewish language. On the other hand, the missionaries themselves, while using Yiddish as a linguistic tool for conversion purposes, consciously sought to undermine the legitimacy of this same language as a literary medium. Furthermore, using Yiddish as a language of conversion would lead to its eventual demise: if the Christian mission in Yiddish were to achieve its final objective and bring about Jewish conversion, it would entail the decline and eventual disappearance of the Jewish language, together with other manifestations of Jewish culture.[40]

The project undertaken by early modern Protestant missionaries, to approach the Jews in their own language in order to convert them, did not achieve its goal. The evidence we have suggests that by using Yiddish the missionaries did succeed in attracting Jewish attention, conversing with Jews on religious matters, and introducing Jews to Christian writings. But the number of Jews who actually converted was much smaller than was hoped for by the missionaries. During the second half of the eighteenth century, with the rise of the secularizing ideological forces of the Enlightenment on the one hand, and the growing subordination of the church to the political power of the state on the other, the missionary cause rapidly lost ground in the German lands. General interest in missionary work deteriorated significantly, and missionary institutions lost much of their previous influence to the state, including their former dominant role in the integration of the Jews into German society.[41] The Germanization of Yiddish and the gradual shift from Yiddish to German, which eventually took place among German Jewry from the late eighteenth century onwards, was not the outcome of mass conversion but of secular dynamics of acculturation and emancipation, bringing about a new chapter in the history of Christian-Jewish relations in the German-speaking world.

Nine Christian Hebrew and Jewish Yiddish in Early Modern Germany

The close relation between Yiddish and Hebrew was critical to the preoccupation of Christian scholars with the Jewish vernacular. First, it was mainly the linguistic affinity of Yiddish to Hebrew—even more than its close relation to German—that aroused the Christian interest in Yiddish, especially in the earlier stages of this interest. Second, the relation to Hebrew played a crucial role in determining the attitudes of Christians toward the Jewish-German language. Considering the deep appreciation and even admiration of the Hebrew language noticeable in many of the writings of Christian Hebraists, one might have expected the relation of Yiddish to the holy tongue to bring about a more positive image of this language, too. However, the exact opposite happened, as we shall now see.

Hebrew and the German Jews

One of the central motifs of the Christian discourse on Yiddish was the claim that the Hebrew language, after being replaced by Yiddish, was no longer the language of the German Jews. An example of this notion can be found as early as 1527 in the words of Sebastian Münster. A prominent reformer, Münster was also a highly influential Christian Hebraist and one of the earliest Christian Yiddishists.[1] In the introduction to his Aramaic grammar, Münster claimed that after the seventy years of Babylonian captivity (in the sixth century BCE), the Jews who returned to Judea brought Aramaic with them as their common language. This situation, Münster maintained, is quite similar to that of "our German Jews" (*Iudaeis nostris Germanis*), for "if they were given today the opportunity to return to the Holy Land and occupy it, they would surely make the German language [that is, Yiddish] their vernacular, since only very few among them know how to speak Hebrew."[2] A similar statement was made by Paulus Fagius in the introduction to his Yiddish translation of the Bible (1544), in which he claimed that "they are called the Hebrews [*Hebreer*], and yet there is no other people under the sun that has less understanding of the true, proper Hebrew language."[3]

These examples represent a prevalent notion among early modern Christian—especially Protestant—scholars, which played an important role in their discussions on the Yiddish language.[4] In their attempt to demonstrate the fact that the German Jews of their time no longer mastered the Hebrew language, and thus to undermine the traditional association between this language and the Jewish people, the authors claimed that "the common Jews understand only a little Hebrew; they learn from childhood a few words that they distort and corrupt and mix inside their German. . . . Of the Hebrew Grammar and the true essence [*Genio*] of the Hebrew language, even their most educated rabbis rarely have any knowledge."[5] Thus, when they tried to speak the holy tongue—either the language itself or the Hebrew words they incorporated in Yiddish—it came out false and distorted, "entirely contrary to the grammar and nature of the language."[6] The authors explained for instance that the Jews pronounced "a" like "o" or "e," "o" like "ou," and "t" like "s." They also offered many examples to show how a Hebrew word should be pronounced, and conversely the way it was pronounced by the German Jews according to their "peculiar pronunciation" (*besondere Aussprache*): for "*Betulah*" (virgin) they said "*B'suleh*"; for "*Olam*" (world), "*Oulem*"; for "*Mescharet*" (servant), "*Meschores*"; and so on. In his Yiddish-German lexicon from 1773 the Hebrew censor Leopold Thirsch explained that because his aim was to teach Christians the *Jews'* language, he did not transcribe the Hebrew words in the lexicon according to "the true, genuine [pronunciation], which is customary among those who are knowledgeable in the Hebrew language," but according to "the one which is indeed faulty, but these days is nonetheless in common use among the Jews."[7]

A further example given by the authors for the way the German Jews "corrupted" the Hebrew language by using Yiddish, in either speaking or writing, was their habit of conjugating Hebrew verbs in German forms and of adding German suffixes to Hebrew nouns; for example, "*gaslen*" (*rauben*, to rob) from גזל (*gazal*), "*rohnen*" (*sehen*, to see) from ראה (*ra'ah*), and "*schächten*" (*schlachten*, to slaughter) from שחט (*shahat*), as well as *draschle* (a small oration) from דרשה (*derashah*), and *seferchen* (a small book) from ספר (*sefer*).[8] These and similar examples were repeated in almost all the Christian writings on Yiddish, usually accompanied by the authors' disapproval of such linguistic usage: they presented it as a "corruption" (*verderben*, *corrumpieren*) of the Hebrew language and in some cases even referred to Yiddish as a "barbaric" form of Hebrew (*Hebräo-barbarisch*, *barbara & Pseudo-Hebraea*).[9] The Jews' corrupting and even mutilating (*verstümmeln*) the Hebrew words they incorporated into Yiddish, it was argued, rendered the Hebraisms in their language completely incomprehensible for Christians, even those who were highly proficient in the Hebrew tongue.

Another central point in the authors' demonstration of how ignorant the German Jews were of Hebrew was their inability to read the language. This claim had serious theological implications, for it meant that they could not read the Bible in the original, or that they read it without understanding the text correctly. "The Jews of our time are ignorant of the Hebrew tongue," lamented Johann Wagenseil in 1705, "and because of that, among other things, the veil hangs in front of their eyes, which prevents them from truly understanding the writings of Moses and the prophets."[10] This association between the Jews' lack of proficiency in Hebrew and their insufficient knowledge of the Bible already appeared in the writings of Paulus Fagius, who interpreted both disadvantages as God's punishment of the Jewish people: "And so we can see how dreadfully the Lord has punished and afflicted them, in that He took from them not only the correct and true understanding of the Holy Scripture, but also the means by which they could have attained such understanding."[11]

The Christian assertion that the Jews understood the Bible in a false manner had a long tradition, and here it was given renewed validity through the linguistic argument. For the Protestant authors, who saw the Bible as the ultimate source of religious truth, the Jews' ignorance in this field constituted decisive proof of their mistakes and blindness in questions of faith. If the Jews could not read the source of the holy truth, how would they ever reach it?

The authors were of course well aware of the fact that the Jews possessed various Yiddish translations of the biblical text.[12] However, from their perspective, this was merely further proof that the Jews had lost their traditional claim over the Hebrew Bible. Furthermore, despite their Protestant stance in favor of biblical translations in the vernacular, the Christian authors hardly considered these translations appropriate for transmitting religious truth. In the 1730s Johann Callenberg pointed out that in all the existing Yiddish translations of biblical texts, the Jewish translators "did not pay enough tribute to either the clarity [*perspicuitas*] or the accuracy [*integritas*] [of the text]. [Moreover,] the same translators always incorporated excessively verbose interpretations in the text, by which the reader is led away from the beneficial use of the divine Word, and especially from the acknowledgment of Christ." And so, Callenberg concluded, "many Jews are not in possession of a decent [*integro*] Bible in their vernacular."[13]

The insufficient knowledge of Hebrew among the Jews further implied that they did not understand their Hebrew prayers. Thus, they prayed in the holy tongue without understanding what they were actually saying. This practice was severely criticized by the Protestant authors, who attached great value to praying in an intelligible language. Moreover, the authors often used the discussion on the Jewish language of prayer for emphasizing the Jews' lack of devotion, or *Andacht*, in their religious practices, and hence the worthlessness and superstitious nature of those practices. According to the Protestant authors, the Jews prayed only with their lips, not with their hearts; they babbled (*plappern*) the words out of habit rather than true reverence, without devotion, soul, and faith (*ohne Andacht, Geist und Glauben*). No wonder, therefore, that their prayers were not being heard.[14]

In his extensive ethnographic work *Jüdische Merckwürdigkeiten* from 1714, the Frankfurter Hebraist Johann Jacob Schudt related that he once discussed this point with some Jewish women. When he said to one of them, "you read [your prayers] like the nuns read the Latin psalms, in that you just say the words, without knowing what they mean or what it is you pray," she answered, "I don't understand it, but God does."[15] Another woman, whom Schudt asked how exactly would praying without understanding help her, answered: "oh, it helps a lot. It is the same as when the doctor writes me a prescription. I cannot understand that either, but it helps me nonetheless."[16] The idea presented in this passage, regarding the Jews' stubbornness and superstition in their insistence on praying in Hebrew, even at the expense of understanding, was quite popular among Protestant scholars. In order to stress this point, these scholars provided their readers with more Jewish assertions, such as the notion that God prefers to hear the prayers in the holy tongue, or that the angels, who deliver the prayers to God, understand Hebrew better than Yiddish.[17] The comparison of the Jewish women with the nuns who pray in Latin, cited above, is also worth noting, for it is a telling example of the way Protestant authors incorporated intra-Christian polemics into their writings on Jewish matters.[18] Of course, not all authors exposed their anti-Catholic bias as blatantly as Schudt. As Protestant readers were familiar with anti-Catholic criticism of the use of the Vulgate instead of the original Hebrew Bible, and of the practice of praying in Latin instead of the vernacular, indirect comparisons between Jews and Catholics on these issues were probably sufficient to deliver the desired message.

Biblical Hebrews and Yiddish-Speaking Jews

Critical discussions about the decline in the knowledge of Hebrew among the majority of Ashkenazi Jews took place inside the Jewish communities, too, as educated Jews and members of the rabbinical elite pointed out the problematic repercussions of this situation and proposed possible solutions, such as the use of Yiddish for the dissemination of religious knowledge.[19] What is not clear, however, is why this would be of any concern to the *Christian* authors? Why would Protestant writers choose to emphasize that Hebrew, after being replaced by Yiddish, was no longer the language of the German Jews? The answer appears to be that apart from the direct theological criticism of the Jews with regard to reading the Bible and praying in the synagogue, the separation of the Jews from the Hebrew language also enabled the Protestant authors to draw a distinct line between the ancient, biblical Hebrews and the Jews of their time. In the years following the Reformation, the rising importance of the Old Testament among Protestant scholars brought with it a sense of respect and high regard for the biblical Jews as God's Chosen People, leading to incongruity between the admiration of the biblical Jews on the one hand, and the contempt towards contemporary Jews on the other. This dissonance was resolved in most cases by means of a strict separation between different periods in Jewish history, so that the Christian scholars could admire and idealize the Jews of one period, while despising those of another.

The distinction and even contrast between biblical and modern Jews was repeatedly emphasized in Protestant writings on Jews and Judaism, usually by making the assertion that the modern Jews replaced Scripture with the Talmud as their major source of religion, and the Mosaic Law with the laws of their rabbis.[20] Here we are presented with another claim of replacement, that of Hebrew with Yiddish. If Hebrew was the holy language of the ancient Children of Israel, the fact that the German Jews of the early modern era no longer mastered this language was considered by the Protestant scholars as proof of how far these Jews had strayed from the biblical ideal. With their despised and corrupted Jewish-German language, the Jews of the Holy Roman Empire were no longer the Chosen People but the "removed Israel," condemned to be dispersed among the Gentiles.

Yet the transition of the Jewish people from biblical Hebrews to modern Jews was not confined to the temporal dimension. It also entailed a geographical dimension, of a transition from the Orient to Europe. In the process, the Jews lost their original Oriental language (Hebrew), but did not replace it with an entirely European one. Rather, they maintained a conspicuous Hebrew component in their modern language: Yiddish is written in Hebrew characters, from right to left, and contains many Hebrew words. The Hebrew component lent Yiddish, in Christian eyes, an unmistakable "Oriental note," and together with the prevalent understanding of Jews as stemming from Oriental stock,[21] emphasized the Jews' liminal place as Orientals on European soil.[22]

The notion regarding the "Oriental connection" of Yiddish was further reinforced by the functions fulfilled by the Jewish language in the service of Christian theology.[23] The idea that languages related to Hebrew could help in achieving a better understanding and interpretation of the Bible was, alongside missionary purposes, the main force behind early modern Orientalist scholarship.[24] Indeed, it is no coincidence that Christian scholarship on Yiddish was practiced in the great German centers of Oriental studies of the time, such as Leipzig, Wittenberg, Hamburg, and Halle, and found its way into the works of leading German Orientalists. From the inclusion of Yiddish terms in Christian dictionaries of Hebrew and Aramaic, through the incorporation of chapters on Yiddish in works on Oriental languages, and up to the institutionalization of Yiddish studies in the Pietistic center for Orientalist scholarship in Halle, the study of the Jewish-German vernacular was closely associated with early modern Oriental studies.

Most important, it was precisely the Hebrew component that provoked many of the negative representations of Yiddish among Christians. Formulated in terms we shall encounter in latter-day Orientalist discourse, with regard to the "cultural backwardness" of modern Orientals, these representations stigmatized Yiddish as degenerate, barbaric, uncultivated, and essentially foreign.[25]

An illuminating example of this notion comes from Wagenseil's famous indictment of Yiddish in his *Belehrung* from 1699. Listing the different ways in which the Jews, by speaking Yiddish, violated and corrupted the German language, Wagenseil emphasized that "they mixed countless numbers of Hebrew words and phrases into German, so that whoever hears them speak German [Yiddish] cannot but believe that they are speaking nothing but pure Hebrew, since hardly a single comprehensible word comes out."[26] The scholars' discontent with the Hebrew component in Yiddish also emerges in their criticism of the literary style of Yiddish works. In this case, too, the presence of Hebrew loanwords in what were perceived as basically German texts was considered a dominant reason for the "horrible/uncouth and unrefined style" or "barbarity of style" (*stylo horrido & inculto*, *styli barbariem*) of Yiddish works.[27] In the following decades, this notion became ever more prevalent. In 1784 the professor of theology in Altdorf and Jena, Johann Christoph Doederlein, criticized the language of Yiddish biblical translations, denouncing it as "utterly impure, barbaric, and, because of the intermingling of Hebrew and rabbinic words with German suffixes, completely incomprehensible to the German reader, often ridiculous, and conducive to the maintenance of the language-barbarism [*Sprachbarbarey*] among the Jews."[28]

Other reasons for the scholars' harsh criticism of Yiddish and its function as a literary medium were also related to the notion that the

Jews could not detach themselves from their old language. Caspar Calvör, for instance, noted that "the Jews write their German according to the manner of Hebrew [*nach Hebräischer Art*] without vowels, either entirely or to a large extent," as one of the characteristics that turned Yiddish into a corrupt and incomprehensible language[29]; whereas Wagenseil criticized Yiddish poetry for its tendency to imitate certain Hebrew poetic structures, foreign to German literary tradition.[30] Of much graver consequence, however, was, in the eyes of Christian authors, the Jewish practice of translating biblical works from Hebrew into Yiddish in a strictly verbal, word-for-word manner. Emerging from a point of deep respect for the sanctity of the biblical text, the Yiddish Bibles aimed to keep the translation as close as possible to the literal meaning of the Hebrew original, without taking into account the syntactic and lexical rules of spoken Yiddish, which were closer to German. For the Christian scholars, the Jewish custom of translating word-for-word from Hebrew into Yiddish, "regardless of how bad it sounds in German," rendered the Yiddish translations of the Bible stylistically inferior and hardly comprehensible.[31] Moreover, it was commonly seen as indicative of "Jewish superstition." The Lutheran theologian Johann Fecht, for example, noted in 1700 that "since the people of the Holy God spoke Hebrew and Greek, it would be ridiculous to translate in a word-for-word [*verba verbis*] manner as the Jews have done in their German [Yiddish] Bibles out of great superstition [*ex magna superstitione*]."[32] These condemnations appear very clearly in the words of Johann Buxtorf, the most influential Christian Hebraist and Yiddishist of the seventeenth century. Discussing the Jewish custom of translating from Hebrew into Yiddish, Buxtorf pointed out that

> this is, however, a flaw common to them [the Jews] all: that what they translate from Hebrew, they translate too literally. The Hebraisms are so persistent that they obscure the German idiom. They superstitiously [*superstitiose*] hold so closely to preserving the extraneous and literal word that they sometimes leave no sense at all; sometimes the sense is obscure, sometimes disagreeable. The more ignorant a person is, the more superstitious he is in this regard.[33]

Criticizing word-for-word translation (*verbum pro verbo*) as "superstitious" and inferior to translating the sense of a given text (*sensum de sensu*) was quite prevalent in early modern discussions on the art of translation.[34] In the Jewish context, however, this notion also alluded to a long-established motif in Christian anti-Jewish polemics, regarding the Jews' "superstitious" adherence to the literal meaning of the biblical text at the expense of a deeper and more spiritual understanding. The claim that the Jews were captives of the letter rather than the spirit of the Bible goes back to the Church fathers, but it became especially prevalent in Protestant circles. As an unshakeable expression of the Jews' literal-mindedness, the Jewish practice of translating the Bible in a word-for-word manner was presented in sharp contrast to the "spiritual" interpretation of the Bible in Christian, primarily Protestant, tradition.

The comments regarding Yiddish translations illuminate the intersection of theological and cultural evaluations in Christian criticism of Yiddish literature. This is true of the Christian scholars' comments on the literary style of Yiddish works and also, as we have seen above, of many of their statements regarding the content of these works, which they denounced as both intellectually inferior and religiously erroneous.[35] Indeed, the derogative terms in which the Christian authors chose to describe Yiddish writings—ridiculous, foolish, distasteful, and superstitious—referred to what they considered to be its crude literary style, poor intellectual and scholarly level, and degenerate religious teachings, thus creating an important confluence between cultural inferiority and theological error, which in their eyes dominated contemporary Ashkenazi Jewish culture. The Jewish "falling from grace," from Hebrew to Yiddish, from the biblical Orient to modern Europe, was thus presented as a religious *and* a cultural process of degeneration. It was against this degenerative model that the Protestant Hebraists could then devise a contrasting model—one of cultural evolution and religious succession.

Hebrew, Yiddish, and the Question of the "Chosen People"

The Hebrew language that declined among the German Jews, according to some of the authors, did not disappear altogether but was preserved in its original and pure form among one group in Germany and one only—the Protestant Hebraists, including the authors themselves.

In contrast to their opinion of the German Jews and their corrupted language, the Hebraists claimed that the Italian Jews did preserve the Hebrew in its original, pure form, according to its grammar and correct pronunciation. And since Johannes Reuchlin, who brought the knowledge of Hebrew to the German Christians at the beginning of the sixteenth century, acquired the language from Italian Jews,[36] it was the Christian Hebraists who thereafter maintained the finest and purest form of Hebrew.[37] In addition, the authors elaborated on the dedication of Christian scholars to the learning of Hebrew, and the thriving of Hebrew scholarship in Protestant territories, placing in sharp relief the neglect of Hebrew among the German Jews, who replaced it with Yiddish.[38] "We Christians," declared Johann Wagenseil in a triumphant manner, characteristic of many of the Hebraists' writings, "greatly surpass the Jews as far as the true understanding and knowledge of the Hebrew language is concerned." After elaborating on the Jews' insufficient knowledge of the holy tongue, Wagenseil further stressed the Christian advantage in Hebrew studies, which was achieved by virtue of "the praiseworthy men, [the seventeenth-century Protestant Hebraists] Buxtorf and Glassius, [who] provided us with Hebrew grammars, and by so doing put all the *Baale Dikduk* or Jewish grammarians to shame."[39]

As a clear case of an "appropriation of one culture by another, apparently stronger one"—to use Edward Said's terminology[40]—the attempt made by early modern Protestant scholars to expropriate the knowledge of Hebrew from the Jews and to assert their own claim over it in many ways anticipates the Orientalist project of modern European colonialism. As in latter-day Orientalism, in our case as well European philologists actively pursued the goal of disinterring an ancient Oriental language and its texts, neglected due to the inertness of their former possessors, and integrating them into modern European culture and scholarly institutions. This act symbolically defined the power relations between Occident and Orient, as well as (within Europe) between Christians and Jews; and from a Western perspective, it symbolized the notion that civilization moves from the passive East to the active, dynamic West, culminating in European superiority over "Oriental backwardness."

Referring to the context of modern colonialism, Said described this process of appropriation: "Faced with the obvious decrepitude and political impotence of the modern Oriental, the European Orientalist found it his duty to rescue some portion of a lost, past classical Oriental grandeur. . . . What the European took from the classical Oriental past was a vision (and thousands of facts and artefacts) which only he could employ to the best advantage."[41] In the eyes of Christian Hebraists, Hebrew, too, was redeemed from its degenerate state among the German Jews to be cherished and dignified again via European Christian scholarship, and for the latter's benefit. As opposed to the Jews' passive loss of Hebrew as part of their general process of degeneration, the process of Christian acquisition of the language was triumphantly constructed as an evolutionary progress, a scholarly achievement that became possible due to the efforts of active Hebraists. Hebrew, the ancient Oriental language, was now part of Christian, European culture, leaving contemporary Jews with their debased European-Oriental language, a pale shade of past grandeur and a constant reminder of their decline.

But apart from the cultural-colonial issues, the appropriation of Hebrew by Protestant scholars had profound theological implications that related to the core of traditional Christian-Jewish polemics. Underlying the Hebraists' claim to be the present guardians of the Hebrew language lurked the idea that the Protestant Church was in fact the "New Israel."

Protestant interest in Jews and Judaism, as it expressed itself in Germany from the Reformation onwards, was not limited to the revived interest in the Bible or to the will to convert the Jews. It was part and parcel of a more comprehensive cultural process that aimed to construct Protestant identity as a substitute for the Jewish one. Since the Protestant Church considered itself to be the "New Israel," it had first to deny the Jews their claim of being the "Chosen People," and then present itself as their successor.[42] By writing on the Jewish language, Protestant scholars were seemingly trying to achieve precisely this. Just as the Jews lost their holy language to the Protestant scholars, so did they lose their status as the Chosen People to the Protestant community. The Protestant Hebraists, who inherited the holy language from the Jews, also inherited their preeminence in the eyes of God: symbolically, as the new bearers of the holy tongue; and practically, as the sole holders of the key to religious truth, the means to a correct understanding of the Hebrew

Bible.[43] Both of these points were of special importance to Protestant Hebraists, since their polemics could be directed not only at the Jews but also at the Catholic Church and its adherence to the Latin Vulgate.

In his book *Jewish Self-Hatred*, Sander L. Gilman claims that "Yiddish became important to the Christian community only after the complete expropriation of Hebrew by the world of Protestant theology."[44] Yet it is my contention that Yiddish in fact played an important role in the Christian project of appropriating Hebrew, and not only as an aid in the learning of the holy tongue. Rather, it seems that for the Christian Hebraists, Yiddish language and literature also fulfilled an important discursive function. Entering the field of Hebrew studies in the late fifteenth century, Christian scholars were competing for a domain of expertise traditionally dominated by Jews. Against the notion that the Jews enjoyed a "natural advantage" in the rivalry for the hegemony over the knowledge of Hebrew, the Christian Hebraists had only their scholarship to offer.[45] Moreover, the Christian ambition to gain mastery of Hebrew without Jewish mediation proved difficult to achieve, and especially in the sixteenth and seventeenth centuries Christian Hebraists often had to rely on Jews or converts from Judaism as Hebrew tutors, editors, proofreaders, and compositors. By debasing the cultural and intellectual image of their Jewish rivals through negative representations of the latter's contemporary culture, Christian Hebraists could make their own scholarly achievements stand out in full glory. From a Christian perspective, the study of Yiddish was therefore an important element in constructing the hegemony of Christian scholarship over that of the Jews.

The traditional association between Hebrew and the Jewish people had even graver consequences from a theological perspective, as it rendered the Protestant attempt to appropriate this language highly problematic. Erasmus had already expressed his concern "that the rebirth of Hebrew studies may give Judaism its cue to plan a revival . . . I watch our great hero Paul toiling to defend Christ against Judaism, and I feel that some men I could name are slipping back into it secretly."[46] Indeed, from the very beginning of the Reformation, the intense preoccupation of Protestant scholars and reformers with the Hebrew language and its literature made them highly vulnerable to accusations of Judaization. With the aura of suspicion surrounding Christian Hebrew studies, such accusations as "those who study Hebrew become Jews" or that Hebrew scholarship would lead to the "Judaization of Christianity" were frequently directed at Protestant Hebraists, both from Catholic opponents and from inside the Protestant camp.[47]

In this respect, the claim promoted in Protestant works about Yiddish, that the Jews had lost their traditional hegemony over the holy tongue to the Protestant Hebraists, and that Yiddish, and not Hebrew, was in fact the language of contemporary Jews, should be seen as a means used by Protestant scholars to reaffirm linguistic difference as a marker for distinguishing themselves from the Jews. Since the desired outcome of the Christian appropriation of the Hebrew language was certainly not to assume a hybrid Christian-Jewish identity, the dichotomy the Hebraists created between the praiseworthy Christian Hebrew and the denigrated Jewish Yiddish was necessary in order to reassert the boundaries between themselves and the Jews, and thus to maintain Christian theological order. The study of Yiddish, in other words, was important for both the practical acquisition and the ideological appropriation of the Hebrew language: it helped Christian Hebraists to liberate themselves from their dependence on Jewish tutors, and even more fundamentally, to liberate the field of Hebrew studies from its centuries-old Jewish tradition.

Conclusion

Yiddish-Speaking Orientals: Language Shift and the "*Verbesserung der Juden*"

The principal notions underlying the Christian presentations of the relation between Hebrew and Yiddish remained relatively constant throughout the early modern period. In fact, the main ideas propagated in these presentations persisted well into the late eighteenth and nineteenth centuries. Yet from the second half of the eighteenth century we can detect a certain shift of emphasis in the Christian discussions on this topic, from a more theological to a more cultural one. This is not to say that the religious element wholly disappeared. However, with the growing skepticism regarding the divine origin of both the Hebrew language and the biblical text on the one hand, and the German philosopher Johann Gottfried Herder's influential writings on the exalted poetry of the ancient Hebrews on the other, the cultural implications of the Jews' historical shift from Hebrew to Yiddish moved to the center of attention and were formulated in ever more explicit Orientalist terms.

Early traces of a more cultural approach to the Jewish "falling from grace" can be found already at the beginning of the eighteenth century in a short tractate by Johann Jacob Schudt. Like most of the other authors under discussion, Schudt usually focused on the theological implications of the Jews' historical shift from Hebrew to Yiddish. But in a small work from the year 1716, dealing with the Frankfurt Jews of his time, Schudt chose to focus on the *cultural* implications of this shift. "For the amusement [*Belustigung*] of the benevolent reader" Schudt added an appendix to the work, including examples of Jewish riddles and fables of two kinds: those common among the ancient Hebrews, taken from the Bible, and contemporary Yiddish ones.[1] Drawing a distinct line between the old *Hebrews* (*Hebräer*) and present-day *Jews* (*Juden*), Schudt elaborately praised the custom of the old Hebrews, as well as other ancient Oriental peoples, to express their worldly and divine wisdom in fables and riddles, so as to gain both useful edification and a sharpening of the intellect, as well as graceful amusement. In stark contrast to his admiration of the cultural and intellectual practices of the ancient Hebrews, Schudt presented the Yiddish riddles with the following words: "The Jews of our time, who are no more than the foam and yeast [*Schaum und Hefen*, that is a pale shadow] of the ancient, wise Hebrews, wish to imitate their ancestors also in this aspect, that they amuse themselves in company with riddles and complicated questions; but they do not measure up to their ancestors by far."[2]

But the most celebrated and influential example of the focus of a Christian author on the *cultural* deterioration of the Jews, rather than on their theological "falling from grace," appeared only seven decades later in the work of the Enlightenment philosopher Johann Gottfried Herder. In his works on poetic language and national consciousness from the early 1780s, and also in his later works, Herder identified a process of linguistic and cultural decay in the Jewish people, which he ascribed to their transition from the biblical Orient to their contemporary existence in the Diaspora. Possessing the Hebrew language in its purest, most pristine form, the ancient Hebrews had created poetry imbued with divine spirit and deep aesthetic values; the Jews of his time, however, separated from their original homeland, possessed only a degenerate culture and language, described by Herder as "a sad mixture" (*ein trauriges Gemisch*). The Jews' decline from their past days of glory as noble Orientals to their debased state as "the Asiatics of Europe" was, according to Herder, irreversible. Therefore, the only way for them to redeem themselves would be to abandon their inappropriate moral and ethical codes, as well as their equally inappropriate Jewish language and culture, and integrate into European culture and society. The "Jewish question" should thus be resolved not through religious conversion but through a linguistic and cultural one.[3]

The shift of gravity in the Christian discourse on the Jews' language from a more theological perspective to a more cultural one had far-reaching implications for the position of the Jews in the German lands. Just as the notion that contemporary Jews had no true, "decent" religion justified Christian mission to this minority, so did the notion that contemporary Jews had no true, "decent" language and culture pave the way to a "civilizing mission" among them.[4] Aiming to deorientalize the Jewish population living in their midst, German reformers and bureaucrats considered the replacement of Yiddish with German to be a key element in the "improvement" (*Verbesserung*) of the Jews, a vision they promoted by means of legislation.[5] In the various tolerance patents and edicts of emancipation granted to the Jews in Austria and the German lands during the late eighteenth and nineteenth centuries, the Jews were required to abandon their old language and adopt German as a precondition for gaining the benefits promised in the edicts. Seeking to strengthen central government control and at the same time to promote their enlightened educational ideals, German legislators did not merely order the Jews to conduct business and keep their commercial records in German. They also required them to use the German language in all public and private correspondence, assume German names, and become educated in German. In order "to make the Jewish nation useful and serviceable to the state, mainly through better education and enlightenment of its youth,"[6] the Jews were directed to send their children to German-language schools or to open such schools for them. Thus, the requirement that Jews earn legal equality through re-education, especially through full acquisition and usage of the German language, became a central element in the German Enlightenment project of "internal colonization," which promoted the cultivation of the Jewish minority in the service of the state.[7]

By the time their English and French counterparts had launched their fully fledged *mission civilisatrice* in overseas colonies for the improvement and benefit of their "culturally backward" Oriental populations in the nineteenth century, the Germans had already been engaged in attempts to civilize their own "Oriental Other"—the Yiddish-speaking Jews of Central Europe. However, the same skepticism regarding the possibility of a true Jewish conversion, which for centuries had accompanied missionary endeavors, persisted in the debates in nineteenth-century Germany over the possibility of Jewish regeneration. The question whether the Jews could be civilized and truly integrated into German society became paradigmatic in the Dohm-Michaelis debate in the early 1780s over the civil status of the Jews.[8] While both men agreed on the "degeneration" of contemporary German Jews, they differed in their opinions as to the causes of this degeneration, and hence in their respective solutions to the problem. Dohm and other liberal reformers argued that the degenerate state of the Jews—"these unfortunate Asiatic refugees" (*unglücklichen asiatischen Flüchtlinge*), as Dohm referred to them[9]—was not inherent in the character of the Jews or their religion but the result of centuries of Christian persecutions. Granting the Jews equal rights, therefore, would remove the cause of Jewish degeneration and would necessarily lead to their improvement. In opposition to this view, Michaelis and later German nationalists from conservative and anti-Semitic circles rejected the possibility of Jewish regeneration. Insisting on the Jews' immutable, "Oriental nature" (*orientalischen Wesen*), the opponents of emancipation maintained that the degenerate character of the Jews could not be altered. As a foreign and Oriental people, it was argued, the Jews would always retain their essential difference, and would never be able to integrate into European culture.[10]

The question about the possibility of Jewish cultivation and eventual integration into German culture informed the discussions on the Jewish language, too, as doubts were raised regarding the capability of Jews to relinquish their Yiddish and Jewish speech patterns and truly master the German language. As historian Shulamit Volkov claims, "Full mastery of the German language . . . became the essence of the acculturation of the Jews, and was the most conspicuous aspect of their success; but, at one and the same time, it was also the most sensitive site for criticizing and attacking them."[11] Going back to Herder's linguistic nationalism and the Romantic tradition, the notion that language bears the imprint of a person's born identity found many supporters in nineteenth-century Germany. With the implication that *adopting* a language can be no more than a superficial achievement, this notion created almost insurmountable obstacles for the admission of the Jews into the German *Kulturnation*.[12]

During the nineteenth century, Jews were frequently accused that their German was too "Jewish," too foreign, or simply artificial. Popular theater plays at the beginning of the century mocked Jewish aspirations to enter German culture by ridiculing their language.[13] In such plays, the figures of acculturated Jews, like Isidor Morgenländer ("Oriental") and others, attempt to demonstrate their successful acculturation by speaking High German. However, their flawed German, Jewish intonation, and recurrent lapses into Yiddish betray their failure and stigmatize them as essentially foreign. In a famous tractate from 1850, *Das Judentum in der Musik*, Richard Wagner emphasized the foreignness of European Jews, as conveyed by their language. Branding Jewish speech patterns as "completely alien" (*durchaus fremdartig*), the great composer rejected any possibility of Jewish assimilation. According to Wagner, "The Jew speaks the language of the nation in whose midst he dwells from generation to generation, but he speaks it always as an alien. . . . [He] talks the modern European languages merely as learnt, and not as mother tongues."[14] Bolstered by the emerging racial discourse of the later part of the century, the idea that the "corrupt" language of the Jews was part of an immutable Jewish nature continued to undermine the basic assumptions of emancipation. Due to his alien, non-European origin, it was argued, the Jew would never be able to truly master the German tongue. Any attempt to do so would be no more than an unauthentic mimicry.

Most of the Christian Yiddishists discussed in this study did not live to see the emancipation edicts or to participate in the debates on the Jewish language that followed them. But in their own writings on Yiddish, they often touched upon the topic of Jews and the German language and to a large extent anticipated the major outlines of the debate in the later period.

Especially illuminating in this respect are the reasons provided by the various authors for the Jewish "corruption" of the German language.[15] As we have seen, the most common assertion was that the Jews *chose*, consciously and deliberately, to reject the German language of the general population and cultivate a special dialect of their own: either because they despised German, as a *goyim* language, and did not ascribe to its learning any importance; or because they wished to distinguish themselves from their surroundings and preserve their separate existence; or because they preferred to cultivate a "secret language" as a means to conceal their illicit dealings. A different opinion, advocated by Johann Wagenseil at the turn of the eighteenth century, laid the cause for the Jews' poor German with the social conditions imposed on the Jewish minority in the German lands. Focusing on the environmental origins of the Jews' vices rather than on some innate Jewish evil characterized the meliorist discourse on the Jews that emerged in the German lands from the late seventeenth century, especially with regard to Jewish economic behavior.[16] An active participant in this discourse, Wagenseil saw the language situation of the Jews as environmentally induced, too. The German Jews, he argued, did not speak or write correct German, simply because they were not educated in German schools and could not take a German tutor for their children.[17] The Jews, in other words, could theoretically acquire the German language, once given the possibility to do so.

From Wagenseil's perspective, therefore, the emancipation edicts of the following century, which offered the Jews the opportunity to educate their children in German, could certainly be viewed as the right solution to the Jewish language problem. And since the edicts in fact *required* the Jews to do so, they could also be viewed as an appropriate solution from the point of view of those who ascribed the Jews' corrupt language to their reluctance to learn and use German. Yet a third reason for the Jews' "corruption" of the German language was also expressed in the early modern literature. In the introduction to his bilingual missionary tractate *Gloria Christi* (1710), the Lutheran theologian Caspar Calvör discusses this issue at great length. Among other things, Calvör also raises the argument that the Jews "corrupt" the German language because, "as a foreign and, according to their origin an Oriental people [*als ein fremdes und dem Ursprung nach orientalisch[es] Volck*]," the Jews have hardly any common ground with "our German mother tongue." A few pages later, Calvör again emphasizes this point. The German Jews, he asserts, "do not have a fixed German grammar, and indeed can hardly have one, since, as a foreign-Oriental people [*als ein fremd-orientalisch[es] Volck*], they do not understand the German language correctly."[18] Pointing to the Jews' alien, Oriental origin as a cause of their corrupt language, Calvör in fact rules out the possibility that Jews would ever be able to master the German language. As an "Oriental people," according to his logic, the German Jews can only speak Yiddish, not proper German. Although he does not formulate his assertion in the terminology that would come to dominate the discourse on language and race in the later period, Calvör nonetheless introduces a racialist dimension into the discussion on the Jews' language, thus providing an important early example of a notion that would become so crucial in later generations.

Conclusion

In recent years there has been a growing tendency among scholars to replace older views of medieval and early modern Christian-Jewish relations with a more complex historical understanding. Instead of formulating these relations solely in terms of isolation, persecution, and toleration, newer historiography also emphasizes the cultural, social, and intellectual *interaction* between Jews and Christians. For historians looking to highlight the aspect of contact and cultural exchange in early modern Christian-Jewish relations, the field of Christian Hebraism seems to be particularly attractive. The engagement of Christian Hebraists with Jewish texts, as well as their cooperation with Jewish translators, compositors, and proofreaders, present this field as a natural site for encounters between Jews and Christians.[1] The question of course is how to interpret these encounters. One approach is presented for example in some of the essays collected in the volume *Hebraica veritas?* from 2004, in a section entitled "Negotiating Dialogue." Although it by no means disregards the polemical and missionary impulses that characterized the work of many Christian Hebraists, this approach nonetheless seeks to emphasize the more positive implications of Christian Hebraism for Christian-Jewish relations in early modern Europe. The relevant essays in *Hebraica veritas?* thus point out "the efforts—on both Jewish and Christian sides—to forge some form of dialogue that bespeaks the potential (if not the reality) of mutual respect," as well as the idea that "the engagement of Christians with Jews and Jewish texts could lead to a greater sympathy between the two groups and contribute to emerging ideas of ecumenism and tolerance."[2] Another approach, promoted for instance in the works of Jonathan M. Hess and Susannah Heschel,[3] defines Christian-Jewish relations in terms of power, domination, and control. Drawing upon the insights of postcolonial studies, they suggest viewing the history of European Jewry as a colonized population within Western Christendom. In this context of asymmetrical power relations that characterized the Christian-Jewish encounter for centuries, such works interpret Christian Hebrew and biblical scholarship in late eighteenth and nineteenth-century Germany in the light of Edward Said's Orientalist paradigm, with its emphasis on the close linkage between intellectual authority and colonial power in Western discourse of the Orient. According to this interpretation, the scholarly investigation of Judaism should also be seen as an effort to express and justify Christian hegemony over the Jews, an effort "whose political ramifications entailed not an overseas colonization, but a domestic one."[4]

Like other instances of Christian study of Judaism, the field of Christian Yiddishism offered an important site for Christian-Jewish encounter in early modern Germany, a function that was further reinforced by its subject of study, the Yiddish language itself. In contrast to other Jewish subjects of study, such as Hebrew or rabbinic literature, Yiddish was not entirely "Jewish" nor a remnant of a culture remote in both time and space. It was a language that emerged and developed on German territory as the result of (at least partial) assimilatory processes of absorption and adaptation of the dialects of the non-Jewish surroundings. Therefore, if Yiddish indicated Jewish separation and isolation, it also indicated that the German Jews were not completely alienated from their surroundings, and thus could certainly serve to mitigate the image of the Jew as a complete foreigner.[5] Further than that, as a "third space" between Hebrew and German, Yiddish presented itself as a linguistic mediator between the Jews and their non-Jewish surroundings. At least in Western and Central Europe, where Yiddish never lost contact with its German progenitor, we may certainly assume that it was not completely unintelligible to non-Jews, but enabled the Jewish minority to maintain contact with the speakers of other German dialects.[6] Thus, despite its function as a marker of separate Jewish identity, Yiddish nonetheless provided Jews with a valuable means of communication and interaction with their Christian neighbors.

The Christian corpus of Yiddish textbooks, dictionaries, grammars, and translations significantly contributed to the function of the Jewish-German language as a bridge between the two sides of the religious divide. Instructing their readers in the Yiddish language and the Hebrew alphabet, most of the Christian works were specifically designed to facilitate communication between Jews and non-Jews, and support Christians in their interactions—commercial, missionary, or otherwise—with members of the Jewish community. Moreover, by exposing their coreligionists not only to the Yiddish language but also to the vast literature written in it, Christian Yiddishists promoted the acquaintance of non-Jews with contemporary Jewish culture. Reading Jewish texts in Yiddish offered a window to the closed world of Ashkenazi Jewry and contributed to the familiarity of Christians with the religious and cultural world of their Jewish neighbors.

However, as becomes apparent from this study, early modern Christian scholarship on Yiddish was rarely motivated by pure interest in Jewish culture, nor did it seek to facilitate a true dialogue between Jews and Christians. Christian Yiddishists did not attempt to understand Jewish culture on its own terms, let alone to accept it, and the body of linguistic and philological literature they produced was hardly an expression of neutral, disinterested knowledge. Instead, the scholarly investigation of the Yiddish language and literature was part of a Christian attempt to achieve intellectual domination of Jewish culture, inextricable from their ambition to exert control over the Jewish minority in the German lands.

Encompassing both the religious domain and the more secular, socioeconomic one, the Christian preoccupation with Yiddish reveals an attempt to achieve two forms of control over the Jews. The first was an active, if not an aggressive form of control, as manifested in the ambition to utilize Yiddish for anti-Jewish polemics and missionizing among the Jews. Recognizing the social function of Yiddish as the Jews' *private* language, theologians and missionaries came to the conclusion that mastering it would enable them not only to penetrate the closed Jewish world but also to offer the Jews the Christian religion via a friendly and more familiar medium—two important prerequisites for a successful mission. The second form of control was a defensive one, which aimed to fight Jewish blasphemy, deception, and other forms of deviant and illicit behavior believed to prevail among the Jews. The underlying assumption was that Yiddish was the Jews' *secret* language, deliberately used to conceal Jewish affairs from Christian eyes. Identifying Yiddish as the private language of the Jews on the one hand, serving them as a means to maintain their separate existence and resist conversion to the dominant Christian society, and on the other hand, perceiving it as the Jews' secret language, serving them as a means to subvert the Christian religious and social order from within, suggests that the Christian authors viewed Yiddish as what we would term today an "antilanguage," the language of an "antisociety." Intentionally created by subordinated and marginalized groups antagonistic to the dominant society, an antilanguage is the language of social conflict, and as such presents a threat to the existing social order.

By offering instruction in the Yiddish language and acquaintance with its literature, Christian Yiddishists provided their readers with concrete tools for achieving a direct, practical control over the Jewish minority. But the Christian works on Yiddish supported the conjunction of knowledge and power also in a less direct manner. In their discussions on the Jewish language, the Christian authors participated in a broader discourse on Jews and Judaism in early modern Germany, a discourse that both reflected and sustained the power relations between Jews and Christians that prevailed at the time, and emphasized the marginal place of the Jew within German culture and society. This form of domination, which we may designate as "discursive" or "ideological," involved creating a denigrating image of the Jew, in contrast to which the authors could then construct a self-glorifying image of Christian culture and society. The Jew was thus made to function as the inferior Other, who by serving as an antithesis to the Christian created the contrast needed by the Christians to affirm and elevate their own identity.

This form of discursive domination comes forward already in the Christian discussions on the practical uses of Yiddish for non-Jews, examined in the first two parts of the book. The religious and cultural inferiority of the Jew emphasized in the theological and missionary writings was supplemented by the notions of Jewish subversiveness, apparent in both the theological and the more secular writings on the Jewish language. Mobilizing prevalent stereotypes of the Jew as a defrauder and a thief, the writings on Yiddish as the language of Jewish businessmen and criminals constructed the image of the Jew as an antithesis to law-abiding (and German-speaking) Christian society. The Christian writings on the Jewish language thus contributed to the marginalization of the Jew on various interrelated levels—the theological-cultural and the socioeconomic—and promoted the understanding of the Jewish minority as an "antisociety" which needed to be subjugated.

Yet it is especially when we examine the different ways in which the Christian authors depicted Yiddish via its relations to German on the one hand, and to Hebrew on the other, that the element of discursive domination becomes evident. As shown in the third part of the book, the depictions of the relation between Yiddish and its parent languages were hardly impartial, matter-of-fact linguistic presentations. Rather, they served the Christian authors as a forum to promote their own agendas regarding the Jews, the latter's place in German society, and the intricate relations between Christianity and Judaism. A close reading of these texts, therefore, reveals not only the way their authors perceived and defined Jews and Judaism, through the unique perspective of language, but also the way they perceived and defined their own language, religion, and culture, in contrast to those of the Jews.

Although one might have assumed that due to its great affinity with German, Yiddish would help mitigate the image of Jewish Otherness, it seems that the opposite happened. Instead of inserting an element of familiarity that would bridge the gap between Christians and Jews, the "third space" created by Yiddish seems to have enhanced Christian fears of hybridity and contamination, creating the need to control and contain the close relation between the two languages. As "almost the same, but not quite," to use Homi Bhabha's famous designation of the "westernized colonial," Yiddish presented a serious challenge to the Christian scholars, who considered language an essential trait of a German collective identity. Their attempts to struggle with this challenge, which became especially evident in the late seventeenth and eighteenth centuries, included two important strategies. The first was constructing a derogatory image of Yiddish as a deformed and corrupt German or alternatively as a mixed and confused mongrel language (*Mischlingssprache*). The second strategy aimed to draw a distinct line between "our German" and "the German of the Jews," despite the linguistic affinity between the two variants on the one hand, and the dialectal fragmentation of German at the time on the other. From a social perspective, these strategies enabled the Christian authors to support and affirm the existing social order. Since in every society the *social* hierarchy is reflected and sustained by the *linguistic* hierarchy,[7] the marginalization of Yiddish stood as a metaphor for the marginalization of its Jewish speakers inside German society. From a nationalistic perspective, they enabled the authors to exclude the Jews from the vision of a consolidated German nation, and at the same time to define their own German language in opposition to Yiddish, and hence to constitute German identity in opposition to the Jewish one. This form of "oppositional" or "reactive" identity was especially important because of the paradox inherent in the German national consciousness at the time, in which the major constituent of this consciousness, the German language, was itself a somewhat vague and not clearly defined concept.

The ways in which the derogatory image of Jewish religion and culture constituted a crucial component of Christian self-affirmation were further explored in the last chapter of the book, dedicated to the Christian representations of the relation between Yiddish and Hebrew. The central claim put forward in the authors' discussions on this subject is that Hebrew, after being replaced by Yiddish, was no longer the language of the German Jews. Of special significance here is not simply that the Christians noted this historical linguistic shift but the value and meanings they assigned it, and the ideological postures it was made to support and justify, most notably, the claim of Christian Hebraists to have superseded the Jews as the bearers of the holy tongue. By presenting their own Hebrew scholarship in sharp relief to the neglect of Hebrew among Ashkenazi Jews, who replaced it with Yiddish, the Christian authors asserted their cultural superiority over the Jews and reaffirmed the idea that the Protestant community was in fact the "New Israel." As demonstrated throughout the chapter, the Christian discussions on this topic show strong resemblance to what we would term today an Orientalist discourse. The characteristics of this discourse, which in many ways anticipate the later Orientalist project of modern European colonialism, would become ever more dominant in the German-Christian discourse on Jews and Judaism, as well as on the Jewish language, throughout the late eighteenth and nineteenth centuries.

The derogatory discourse on the Jews' language in the German lands, which had been for centuries in the making, continued both to construct and to reflect the image of Jews and Judaism in Germany well into the twentieth century. While other European vernaculars have been triumphantly established as national standards and highly praised media of culture and scholarly activity, Yiddish continued to be dismissed as a denigrated *jargon*, inappropriate for respectable, educated individuals in modern Europe. The discussions on the Jewish-German language that took place in scholarly circles and the popular culture in Germany from the late eighteenth century onwards were, undoubtedly, a product of their time. They were shaped by the changing intellectual climate of the Enlightenment and its aftermath, and by the transformations in the status of the Jews in the German lands. Like the "Jewish question" in general, the question of the Jews' language became less of a theological concern and more of a social one, inextricable from contemporary debates on Jewish cultural improvement and political emancipation. However, as this book has aimed to demonstrate, the Christian discourse on Yiddish in the German lands has a long history that predates the debates of the Enlightenment and goes deep into the centuries preceding the modern period. It was during that earlier period that the foundations were laid, not only for a scholarly investigation of the Yiddish language and literary achievements but also for the discourse that would become a key component in the processes that led to the decline and eventual demise of the Jewish language in Western and Central Europe.

Epilogue: Christian Yiddishism—and the Jews?

This book has focused on early modern Christian literature on Yiddish on two interrelated levels: that of Christian-Jewish polemics and that of intra-Christian debates. As perceptions of Yiddish were closely linked to almost each and every one of the many Jewish stereotypes prevalent in early modern Germany, the study has addressed a wide array of questions, ranging from religious polemics to socioeconomic prejudices, from the evaluation and rating of languages to national consciousness, and from missionary endeavors to Orientalist concepts. But many other questions arise from this study, concerning the *Jewish* responses to early modern Christian literature on Yiddish. Did the Jews attempt to refute the main notions that came forward in the Christian writings? Did they accept or even internalize them? Or did they ignore this genre altogether? Although further research is still needed, it seems that on the whole the Christian literature on Yiddish did not evoke a special response inside the Jewish communities, at least not a public one. We could of course assume that Jews were simply not exposed to this kind of literature, or alternatively, that even if they *were* aware of the Christian discourse on Yiddish they lacked the political power to publicly polemicize with its content. In this case, one can view the fact that Yiddish and the literature written in it persisted in the German lands well into the nineteenth century, in spite of Christian denunciations, as a response in its own right. Like many other aspects of Jewish existence in the German lands, the persistence of Yiddish can be certainly viewed as a passive resistance to hegemonic Christian representations, a "revolt of the colonized" who insists on maintaining his own culture and identity in the face of authoritative attempts to subdue and eliminate them.

But these suggestions seem insufficient. Jewish history in the German lands does present us with instances of Jewish public responses to Christian works and authors that were perceived as a threat to the Jewish community. The publication of Eisenmenger's *Entdecktes Judenthum* was postponed for a decade due to the objections of the Frankfurt Jews; Moller's Yiddish translation of the New Testament became a rarity after Jews had burned all the copies they could get; and Brenz's anti-Jewish *Jüdischer abgestreiffter Schlangen-Balg* initiated a Jewish apologetics already in the year after its appearance—to mention only very few examples.[8] It would appear more likely that Jewish authors simply did not consider it important enough to respond to the Christian attacks on the Yiddish language and literature. After all, Yiddish was not viewed by Jewish scholars as a pillar of Jewish existence, nor as an essential component of Jewish self-image or self-definition. It was not considered holy, like Hebrew, and in the vast corpus of early modern anti-Jewish polemics, the writings of Christian Yiddishists were certainly not the fiercest. The attacks on Yiddish culture, therefore, were probably not considered a serious threat to the Jewish community. Finally, we should also consider the possibility that Jews did not attack or refute Christian notions of Yiddish culture simply because many Jewish scholars, religious leaders, and educational reformers in fact *shared* many of the ideas presented in the Christian discourse, especially with regard to the theological and cultural criticism of Yiddish and its literature.

During the early modern period, discussions on the value of Yiddish language and literature took place inside the Jewish communities of Ashkenaz, focusing on the place and function of the vernacular in Jewish religious culture.[9] Comparing the two discourses makes it clear that certain similarities existed between the Jewish and Christian discourses on the Ashkenazi Jews' language situation in general, and on the Yiddish language and literature in particular. Complaints regarding the decline of Hebrew in Ashkenazi communities, resulting in the incapability of many Jews to adequately read the Bible or understand their prayers; admiration of the Sephardi Hebrew and the cultivation of the holy tongue among the Sephardim; ascribing lower social and cultural status to the Yiddish language and literature; criticism of the *khumesh-taytsh* tradition of scriptural translation and dissatisfaction with the Polish *melamdim* and their "corrupt language"—all these points and more, which came forward in the *Christian* discourse on Yiddish, were also present in the *Jewish* one throughout the early modern period.

The resemblance between the two discourses raises some interesting questions regarding the possible existence of cultural feedback between Jews and Christians in early modern Germany: were the shared motifs an outcome of some form of interaction between the two groups? If so, to what extent was each discourse influenced, directly or indirectly, by the other? How did this exchange take place? Or is it a case in which each discourse developed independently from the other, the common features resulting from the fact that both communities shared basically the same cultural and religious values, operated in the same political and intellectual climate, and responded to the same social and educational challenges? These questions are of major importance since they touch upon a long-standing controversy in Jewish historiography in general, and the history of the Jews in pre-emancipation Europe in particular: to what degree was Jewish culture an autonomous entity, developing in isolation from its non-Jewish surroundings, and to what extent was its development shaped by external influences, first and foremost by its contact with the dominant Christian culture?

Questions regarding the possible influence of the Christian discourse on its Jewish counterpart become even more pertinent with the rise of the *Haskalah* movement in the late eighteenth century, when the similarity between the Jewish-*maskilic* discourse on Yiddish and the Christian one is even more striking than before. Condemning Yiddish as malformed and aesthetically displeasing, prominent *maskilim* rejected this "impure, mixed jargon" as a medium for intellectual discourse, promoting instead the use of either pure Hebrew or pure German. According to Mendelssohn, Yiddish was incapable of transmitting culture and education, and contributed to "the immorality of the common man." Other *maskilim* went even further than Mendelssohn in their attack on Yiddish. They mocked Yiddish and its speakers, especially traditionalists and east-European Jews, and embarked on a campaign to eradicate all traces of the "corrupt tongue," which they saw as a hindrance to Jewish cultural advancement.[10]

The rejection of Yiddish as a legitimate Jewish language formed an inseparable part of the *maskilim*'s broader attack on what they considered a backward and corrupt rabbinical culture and way of life. By this, as well as by introducing aesthetical criticism on the language itself into the Jewish evaluations of Yiddish, the *maskilic* discourse on the Jewish-German vernacular showed clear resemblance to the Christian discussions of the language—not only to those of the Enlightenment but also to the early modern ones. Indeed, many of the negative images of Yiddish, its literature, and its Jewish speakers that came forward in the early modern Christian literature appeared later in Jewish *maskilic* writings as well, especially with regard to the new "Oriental Jews"—the *Ostjuden* of Eastern Europe.

The question whether, and to what extent, the early modern Christian literature on Yiddish influenced and helped shape the Jewish discourse on the language in both its early modern and *maskilic* phases exceeds the scope of the present book. Any attempt to answer it will have to include a comprehensive research of the Jewish literature on Yiddish, as well as a detailed comparison between the Christian and Jewish discourses on the language, with special attention given to the representation of Christian ideas in the Jewish discourse: did the Jews adopt the Christian notions on Yiddish, polemicize with them, or modify them according to their own agenda? It will also have to consider the possible impact of the Christian discourse on its Jewish counterpart: to what degree was the latter an intra-Jewish development, and to what extent should it be seen as a response to the challenges presented by the dominant, non-Jewish culture? By providing a comprehensive presentation and analysis of the early modern Christian discourse on Yiddish, the present study has laid the foundations for such a future project, which could shed further light on one of the most complex and enigmatic topics of Jewish history—that of Christian-Jewish relations in the German-speaking world.

Reference Matter

Notes

Preface and Acknowledgments

1. Landmann, *Der jüdische Witz*, 446. I would like to thank Dr. Diana Matut from the University of Halle-Wittenberg for bringing this saying to my attention.

2. Boeschenstein, "Elementale introductorium in hebreas litteras teutonice & hebraice legendas."

Introduction

1. "Die Enge, der Schmutz, das Gewimmel, der Accent einer unerfreulichen Sprache, alles zusammen machte den unangenehmsten Eindruck": Goethe, *Dichtung und Wahrheit*, pt. 1 (1811), 235–36.

2. *Ibid.*, 196–97, 200.

3. Indeed, some scholars suggest that Goethe practiced his Yiddish with the work of a theology student, published in Frankfurt in 1709 (Koch, *Brevis manuductio*), from which he also copied the alphabetical list and the grammatical rules to his own "Anweisung zur teutsch-hebräischen Sprache" (ca. 1760; see Figure I.1). See Waldman, "Goethe und das Judendeutsch," 125–27.

4. On the emergence and development of the Yiddish language see Weinreich, *History of the Yiddish Language*. The work was published originally in Yiddish in 1973. See also the discussion in Jacobs, *Yiddish*, chaps. 2 and 3.

5. To be sure, each of these approaches to the Jewish language should be understood in its distinct historical context and ideological framework. For interesting discussions on this topic see Wenzel, "Alt-Jiddisch oder Mittelhochdeutsch?"; and Frakes, *Politics of Interpretation*.

6. See Kerler, *Origins of Modern Literary Yiddish*.

7. On the attitudes of the German-Jewish *maskilim* towards Yiddish see Römer, *Tradition und Akkulturation*; Lässig, "Sprachwandel und Verbürgerlichung"; Grossman, *Discourse on Yiddish*, chap. 2; Gilman, *Jewish Self-Hatred*, 87ff.

8. In modern historiography, the treatise usually taken to represent the shift in the Christian stance towards the Jews in the German lands is Dohm, *Über die bürgerliche Verbesserung der Juden* from 1781–83.

9. Burke, *Languages and Communities*, 15ff.

10. On this point see also Baumgarten, *Old Yiddish Literature*, chap. 1.

11. In the words of language historian William Jervis Jones: "For most of our period [1500–1800], with shining exceptions, German was doubly the underdog. It lacked the traditional (if not unquestioned) status of Hebrew, Greek and Latin; and it was functionally the inferior of French, Italian and Spanish, certainly in the perception of most contemporaries, and arguably also if we choose to apply what might nowadays be regarded as standard criteria for judging language status: selection, codification, elaboration and acceptance": Jones, *Images of Language*, vii–viii.

12. Most of the Protestant authors were Lutherans; the others, Reformed. However, in their writings on Yiddish, as in their general stance regarding Jews and Judaism, there were no essential differences between early modern Lutheran and Reformed theologians, at least in the German world.

13. To this one could also add that in general, the interest in Jews and Judaism at the time was especially noticeable in the Germanic world. For comparison, the aforementioned genre of Christian ethnographies on Jewish customs and way of life was also, to a large extent, a German phenomenon. See Deutsch, *Judaism in Christian Eyes*.

14. Borochov, "Di bibliotek," 78.

15. Although the dissertation itself was not published during his lifetime, Weinreich did publish in the 1920s two revised parts of it in Yiddish, about the sixteenth and seventeenth centuries. See Weinreich, *Shtaplen*, chap. 2; and *idem*, "Di yidishe shprakh-forshung."

16. The larger part of the book is dedicated to reprints of the texts (seventeen in number) and their translation into English.

Introduction to Part I

1. On early modern Christian Hebraism see in particular Friedman, *Most Ancient Testimony*; Manuel, *Broken Staff*; Burnett, *From Christian Hebraism*; and Coudert and Shoulson, *Hebraica veritas?* Two very recent and most welcome contributions to the field are Grafton and Weinberg, *"I have always loved the Holy Tongue"*; and Burnett, *Christian Hebraism in the Reformation Era (1500–1660)*.

2. Chrysander, *Unterricht vom Nutzen*, 21.

3. And see the pioneering work of Grafton and Weinberg, *"I have always loved the Holy Tongue,"* on the celebrated classical scholar Isaac Casaubon.

4. See Chapter 6 below.

5. Altshuler, *Seyfer brantshpigl*, intro., n.p. English trans. from Baumgarten, *Old Yiddish Literature*, 35. On early modern Yiddish literature see esp. Chapter 2 below.

Chapter One

1. Luther, *Jesus Christus*, 315.

2. *Idem*, *Wider die Sabbather* (1538); and *idem*, *Von den Juden und ihren Lügen*

(1543). Luther's stance towards Jews and Judaism received considerable attention in modern research. For a recent bibliographical survey see Kaufmann, "Luther and the Jews," 69n1.

3. On the theory and history of the missionary principle of adaptation in general, and that of linguistic adaptation in particular, see Warneck, *Evangelische Missionslehre*, esp. vol. 3, no. 2; Kraemer, *Christian Message*; and Ohm, *Machet zu Jüngern alle Völker*.

4. Although early modern mission in Yiddish was predominantly Protestant, there were also a few Catholic exceptions, most notably the Jesuit Franz Haselbauer from Prague, who published a missionary tract in Yiddish and German in the years 1719–22.

5. See Warneck, *Evangelische Missionslehre*, vol. 3, no. 2, chap. 35: "Nur das Wort"; and Kraemer, *Christian Faith*.

6. See esp. "Akkommodation, missionarische," in Koch, *Jesuiten-Lexikon*, 1:24–28. In fact, the Jesuits' "accommodation experiment," too, was highly controversial, and was officially ended by a papal bull in 1744.

7. Helic, *Dos nay testiment*. On the translator see Wolf, *Bibliotheca Hebraea*, 2:459.

8. According to some scholars, Paul Helic converted again in 1540 and became a Lutheran, though this fact remains uncertain.

9. On the Helic brothers and their printing activities see Teter and Fram, "Apostasy, Fraud."

10. Quoted in English in *ibid.*, 55.

11. It is not entirely clear why Helic chose to base his translation on Luther's New Testament rather than on a Catholic version. For an interesting discussion on this point see *ibid.*, 59–60.

12. Schadeus, *Fünff Bücher des Newen Testaments*. Quotation from *idem*, *Mysterium*, intro., n.p.

13. *Ibid.* The appendix bears the title "A Certain Account on the German-Hebrew Script That Is Employed by the Jews."

14. See Ben Goryon, *Yosifon*. This edition includes an instruction—in Yiddish—on how to read and write the Yiddish language. On Michael Adam's work as translator see Shtif, "Adams yidishe bikher."

15. The two titles are *Khamishe khumshey toyre im khamesh megiles veha-haftoyres* and *Die fünff bücher Mosis sampt dem Hohen lied Salomonis*. . . . On the two versions of Fagius' Bible see also Weinreich, *Geschichte der jiddischen Sprachforschung*, 73–81.

16. Friedrich, *Zwischen Abwehr und Bekehrung*.

17. See Chapters 2 and 3 below.

18. Wagenseil was a sympathizer of Pietism and is considered one of its forerunners. On Wagenseil's stance concerning Jews and Judaism see Blastenbrei, *Johann Christoph Wagenseil*; see also Dickmann, "Judenmissionsprogramm Wagenseils."

19. The works are: Moller, *Novum Testamentum Hebraeo-Teutonicum* (Moller was exceptional in that his inspiration in this project was Elias Schadeus' work rather

than Wagenseil's); Calvör, *Gloria Christi*; Lebrecht, *Eckstein des wahren Christlichen Glaubens*; and [Müller], *Or le'eys erev*.

20. Chrysander, *Unterricht vom Nutzen*, 47.

21. Although Chrysander puts forward different arguments for learning Yiddish in his *Unterricht vom Nutzen des Juden-Teutschen*, the one advocating mission is by far the most dominant one. His textbook is the *Jüdisch-Teutsche Grammatick*, also from 1750.

22. The best source of information on the institute and its activities are the reports made by Callenberg himself. See esp. his first report (from 1730) on the early years of the institute: Callenberg, *Bericht*, with its sixteen supplementaries. For secondary literature see Clark, *Politics of Conversion*, 47–82; and Rymatzki, *Hallischer Pietismus*.

23. The story of the establishment of the Yiddish course, including its aims and methods, is told in Callenberg, *Bericht*, Andere Fortsetzung (1731), 167–75.

24. *Ibid.*, 169–70.

25. Tychsen owned a vast collection of Yiddish literature (today at the University of Rostock), corresponded in this language with Jews for many years, and often related to Yiddish and Yiddish texts in his own writings. He also composed two short instructions on how to read Yiddish. The first appeared in his *Bützowische Nebenstunden*, 1:41-53 ("Einige Jüdische deutsche Briefe"); the other is found in a manuscript form (*Introductio in linguam Judaeo-Teutonicam*, 1775).

26. Callenberg, *Kurtze Anleitunng*; and *idem*, *Jüdischteutsches Wörterbüchlein*.

27. Callenberg, *Bericht*, Sechzehnte Fortsetzung (1738), intro., n.p.

28. Quotations from Fagius, *Die fünff bücher Mosis*, intro., n.p.; and Callenberg, *Bericht*, Andere Fortsetzung (1731), 168–69, emphasis in the original.

29. Wagenseil, *Belehrung der Jüdisch-Teutschen*, intro., n.p.; see also Calvör, *Gloria Christi*, intro., n.p.; Callenberg, *Bericht*, Andere Fortsetzung (1731), 5–6; Neunte Fortsetzung (1734), 150; Callenberg, *Augustana confessio*, Callenberg's intro., n.p.; and the appendix to Callenberg, *Bericht*, Sechste Fortsetzung (1734).

30. The mission in Yiddish was therefore seen as complementary to that in Hebrew, not as a substitute, and missionary endeavors in the Hebrew language, directed at non-Ashkenazi Jews as well as at Jewish scholars in and outside Europe, continued parallel to the mission in Yiddish throughout the eighteenth century.

31. Callenberg, *Neue summarische Nachricht*, 9, 31; *idem*, *Bericht*, Fortsetzung, 2nd ed. (1733), II Schreiben, 78, 80–81; and Andere Fortsetzung (1731).

32. Chrysander, *Unterricht vom Nutzen*, 4, 25–28, here: 27.

33. Christian Moller, for example, justified his decision to translate the New Testament into Yiddish, adjusting the text to the Jewish manner of writing, by explaining that after all, "I wrote it for the Jews, and especially for the uneducated; neither for Christians nor for the learned nor for scholars": Moller, *Novum Testamentum Hebraeo-Teutonicum*, intro., n.p.; see also [Fagius], *Khamishe khumshey toyre*, intro., n.p.; Callenberg, *Bericht*, Andere Fortsetzung (1731), 187–88; Dreyzehnte Fortsetzung (1735), 36; and *idem*, *Neue summarische Nachricht*, 66.

34. *Idem*, *Bericht*, Andere Fortsetzung (1731), 188. See also Wagenseil, "Hoffnung der Erlösung Israelis," 108.

35. For diverse examples see the papers in Burke and Porter, *Languages and Jargons*. For introductory theoretical framework and a historical survey to the subject see Burke's intro. to *ibid.*, 1–21. On the social attributes and functions of dialects see e.g. Haugen, "Ecology of Language," esp. 329–33.

36. In addition to the references in note 29 see also Schudt, *Jüdische Merckwürdigkeiten*, 2:290; Johann Heinrich Seyfertus' intro. to Lebrecht, *Eckstein des wahren Glaubens*, n.p.; and Callenberg, *Bericht*, Andere Fortsetzung (1731), 89.

37. Quotations from Calvör, *Gloria Christi*, intro., n.p.; Chrysander, *Jüdisch-Teutsche Grammatick*, 3; and *idem*, *Unterricht vom Nutzen*, 5. In other works of converts and Christian Hebraists we also find the claim that the Jews refer in this way to Latin, too.

38. See e.g. Eisenmenger, *Entdecktes Judenthum*, 1:504. Literally, the word *galkhes* signifies something belonging to the *galokhim*, "the tonsured ones," i.e. the Catholic priests. See Weinreich, *History of the Yiddish Language*, 1:185, and *idem*, "*Yidishkayt* and Yiddish," 389n9.

39. Wagenseil, "Hoffnung der Erlösung Israelis," 39. See also Schudt, *Jüdische Merckwürdigkeiten*, 2:283–84. Already Paulus Fagius noted in the introduction to his Latin translation of *Sefer emunah* that "they [the Jews] are repulsed by anything, which is not presented in their own language." Callenberg cites this assertion in his Latin intro. to the Yiddish trans. of the *Epistle to the Romans* from 1733, noting it as a reason for his decision to publish the work in Yiddish. See Callenberg, *Pauli apostoli epistola ad Romanos*, intro., n.p.

40. Fagius, *Die fünff bücher Mosis*, intro., n.p.

41. Gerson, *Des Jüdischen Thalmuds*, 213. On the Jews' reluctance to read non-Jewish languages, and especially German, see also Seyfertus' intro. to Lebrecht, *Eckstein des wahren Glaubens*, n.p.; Wagenseil, "Rabbi Mose Stendels," intro., n.p.; Callenberg, *Bericht*, 3; Neunte Fortsetzung (1734), 150; and *idem*, *Augustana confessio*, intro., n.p.

42. See Chapter 2 below.

43. Helvicus, *Jüdische Historien*, vol. 2, intro., n.p. On this work see also Chapter 2 below.

44. Wagenseil, "Hoffnung der Erlösung Israelis," 36.

45. See Clark, *Politics of Conversion*, 51n79. See also Callenberg, *Bericht*, Sechste Fortsetzung (1734), 91; and Zehnte Fortsetzung (1735), 111.

46. *Idem*, *Neue summarische Nachricht*, 23. Callenberg's reports include numerous accounts of missionaries greeting Jews in Hebrew or Yiddish as a catalyst to start a conversation, or using the Yiddish books they carried with them for this purpose.

47. See Callenberg, *Bericht*, esp. Anderer Theil der dritten Fortsetzung (1732), 77–78; Sechste Fortsetzung (1734), 165; and Achte Fortsetzung (1734), 132, 148–49.

48. Chrysander, *Unterricht vom Nutzen*, 33.

49. See Clark, *Politics of Conversion*, 74.

50. Callenberg, *Bericht*, Andere Fortsetzung (1731), 174.

51. To a large extent, this literature was either produced or republished at Callenberg's institute in Halle. For a literary survey and a bibliographical list see Rymatzki, *Hallischer Pietismus*, chaps. 3.1 and 6.3.1.

52. See Callenberg, *Bericht*, 3; Seyfertus' intro. to Lebrecht, *Eckstein des wahren Glaubens*, n.p.; Moller, *Novum Testamentum Hebraeo-Teutonicum*, intro., n.p.; Calvör, *Gloria Christi*, intro., n.p.; and Callenberg's Latin introductions to Moller, *Evangelium Matthaei*, n.p., and to Callenberg, *Pauli apostoli . . . ad Corinthios*, n.p.

53. Callenberg, "Was bey Austheilung der zum Gebrauch der Juden gedruckten Schriften zu beobachten" (1743), quoted in Carlebach, *Divided Souls*, 168n67.

54. The entire story behind the publication of this work, which eventually brought about the establishment of the missionary publishing-house in Halle, is recounted in detail by Callenberg in his *Bericht*, 4ff. A German translation with an introduction by Callenberg was published eight years later, in 1736, for Christian readers: [Müller], *Licht am Abend*.

55. See Callenberg's intro. to [Müller], *Licht am Abend*, n.p.; and Callenberg, *Neue summarische Nachricht*, 6.

56. *Idem*, *Bericht*, 11.

57. [Müller], *Or le'eys erev*, intro., n.p.

58. Callenberg, *Bericht*, Fortsetzung, 2nd ed. (1733), I Schreiben, 40.

59. Numerous stories on Jewish reactions to missionary conversations and writings in Yiddish are to be found in Callenberg's reports, as well as in autobiographies of converts from Judaism. For the latter source see Carlebach, *Divided Souls*, 166–69.

60. Callenberg, *Bericht*, Fortsetzung, 2nd ed. (1733), I Schreiben, 39. By this the Jew is of course alluding to the well-known tale in Genesis 27, in which Jacob deceitfully obtains Isaac's blessing by pretending to be his brother, Esau; at the same time, he is evoking the old typology of Jacob and Esau, well entrenched in Jewish tradition, as symbolizing Jews and non-Jews.

61. Callenberg, *Bericht*, 13. See also *ibid.*, Andere Fortsetzung (1731), 89; Neunte Fortsetzung (1734), 13; and Eilfte Fortsetzung (1735), 85.

62. Calvör, *Gloria Christi*, intro., n.p.

63. Callenberg, *Bericht*, Andere Fortsetzung (1731), 170–71.

64. For examples see *ibid.*, Achte Fortsetzung (1734), 17; Neunte Fortsetzung (1734), 209; Zehnte Fortsetzung (1735), 58, 122, 174; Eilfte Fortsetzung (1735), 37–38; Zwölfte Fortsetzung (1735), 1–2; Dreyzehnte Fortsetzung (1735), 116; Vierzehnte Fortsetzung (1736), 35; and Fünfzehnte Fortsetzung (1736), 79.

Chapter Two

1. On early modern Yiddish literature see in particular Zinberg, *History of Jewish Literature*, Vol. 7; Shmeruk, *Sifrut yidish*; and more recently, Baumgarten, *Old Yiddish Literature*. For an anthology see Frakes, *Early Yiddish Texts*.

2. Turniansky, "Yiddish Literature," 277. This is not to imply, as was often done in older scholarship on Old Yiddish Literature, that these texts lacked literary or aesthetic value, or did not necessitate any intelligence or education among their readers; it only meant that the required knowledge could be obtained also without formal rabbinic education. On this point see for instance Dauber, *In the Demon's Bedroom*.

3. See in particular Helvicus, *Jüdische Historien*, vol. 1, intro., n.p.; vol. 2, intro., n.p.; Wagenseil, *Belehrung der Jüdisch-Teutschen*, 117; *idem*, "Rabbi Mose Stendels," intro., n.p.; Chrysander, *Unterricht vom Nutzen*, 16, 21; Schudt, *Jüdische Merckwürdigkeiten*, 2:289; Wolf, *Bibliotheca Hebraea*, 2:458.

4. Wagenseil, *Belehrung der Jüdisch-Teutschen*, intro., n.p. English trans. from Frakes, *Cultural Study of Yiddish*, 55.

5. "Dazu aber granum salis gehöret": Chrysander, *Unterricht vom Nutzen*, 21. Seventeenth-century professor of theology and Oriental languages from Leipzig, August Pfeiffer, also recommended Christians to take "small sips" (*praelibare paulum*) from the Jewish literature written "in our vernacular": Pfeiffer, *Critica Sacra*, 377.

6. Callenberg, *Bericht*, Achte Fortsetzung (1734), 197–98; see also *ibid.*, Anderer Theil der dritten Fortsetzung (1732), 13.

7. On Fagius' Yiddish Bible and its two introductions—the one in German and the other in Yiddish—see Chapter 1 above.

8. [Fagius], *Khamishe khumshey toyre*, intro., n.p. English trans. from Baumgarten, *Old Yiddish Literature*, 156.

9. On the negative reactions of the rabbis and community authorities to this kind of literature see *ibid.*, 155–57.

10. Helvicus, *Jüdische Historien*, vol. 1, intro., n.p.; vol. 2, intro., n.p.

11. *Ibid.*, vol. 2, intro., n.p.

12. The earliest extant edition appeared in 1622, apparently in Hanau (rather than in Basel, as stated on the title page). Three earlier editions, from Lublin and Cracow, have been lost.

13. "Chapter XVI: On the German-Hebrew Language of the Jews of Frankfurt and Other [Jews]": Schudt, *Jüdische Merckwürdigkeiten*, 2:281–96; Supplement: 4:113–23.

14. *Ibid.*, 2:289. See also Chrysander, *Unterricht vom Nutzen*, 16.

15. Schudt, *Jüdische Merckwürdigkeiten*, 2:289. Parts of the *Tsene-rene* (from the first portion of Genesis) were in fact translated for Christian readers already in 1660, albeit into Latin rather than German. See Saubert, *Codicis*.

16. Callenberg, *Bericht*, Fünfzehnte Fortsetzung (1736), 136.

17. As attention to the ability to *read* Yiddish was a common feature in Christian tutorials for this language, only the most prominent examples are mentioned here: Johann Buxtorf provides a detailed bibliographical list of Yiddish works, including short descriptions and remarks in his *Thesaurus grammaticus*, 649–51; a detailed bibliography of Yiddish literature is also to be found in Wolf, *Bibliotheca Hebraea*; Christoph Helwig (Helvicus) translated parts of the *Mayse-bukh* into German (*Jüdische Historien*, 1612); Johann Wülfer translated Salman Zvi Hirsch's *Yudisher teryak* into

Latin in his *Theriaca Judaica* from 1681; Wagenseil, *Belehrung der Jüdisch-Teutschen*, and Schudt, *Jüdische Merckwürdigkeiten*, vol. 3, offer a collection of entire works and passages from works from different Yiddish genres, some with German translation.

18. Chrysander, *Unterricht vom Nutzen*, 9, 21.

19. *Ibid.*, 20, and see also 47; Pfeiffer, *Critica Sacra*, 377. With regard to specific Yiddish works see for instance Chrysander, *Unterricht vom Nutzen*, 7–8; Helvicus, *Jüdische Historien*, vol. 1, intro., n.p.; vol. 2, intro., n.p.; Wagenseil, "Rabbi Mose Stendels," intro., n.p.; and Johann Jacob Rambach's intro. to Willemer, *Gebet-Buch derer heutigen Jüdinnen*, n.p. See also Chapter 1 above.

20. On this genre see in particular Deutsch, *Judaism in Christian Eyes*.

21. On Buxtorf's career in Jewish studies see Burnett, *From Christian Hebraism*.

22. Buxtorf, *Thesaurus grammaticus*, 649–51.

23. Burnett, *From Christian Hebraism*, 243. For a thorough discussion of Buxtorf's *Juden Schul* see *ibid.*, chap. 3. An illuminating discussion of this work and its literary sources is also offered by Grafton and Weinberg, *"I have always loved the Holy Tongue,"* chap. 3.

24. In a letter to the theologian Matthias Martinius from 1606, Buxtorf mentions this book as one of the prime sources for his *Juden Schul*: "You ask how I managed to collect these Jewish myths. I reply that the Jews themselves compiled them for me. They did so in the first place by providing me with their book of customs, which is entitled *Minhagim* and is published in Hebrew-German. If you want it, I will give it to you" (quoted in English in *ibid.*, 142–43).

25. Burnett, *From Christian Hebraism*, 78–79.

26. "den Goliath mit seinem eigenen Schwerdt [zu] erwürgen": Chrysander, *Unterricht vom Nutzen*, 20.

27. Wagenseil, "Rabbi Mose Stendels," intro., n.p.; see also his *Belehrung der Jüdisch-Teutschen*, 93, where Wagenseil discusses Jewish Passover-songs in Yiddish.

28. Chrysander, *Unterricht vom Nutzen*, 20–21.

Chapter Three

1. Warren and Laslett, "Privacy and Secrecy," quotation from 43.

2. *Ibid.*; Bok, *Secrets*, esp. 5ff, quotation from 6.

3. Carlebach, "Attribution of Secrecy."

4. On this point see esp. *ibid.*; see also Deutsch, "Polemical Ethnographies"; Carlebach, *Divided Souls*, chap. 9.

5. See Trachtenberg, *Devil and the Jews*, esp. 61–63; and Hsia, *Myth of Ritual Murder*, esp. 6–7, 135–36.

6. On the "demystification of Hebrew" as part of the general disenchantment of Jewish magic in Protestant Germany see *ibid.*, esp. 143, 148. For useful insights on the perception of Hebrew and later on Yiddish as the secret or hidden languages of the Jews see Gilman, *Jewish Self-Hatred*, 22–86. However, Gilman discusses this image of Yiddish almost exclusively within the secular sphere, whereas theological aspects are discussed with regard to Hebrew.

7. Scott, *Domination and the Arts of Resistance*, quotation from 4. See also Seidman, *Faithful Renderings*, 4–5.

8. Cohen, *Friars and the Jews*, 60–76; and Schwerhoff, "Blasphemie," 125–35.

9. On the central role the fear of Jewish blasphemies played in Protestant writings as well as in political policy regarding the Jews from the 1530s and into the eighteenth century see Kaufmann, "Die theologische Bewertung."

10. Carlebach, "Anti-Christian Element," 12–15. For a thorough discussion of *Toledot Yeshu* see Krauss, *Das Leben Jesu*. Krauss mentions several Yiddish works that contained anti-Christian polemic in his *Jewish-Christian Controversy*.

11. Brenz, *Jüdischer abgestreiffter Schlangen-Balg*, chap. 1.

12. Carlebach, "Anti-Christian Element," 16; see also Krauss, *Jewish-Christian Controversy*, 249–50.

13. Rambach's intro. to Willemer, *Gebet-Buch derer heutigen Jüdinnen*, n.p.

14. Chrysander, *Unterricht vom Nutzen*, 25.

15. This was one of two complete Yiddish versions of the Bible published in Amsterdam at the same year. The other translation is that of Joseph ben Alexander Witzenhausen, published at the shop of Joseph Athias in 1679. On these two Amsterdam Bibles see in particular Aptroot, "'In *galkhes* they do not say so'"; *eadem*, "Yiddish Bibles in Amsterdam"; and Timm, "Blitz and Witzenhausen."

16. Kortholt, *De variis scripturae*, 343–44.

17. Carpzov, *Critica Sacra*, 759–61.

18. *Ibid.*, 761–78, and see also Wolf, *Bibliotheca Hebraea*, 4:187–88; and Anon., *Nachrichten von einer Hallischen Bibliothek*, 106.

19. Chrysander, *Unterricht vom Nutzen*, 7–9. See also Anon., *Nachrichten von einer Hallischen Bibliothek*, 107–8. Attacking Blitz for taking the liberty "to include his interpretations and refutation in the text," the anonymous author of the *Nachrichten* asserts that "one cannot say anything else to his [Blitz's] defense besides that he has done what he, as a Jew, felt he had to do": *ibid.*

20. Schudt, *Jüdische Merckwürdigkeiten*, 1:284–85.

21. *Ibid.*, 1:285, and see also Kortholt, *De variis scripturae*, 344. For further discussion on Blitz's translation see Wolf, *Bibliotheca Hebraea*, 2:454–55. For denunciations of Jewish "blasphemies" and anti-Christian expressions in other Yiddish prayer books and biblical translations see Kortholt, *De variis scripturae*, 342; Carpzov, *Critica Sacra*, 753–56; Wagenseil, "Rabbi Mose Stendels," intro., n.p.; Chrysander, *Unterricht vom Nutzen*, 14.

22. Trachtenberg, *Devil and the Jews*, 15.

23. Eisenmenger, *Entdecktes Judenthum*, vol. 1, title page. After the Frankfurt Jews managed to stop the publication of the first edition in 1700, a second edition was printed in Berlin, although the place noted on the cover is Königsberg, which was outside the emperor's jurisdiction.

24. On Eisenmenger and his *Entdecktes Judenthum* see in particular Jacob Katz, *From Prejudice to Destruction*, chap. 1.

25. Like other works in this genre, Brenz's title is quite revealing: *Jewish cast-off*

snakeskin, that is a thorough detection and rejection of all blasphemies and lies that the poisonous Jewish snake-vermin habitually use, partly in the damned synagogues, partly in their homes and in secret gatherings. Both works, Brenz's *Jüdischer abgestreiffter Schlangen-Balg* and Hirsch's *Yudisher teryak* (with Latin trans.), were republished in Wülfer, *Theriaca Judaica*. All further references to Brenz's work are to the paginated reprint in Wülfer, *Theriaca Judaica*.

26. For an interesting discussion on Eisenmenger's work in general, and its relations to the tradition of converts' literature in particular, see Carlebach, *Divided Souls*, 212–21.

27. The full title is *Detectum velum Mosaicum . . . That Is Jewish Cloak of Moses' Law, Under Which the Jews of Our Time Pursue All Kinds of Knavery, Vice, Abomination, and Usury; Removed and Exposed by Dietrich Schwab, Who Turned from Jew to Christian*.

28. *Ibid*., 45–46.

29. Brenz, *Jüdischer abgestreiffter Schlangen-Balg*, 11–12.

30. For an interesting analysis of a sixteenth-century representative of this genre see Deutsch, "Jewish Anti-Christian Invectives."

31. The following discussion is based primarily on the works of Brenz, Schwab, and Eisenmenger as representative sources, but similar examples also appear in other descriptions of Jews and Judaism from the time. Although Eisenmenger draws heavily on Jewish literary sources, he also refers extensively to Jewish oral culture. For this he derives his information mainly from reports of converts, and occasionally from his own experience.

32. Orthography here and in all other quotations is after the way it is written in the Christian sources. As was usually the case with foreign words inserted into German texts, the Hebrew or other non-Germanic words in Yiddish documented in the Christian writings were set in roman characters and the German in gothic ones, thus visually stressing the foreignness of the former.

33. On cursing and its relation to common swearing see Montagu, *Anatomy of Swearing*, 52ff.

34. Matisoff, *Blessings, Curses, Hopes, and Fears*, esp. chap. 9, 71ff. Quotations are from 4, 103. On the psychological functions of swearing in general see Montagu, *Anatomy of Swearing*, esp. chap. 5.

35. Selig, *Lehrbuch*, 202–3, 209, 323. Eisenmenger, too, claims that he has often heard Jews cursing in this way: *idem*, *Entdecktes Judenthum*, 1:628. Indeed, some highly expressive curses of this kind exist in Yiddish until today; see Guri, *Let's Hear Only Good News*.

36. Deutsch, "Polemical Ethnographies."

37. This example is from Chrysander, *Unterricht vom Nutzen*, 30. For similar examples, sometimes in slight variations, see Deutsch, "Polemical Ethnographies," 215–17.

38. Chrysander, *Unterricht vom Nutzen*, 28–31, esp. 30.

39. Weinreich, *History of the Yiddish Language*, 1:193–95, here: 194.

40. In a chapter dedicated to this topic, Eisenmenger enumerates no less than thirty-eight designations of this kind: "How the Jews usually call the Christians, and what kind of names, in most cases derisive, do they give them": Eisenmenger, *Entdecktes Judenthum*, vol. 1, chap. 16.

41. *Ibid.*, 1:716; and Brenz, *Jüdischer abgestreiffter Schlangen-Balg*, 9.

42. "When the Jews notice that one wishes to give a Christian the Lord's Supper, they say: *Er habe den Thola geachlet*, that is, he ate the hanged one": *ibid.*, 10; and Schwab, *Detectum velum Mosaicum*, 45.

43. Eisenmenger, *Entdecktes Judenthum*, 1:279, 535–36.

44. *Ibid.*, 1:553–54; see also Brenz, *Jüdischer abgestreiffter Schlangen-Balg*, 10; and Schwab, *Detectum velum Mosaicum*, 44.

45. Dovid Katz, "On Yiddish," 26–27; Baumgarten, *Old Yiddish Literature*, 19; Borochov, "Di bibliotek," 83. On this genre see also Ave-Lallemant, *Das deutsche Gaunertum*, 3:230–40 ("Die jüdischdeutsche Volksgrammatik"); and Weinreich, *Geschichte der jiddischen Sprachforschung*, 164–79.

46. Now available with English trans.: see Finkin, *Eighteenth-Century Language Text*.

47. J.W., *Jüdischer Sprach-Meister*, intro., n.p. English trans. largely from Finkin, *Eighteenth-Century Language Text*, 21.

48. Although Ave-Lallemant and especially Weinreich give the impression that PhilogLottus and Bibliophilus were also converts, we have in fact no indication for that.

49. Bibliophilus, *Jüdischer Sprach-Meister*, 75. An earlier and more famous mention of this Jewish pun was made at the beginning of the sixteenth century by the convert Johannes Pfefferkorn, in his influential tractate *Der Juden Veindt*, n.p.

50. Bibliophilus, *Jüdischer Sprach-Meister*, 74.

51. This view is represented, for example, by Carlebach, "Anti-Christian Element."

52. This point is suggested by Seidman, *Faithful Renderings*, 5.

53. An important representative of this scholarship is Yuval, *Two Nations in Your Womb*.

54. *Ibid.*, chap. 3.

55. Two interesting studies are: Burke, *Historical Anthropology*, chap. 8; and more recently Horodowich, *Language and Statecraft*. Quotation from Burke, *Historical Anthropology*, 96.

56. *Ibid.*, 101.

57. See Horodowich, *Language and Statecraft*, esp. chaps. 2 and 3; see also Levy, *Blasphemy*, esp. chap. 5; and Loetz, *Mit Gott handeln*. The fear of becoming complicit in the Jews' "crimes" was explicitly stated by Luther: "We dare not tolerate their conduct . . . If we do, we become sharers in their lies, cursing, and blasphemy": *idem*, *Von den Juden*, 522 (quoted in English in Price, *Johannes Reuchlin*, 218).

Chapter Four

1. On the efforts to promote Hebrew and biblical studies among Protestant scholars see in particular Friedman, *Most Ancient Testimony*; Burnett, *From Christian Hebraism*; and *idem*, "Dialogue of the Deaf," esp. 182ff.

2. An opposition to this practice was presented by the Jesuit Caspar Kümmet, who argued in his Yiddish appendix that "If anyone were to wish to learn to read Hebrew-German before Hebrew, he is clearly deceiving himself: for he would cause himself nothing but confusion and he would not gain any knowledge of reading Hebrew. This is the reason that I postponed this appendix until the very end": Kümmet, *Schola Hebraica*, 310. English trans. from Frakes, *Cultural Study of Yiddish*, 203.

3. See esp. his works *Compendiaria isagoge in linguam hebraeam* and *Prima quatuor capita Geneseos hebraice*, both from 1543. On Fagius' work as a Hebraist see Friedman, *Most Ancient Testimony*.

4. Fagius, *Prima quatuor capita Geneseos*, intro., n.p.

5. Chrysander, *Unterricht vom Nutzen*, 4, 53.

6. *Ibid.*, 21.

7. Buxtorf, *Thesaurus grammaticus*, dedicatory epistle, n.p., and 648. English trans. from Frakes, *Cultural Study of Yiddish*, 46, 157.

8. See Chapter 7 below.

9. According to Ave-Lallemant, the author's real name is J. P. Lütke, but he does not mention his source of information: *idem*, *deutsche Gaunertum*, 3:233. According to Weinreich, the place of publication noted on the title page, Freyberg, refers to Freiburg. It is more likely, however, that it refers to Freiberg (in Saxony), as indicated by Ave-Lallemant.

10. PhilogLottus, *Kurtze und gründliche Anweisung*, intro., n.p.

11. Wagenseil, *Belehrung der Jüdisch-Teutschen*, 117; and J.W., *Jüdischer Sprach-Meister*, intro., n.p.

12. PhilogLottus, *Kurtze und gründliche Anweisung*, intro., n.p.

13. The quotation is from Burnett, *From Christian Hebraism*, 168, with regard to Buxtorf. This position however stood at the heart of Protestant Hebraism in general.

14. Baumgarten, *Old Yiddish Literature*, 22; see also Röll, "Die Bibelübersetzung ins Jiddische."

15. This is the first known Yiddish printed book.

16. Baumgarten, *Old Yiddish Literature*, 22–23. For an elaborate discussion on the teaching method in the *kheyder* and its close relations to the Yiddish lexicographical tradition see Turniansky, "Ha-limmud ba-heder," esp. 22ff.

17. In his Hebrew Grammar from 1524 Münster offers "A short instruction how to write the vernacular language with Hebrew characters," including explanations regarding the Yiddish alphabet and a small Yiddish-Hebrew-Latin dictionary: Münster, *Institutiones Grammaticae*, n.p. On Münster's work as Hebraist see esp. Friedman, *Most Ancient Testimony*.

18. Münster, *Dictionarium Hebraicum*, intro., n.p.; and *idem*, *Dictionarium Chaldaicum*, intro., n.p. We encounter the practice of using Yiddish lexemes for explaining Hebrew and Aramaic ones also in works of later Orientalists, such as Johannes Coccejus (1603–69). See Bobzin, "Vom Sinn des Arabischstudiums," 26.

19. On the first point see Wolf, *Bibliotheca Hebraea*, 2:458; on the second point see Price, *Johannes Reuchlin*, 65; on the third point see Baumgarten, *Old Yiddish Literature*, 22n70.

20. Wagenseil, *Belehrung der Jüdisch-Teutschen*, intro., n.p.

21. Buxtorf recommends specific Yiddish lexicons in the bibliographical list in his *Thesaurus grammaticus*, 649–51, and in his *Bibliotheca rabbinica nova* from 1613.

22. On Oriental studies in early modern Germany see Bourel, "Die deutsche Orientalistik im 18. Jahrhundert"; Mangold, *Eine "weltbürgerliche Wissenschaft,"* esp. 29–31; Marchand, *German Orientalism*, 1–38; and Ebert and Hanstein, *Johann Jacob Reiske*.

23. PhilogLottus, *Kurtze und gründliche Anweisung*, intro., n.p. and 1.

24. "*taytsh-khumesh*" is the name of the Yiddish translations of this kind; "*khumesh-taytsh*" (or simply "*taytsh*") is the language of translation. On the *taytsh-khumesh* tradition see Turniansky, "Le-toldot ha-'taytsh-khumesh'"; *eadem*, "Ha-limmud ba-heder," esp. 22ff.; Timm, *Historische jiddische Semantik*; and Baumgarten, *Old Yiddish Literature*, chap. 5.

25. See Chapter 9 below.

26. See Buxtorf, *Thesaurus grammaticus*, 652; Wagenseil, *Belehrung der Jüdisch-Teutschen*, intro., n.p.; and Chrysander, *Unterricht vom Nutzen*, 19.

27. Schadeus, *Mysterium*, Yiddish Appendix, n.p. English trans. from Frakes, *Cultural Study of Yiddish*, 137.

28. See Chapter 3 above.

29. Quotation from Anon., *Nachrichten von einer Hallischen Bibliothek*, 108.

30. Bodenschatz, *Kirchliche Verfassung*, pt. 4, 94. For similar opinion see Wagenseil, "Rabbi Mose Stendels," intro., n.p. On the Christian criticism regarding the insufficient knowledge of the German Jews in Hebrew see Chapter 9 below.

31. See Kortholt, *De variis scripturae*, 342–43, and esp. Carpzov, *Critica Sacra*, 753–56, 759.

32. Schudt, *Jüdische Merckwürdigkeiten*, 1:285; and Anon., *Nachrichten von einer Hallischen Bibliothek*, 98–102, 108.

33. Chrysander, *Unterricht vom Nutzen*, 6; and Wolf, *Bibliotheca Hebraea*, 2:454.

34. Although Glüsing's name does not appear on the work, modern scholars seem to agree that this prominent figure in the radical Pietistic circles of northern Germany, who published several works in the print-shop of his friend Holle, was also the editor of the *Biblia Pentapla* and the author of its introductions. On the *Biblia Pentapla* see in particular Schrader, "Lesarten der Schrift."

35. [Glüsing], *Biblia Pentapla*, vol. 1, title page, intro., and Holle's dedication, n.p.; vol. 2, intro., n.p.

36. *Ibid.*, vol. 1, intro., n.p.; and vol. 2, intro., n.p. A similar notion is in Chrysander, *Unterricht vom Nutzen*, 6.

37. [Glüsing], *Biblia Pentapla*, vol. 1, intro., n.p.

38. Wagenseil, *Belehrung der Jüdisch-Teutschen*, intro., n.p.

39. *Idem*, "Rabbi Mose Stendels," intro., n.p.

40. *Idem*, *Belehrung der Jüdisch-Teutschen*, intro., n.p. See also Wolf, *Bibliotheca Hebraea*, 2:458.

Conclusion to Part I

1. On the two tendencies regarding the "Jewish question" in early modern Protestantism see Kaufmann, "Die theologische Bewertung"; and Friedrich, *Zwischen Abwehr und Bekehrung*.

2. On this aspect of Christian ethnographies see in particular Hsia, "Christian Ethnographies"; Carlebach, *Divided Souls*, chap. 9; and Deutsch, "*Von der Iuden Ceremonien*."

3. Hsia, *Myth of Ritual Murder*.

Chapter Five

1. Wagenseil, *Belehrung der Jüdisch-Teutschen*, intro., n.p.

2. Chrysander, *Unterricht vom Nutzen*, 25, 28.

3. It was especially in these cases that examples of *handwritten* Yiddish were presented in Christian literature on the Jewish language. Yiddish handwriting was considered less important for scholars but very useful for businessmen. See e.g. Schudt, *Jüdische Merckwürdigkeiten*, 2:288.

4. Some works concentrated solely on this aspect of spoken Yiddish, namely the Ashkenazi pronunciation of the Hebrew words. See e.g. the works of the converts C.G.C. and L.L.O., *Jüdischer Dolmetscher*; and Osterchrist, *Hebräisch- und Teutsches Sprach-buch*. See also Klayman-Cohen, *Die hebräische Komponente*, 22, 26–27.

5. The same Paul Helicz was the publisher of the Yiddish New Testament in Cracow, 1540 (see Chapter 1 above).

6. Late seventeenth-century authors of Yiddish tutorials sometimes mention the advantage of reading Yiddish for business dealings with the Jews, but this is not the main purpose of their tutorials.

7. According to Schröder, Selig also taught Yiddish; see Schröder, *Biographisches und bibliographisches Lexikon*, 2:152.

8. Dovid Katz, "On Yiddish," 25. On these works and their authors see Weinreich, *Geschichte der jiddischen Sprachforschung*, 175–83, 195–220.

9. See Guggenheim-Grünberg, "The Horse Dealers' Language."

10. English trans. from *ibid.*, 49n8.

11. On these works see Chapter 3 above.

12. J.W., *Jüdischer Sprach-Meister*; PhilogLottus, *Kurtze und gründliche Anweisung*; and Bibliophilus, *Jüdischer Sprach-Meister*.

13. Ammersbach, *Neues ABC Buch*, 29.

14. Callenberg, *Jüdischteutsches Wörterbüchlein*, intro., n.p.

15. On this point see Burke's intro. to Burke and Porter, *Languages and Jargons*, esp. 5.

16. Liberles, "Threshold of Modernity," 54–69; and Jersch-Wenzel, "Jewish Economic Activity."

17. Liberles, "Threshold of Modernity," 54–69, 87–92.

18. Selig, *Kurze und gründliche Anleitung*, dedicatory epistle, n.p.

19. PhilogLottus, *Kurtze und gründliche Anweisung*, intro., n.p.

20. Chrysander, *Unterricht vom Nutzen*, 28. English trans. from Grossman, *Discourse on Yiddish*, 128.

21. Quotation from Wagenseil, "Rabbi Mose Stendels," intro., n.p.

22. See Chapter 3 above.

23. Schudt, *Jüdische Merckwürdigkeiten*, 2:211. More examples can be found in Degani, "Hofa'at ha-markiv 'ha-plili.'"

24. Penslar, *Shylock's Children*.

25. See Eibach, "Stigma Betrug"; Penslar, *Shylock's Children*, esp. 13ff.; Jersch-Wenzel, "Jewish Economic Activity"; and Liberles, "Threshold of Modernity," 54–69.

26. On these converts and their anti-Jewish works see also Chapter 3 above.

27. See Chapter 3 above.

28. J.W., *Jüdischer Sprach-Meister*, intro., n.p.

29. Schwab, *Detectum velum Mosaicum*, 131–32. Quotation after the shorter version found in Chrysander, *Unterricht vom Nutzen*, 28–29.

30. *Ibid.*, 29–30.

31. *Ibid.*, 30; see also Schwab, *Detectum velum Mosaicum*, 133; and Wucherfeind, *Der verdammliche Juden-Spieß*, intro., n.p.

32. On this topic see also Chapter 3 above.

33. Eisenmenger, *Entdecktes Judenthum*, 2:582, after Brenz, *Jüdischer abgestreiffter Schlangen-Balg*, 21. In the German translation the word *nephesch* (soul) is mistranslated as "body," which indeed makes more sense in this sentence.

34. For fascinating analyses of the performative qualities and functions of Yiddish in the context of the post-Holocaust era see Seidman, *Faithful Renderings*, intro.; and Shandler, *Adventures in Yiddishland*, chap. 4.

35. Schudt, *Jüdische Merckwürdigkeiten*, 2:213. See also Wucherfeind, *Der verdammliche Juden-Spieß*, 81–82; and PhilogLottus, *Kurtze und gründliche Anweisung*, intro., n.p. As noted by Johann Wagenseil and following him, Johann Schudt, this was the case with other languages as well. As example they mention the practice of Italian Jews to keep their business transactions in Italian written with Hebrew letters, later forbidden by the Italian authorities: Wagenseil, *Belehrung der Jüdisch-Teutschen*, intro., n.p.; and Schudt, *Jüdische Merckwürdigkeiten*, 2:291.

36. Schwab, *Detectum velum Mosaicum*, 143.

37. Schudt, *Jüdische Merckwürdigkeiten*, 2:214.

38. *Ibid.*, 2:214–16. Wagenseil's assertion is found in his *Belehrung der Jüdisch-Teutschen*, intro., n.p. As Schudt correctly points out, the growing tendency among

Jewish parents to hire Christian tutors for their children in order to teach them German and other European languages was acknowledged by Wagenseil himself, in his "Hoffnung der Erlösung Israelis," 55.

39. Schwab, *Detectum velum Mosaicum*, 142–43; and Eisenmenger, *Entdecktes Judenthum*, 2:584. It is however uncertain if these authors meant that the Jews themselves should write the documents in German or, as Schudt once suggested, employ a Christian notary for the job; see Schudt, *Jüdische Merckwürdigkeiten*, 2:217.

40. *Ibid.*, 2:216. On the issuing of edicts of this kind already before the tolerance patents of the late eighteenth century see Chapter 6 below.

41. Shochat, *Im hillufei tekufot*, 58–62.

42. *Ibid.*, 59–60.

Chapter Six

1. Penslar, *Shylock's Children*, 19–20, and see also *ibid.*, 35–38. On Jewish poverty and vagrancy in early modern Germany see also Guggenheim, "Meeting on the Road"; Glanz, *Geschichte des niederen jüdischen Volkes*; and more recently Kühn, *Jüdische Delinquenten*. On poverty, deviance, and criminality in early modern Europe in general, and in the German lands in particular, see Jütte, *Poverty and Deviance*; and Evans, *German Underworld*.

2. Ulbricht, "Criminality and Punishment"; Glanz, *Geschichte des niederen jüdischen Volkes*.

3. Citation from Danker, "Bandits and the State," 99.

4. Glanz, *Geschichte des niederen jüdischen Volkes*, 248. The "*Kocheme*," or "the clever ones," was the name given in *Rotwelsch* to the members of the underworld, as opposed to the "*Wittstöcke*," or "the stupid ones," referring to the members of the "straight," noncriminal world; see Danker, "Bandits and the State," 98.

5. Citations from Jütte, *Poverty and Deviance*, 182, 184; see also *idem*, *Abbild und soziale Wirklichkeit*, 47–51; Burke's intro. to Burke and Porter, *Languages and Jargons*, 14–15; Danker, "Bandits and the State," 98.

6. Jütte, *Abbild und soziale Wirklichkeit*, 146ff., 163ff.; *idem*, *Poverty and Deviance*, 182–83.

7. Guggenheim, "Meeting on the Road," 131–33; Jütte, *Abbild und soziale Wirklichkeit*, 34, 165–67; Glanz, *Geschichte des niederen jüdischen Volkes*, chaps. 11 and 13.

8. Brant, *Narrenschiff*, chap. 63: "Von Bettlern" (of beggars); Moscherosch, *Gesichte Philanders von Sittewald*, chap. 6: "Soldaten-Leben" (soldiers' life). The chapter contains a small lexicon under the title "Feld-Sprach" (field- [i.e. soldiers'] language); and Scherffer, "Teutsche Ordonantz, mit gewöhnlicher Feld: oder Rotwälschen Spraache" (German orderly, with common field- or Rotwelsch-language) in *Geist- und weltlicher Gedichte*. Scherffer, too, appended a *Rotwelsch*-German glossary to his text. The soldiers' language (*Soldatensprache*, *Feldsprache*) was a variety of *Rotwelsch* and shared much of the latter's vocabulary.

9. Luther's intro. to *Von der falschen Betler büberey*, 638.

10. de Sunde [Schwenter], *Steganologia et Steganographia aucta*, 18–20. In 1608

Schwenter became professor of Hebrew at the University of Altdorf, where he later became professor of Oriental languages and mathematics.

11. Reyher, *Mathesis Mosaica*, 209; see also Schudt, *Jüdische Merckwürdigkeiten*, 1:479, where he reasserts that "diejenigen, so das Rottwelsche zu erst auffgebracht, aus den Juden entsprungen gewesen."

12. Wagenseil, *Buch von der Meister Singer*, 435, 438.

13. *Ibid.*, 443.

14. Wagenseil's failure to adequately differentiate between the language of the Gypsies and *Rotwelsch* was already noted by eighteenth-century critics. See e.g. Schudt, *Jüdische Merckwürdigkeiten*, 1:477ff.

15. Wagenseil, *Buch von der Meister Singer*, 445.

16. Quotation from Penslar, *Shylock's Children*, 20.

17. Ulbricht, "Criminality and Punishment," 49–50.

18. On robber-bands in eighteenth-century Germany, including Jewish ones, see Küther, *Räuber und Gauner*; Danker, *Räuberbanden im Alten Reich*; and *idem*, "Bandits and the State."

19. See e.g. Anon., *Actenmäßige Nachricht*. An earlier example is the word-list that stemmed from the investigation of the thief Andreas Hempel and his gang in 1687.

20. Glanz, *Geschichte des niederen jüdischen Volkes*, 242–43; Jütte, *Abbild und soziale Wirklichkeit*, 146.

21. For the entire story see Danker, *Räuberbanden im Alten Reich*, 43–53.

22. At the end of the third edition (1735/6) we find a *Rotwelsch* glossary: "For better understanding of the Jewish thieves' dealings, some words and special technical terms that are common among the robber bands will follow, which the thieves are in the habit of using among themselves."

23. [Einert], *Entdeckter Jüdischer Baldober*, title page and intro.

24. On the fact that churches and monasteries were popular targets for burglars, both Jewish and non-Jewish ones, see for instance Danker, "Bandits and the State," 86.

25. Hobsbawm, *Bandits*.

26. See e.g. Ulbricht, "Criminality and Punishment"; Küther, *Räuber und Gauner*; Danker, *Räuberbanden im Alten Reich*. To be sure, this is the way they are presented in Christian sources, such as [Einert], *Entdeckter Jüdischer Baldober*; and Bierbrauer, *Beschreibung*.

27. [Einert], *Entdeckter Jüdischer Baldober*, 592–93; my emphasis. See also Bierbrauer, *Beschreibung*, 10–11.

28. For an elaborate discussion on these and similar expressions from the *lehavdl loshn* vocabulary see Chapter 3 above.

29. Jütte, *Abbild und soziale Wirklichkeit*, 50.

30. Krackherr, *Bequemes Handlexicon*.

31. *Idem*, *Des Klugen Beamten Hand-Lexicon*, title page.

32. Chrysander, *Unterricht vom Nutzen*, 25, 31–32.

33. *Ibid.*, 31–32.

34. Bibliophilus, *Jüdischer Sprach-Meister*, intro., n.p.

35. See Shochat, *Im hillufei tekufot*, 58–59 (with various references to seventeenth-century sources); Degani, "Hofa'at ha-markiv 'ha-plili,'" 669; Volkov, *Germans, Jews, and Antisemites*, 183; and Römer, "Sprachverhältnisse und Identität," 12.

36. English translation of these edicts appears in Mahler, *Jewish Emancipation*, 18–20, 32–35.

37. For examples see Borochov, "Di bibliotek," 85–86.

38. Grossman, *Discourse on Yiddish*, 136–37, 155.

39. For examples of nineteenth-century criminological literature on Yiddish see Borochov, "Di bibliotek," 87; and Grossman, *Discourse on Yiddish*, 136n7. A prominent example is Thiele, *Die jüdischen Gauner in Deutschland*.

40. Wagenseil, *Belehrung der Jüdisch-Teutschen*, intro., n.p. English trans. from Frakes, *Cultural Study of Yiddish*, 61. See also Schudt, *Jüdische Merckwürdigkeiten*, 2:292; Oppenheimer, *Hodegus ebraeo-rabbinicus*, title page; Osterchrist, *Hebräisch- und Teutsches Sprach-buch*, 4; C.G.C. and L.L.O., *Jüdischer Dolmetscher*, 4–5; Bibliophilus, *Jüdischer Sprach-Meister*, intro., n.p.; Chrysander, *Unterricht vom Nutzen*, 24; Selig, *Lehrbuch*, title page.

41. Both anecdotes appear in Wagenseil, *Belehrung der Jüdisch-Teutschen*, intro., n.p.

42. *Ibid.*

43. See e.g. Degani, "Hofa'at ha-markiv 'ha-plili,'" 677–79.

44. Shochat, *Im hillufei tekufot*, 58–59; Kracauer, *Geschichte der Juden in Frankfurt*, 2:99–100.

45. Selig, *Lehrbuch*, 28.

46. Clark, *Politics of Conversion*, 52.

47. In Prussia, for example, the Jewish oath was practiced until 1869.

48. On the Jewish oath see Stobbe, *Die Juden in Deutschland*, 153–59; Geiger, *Geschichte der Juden*, 2:265–80.

49. Trachtenberg, *Devil and the Jews*, 69.

50. Quotation from Seidman, *Faithful Renderings*, 168.

51. In a letter to Assistant Councilor Ernst Ferdinand Klein, 29 Aug. 1782. See Mendelssohn, *Gesammelte Schriften*, 7:279.

52. Gilman's claim that Wagenseil promoted the use of Yiddish in the Jewish oath, as well as the quotation he provides to support his argument, are incorrect. See Gilman, *Jewish Self-Hatred*, 73, and also 102.

53. Wagenseil, *Belehrung der Jüdisch-Teutschen*, intro., n.p.

54. *Ibid.*

55. Chrysander, *Unterricht vom Nutzen*, 21–22.

56. *Ibid.*, 22–23. On p. 24, after a long explanation on the differences between the Sephardi and Ashkenazi Hebrew, Chrysander demonstrates how the verse is to be read according to the Ashkenazi pronunciation.

57. Wagenseil, *Belehrung der Jüdisch-Teutschen*, intro., n.p.

58. This point is discussed, for instance, in [Einert], *Entdeckter Jüdischer Baldober*, 66, where the author emphasizes the need to use a "*Coscher Sepher Tora*"—i.e. the one the Jews use in the synagogue—when administrating a Jewish oath.

59. Wagenseil, *Belehrung der Jüdisch-Teutschen*, intro., n.p.

60. Chrysander, *Unterricht vom Nutzen*, 21. Wagenseil adds that this will also enable them to ensure that the Jew puts his hand on the right verse while saying the words, another practice considered necessary for a valid oath: Wagenseil, *Belehrung der Jüdisch-Teutschen*, intro., n.p.

Conclusion to Part II

1. Degani, "Hofa'at ha-markiv 'ha-plili,'" 655.

2. The following discussion is based on Halliday, "Antilanguages"; on the concept of "antilanguage" see also Hodge and Kress, *Social Semiotics*, 68ff., 86ff.; Montgomery, *Language and Society*, 96–102.

3. Quotations from Halliday, "Antilanguages," 164, 168, 171, emphasis in the original.

4. *Idem*, "Language and Social Structure," 185.

5. Quotation from *idem*, "Antilanguages," 165.

6. *Ibid*., 181, my emphasis.

7. On this point, and especially on the idea that the Jews *deliberately* deviated from the standard use of German to devise their own language, see Chapter 7 below.

8. See Chapter 3 above.

Introduction to Part III

1. Quotation from Said, *Orientalism*, 36.

2. In recent years there has been a growing recognition of the importance of the Orientalist paradigm, as formulated by Edward Said and others, for the analysis of Western, and especially German, discourse about Jews and Judaism. See in particular Pasto, "Islam's 'Strange Secret Sharer'"; Heschel, "Revolt of the Colonized"; Hess, *Germans, Jews*; and Kalmar and Penslar, *Orientalism and the Jews*.

Chapter Seven

1. On the two dimensions in language description see Haugen, "Dialect, Language, Nation," 242.

2. As Max Weinreich notes, *taytsh* was also the common name of the language in Yiddish itself. See Weinreich, *History of the Yiddish Language*, 1:316–17.

3. The Yiddish translation is that of Joseph ben Alexander Witzenhausen, published by Joseph Athias in Amsterdam (1679, 2nd ed. 1687). On this work see also Chapter 4 above.

4. [Glüsing], *Biblia Pentapla*, vol. 1, title page, my emphasis.

5. Quotations from Chrysander, *Unterricht vom Nutzen*, 4; and Schudt, *Jüdische Merckwürdigkeiten*, 2:288, respectively.

6. Frakes, *Cultural Study of Yiddish*, *passim*, and esp. 8; quotations from 29, 30. Max Weinreich also criticizes Christian Yiddishists on several occasions for not adequately distinguishing between Yiddish and German but relates it mainly to the fact

that these scholars were primarily familiar with literary Yiddish, which at this time was closer to German than the spoken one. See Weinreich, *Geschichte der jiddischen Sprachforschung*, 131.

7. Helicz, *Elemental oder lesebuechlein*, 3. English trans. from Frakes, *Cultural Study of Yiddish*, 103.

8. Buxtorf, *Thesaurus grammaticus*, 657.

9. Wagenseil, *Belehrung der Jüdisch-Teutschen*, title page; Gottfried, *Anweisung zum Jüdischdeutschen*, title page; see also Ernesti, *Die wol-eingerichtete Buchdruckerey*, 138–39; and Friedrich, *Unterricht in der Judensprache*, intro., n.p.

10. Schudt, *Jüdische Merckwürdigkeiten*, 2:289.

11. Buxtorf, *Thesaurus grammaticus*, 657; Sennert, *Rabbinismus*, 65; Meelführer, *Grammaticae hebraeae*, 265; Schudt, *Jüdische Merckwürdigkeiten*, 2:288; Dilherr, *Atrium linguae sanctae*, 61; and Selig, *Kurze und gründliche Anleitung*, intro., n.p.

12. Quotation from Kortholt, *De variis scripturae*, 343.

13. Schudt, *Jüdische Merckwürdigkeiten*, 2:291–92.

14. Selig, *Kurze und gründliche Anleitung*, 35–36. As Baumgarten notes, many of the forms denounced by the Christian authors were in fact features of different German dialects: Baumgarten, *Old Yiddish Literature*, 15–16, 16nn50–52.

15. [Thirsch], *Nützliches Handlexikon*, 6.

16. Gottfried, *Anweisung zum Jüdischdeutschen*, 12.

17. *Ibid.*, 14.

18. Frakes, *Cultural Study of Yiddish*, 8; see also his following note: "At best they [sixteenth- and seventeenth-century depictions of Yiddish] are conceived as minimalist guides to learning the function of the Hebrew alphabet in representing what is always imagined not as an independent Yiddish language or even necessarily as a separate Jewish *dialect* of German but rather simply as a 'corrupted' Jewish style in or version of German": *ibid.*, emphasis in the original.

19. The most notable example is that of Selig, *Kurze und gründliche Anleitung*; and *idem*, *Lehrbuch*.

20. See e.g. PhilogLottus, *Kurtze und gründliche Anweisung*; Callenberg, *Jüdischteutsches Wörterbüchlein*; Bibliophilus, *Jüdischer Sprach-Meister*; Reizenstein, *Der vollkommene Pferde-Kenner*, Yiddish Appendix; Selig, *Kurze und gründliche Anleitung*, and esp. *Lehrbuch*; [Thirsch], *Nützliches Handlexikon*; and Friedrich, *Unterricht in der Judensprache*.

21. On the fusion character of Yiddish see Weinreich, *History of the Yiddish Language*, esp. 1:29–34.

22. Callenberg, *Kurtze Anleitunng*, 1.

23. Chrysander, *Unterricht vom Nutzen*, 5.

24. Gottfried, *Anweisung zum Jüdischdeutschen*, 3.

25. Selig, *Lehrbuch*, viii. In case this was not clear enough, Selig later repeats this idea when he speaks about the "Jewish-German language, which does not deserve to be called a proper and distinct language. It is composed mostly of German words, which are pronounced however in a foul and corrupted manner, and

is mingled with Hebrew, rabbinic, Latin, French, and Polish words, according to every Jew's aptitude and way of life": *ibid.*, 27–28.

26. Such complaints are especially prominent in the works of Calvör, *Gloria Christi*, intro., n.p.; Selig, *Kurze und gründliche Anleitung*; *idem*, *Lehrbuch*; and [Thirsch], *Nützliches Handlexikon*.

27. Quotation from PhilogLottus, *Kurtze und gründliche Anweisung*, title page.

28. Moreover, except for Helicz's *Elemental oder lesebuechlein* from 1543, all works dedicated entirely to Yiddish rather than a chapter in works on Hebrew or Jewish culture in general are from 1699 onwards.

29. Wagenseil, *Belehrung der Jüdisch-Teutschen*, intro., n.p.

30. On the second point see also Gilman, *Jewish Self-Hatred*, 72.

31. Chrysander, *Jüdisch-Teutsche Grammatick*, 3. English trans. from Baumgarten, *Old Yiddish Literature*, 16n48.

32. Quotations from Haselbauer, *Fundamenta grammatica*, 237; Calvör, *Gloria Christi*, intro., n.p.; and Gerson, *Des Jüdischen Thalmuds*, 216.

33. On this common and long-established assertion in the field of sociolinguistics see e.g. Montgomery, *Language and Society*; and Milroy and Milroy, *Authority in Language*. This is certainly true for the early modern era, when pronouncing judgment upon linguistic forms was common also among grammarians, and not only among the general public as is usually the case today. On language evaluation in European intellectual history see in particular Hüllen, *Collected Papers*; and Burke, *Languages and Communities*.

34. Halliday, "Antilanguages," 179; and *idem*, "Language and Social Structure," 184, 186, emphasis in the original.

35. In Weinreich's words: "The principal cultural determinant in the history of Yiddish is the fact that Ashkenazic Jewry came into existence as a community defined by *yidishkayt* . . . it can be firmly stated that *yidishkayt* shaped not only the conceptual world of the Ashkenazic community but its language as well": Weinreich, "*Yidishkayt* and Yiddish," 413. On the intricate symbiosis between Yiddish and *yidishkayt*, a term he uses in order to convey the idea of "Judaism as a civilization," see also Weinreich, *History of the Yiddish Language*, vol. 1, chap. 3: "The Language of the Way of the SHaS."

36. The phrase is from Halliday, "Antilanguages," 179.

37. Hüllen, *Collected Papers*, 189–90, 202–3. As seventeenth-century English playwright Ben Jonson asserted: "Language most shows a man: speak that I may see thee. No glass renders a man's form or likeness as true as his speech": cited in Burke, *Languages and Communities*, 26. According to Burke, the belief of early modern Europeans that language revealed the nature of its speakers was one of the reasons for the growing interest in linguistic diversity, characteristic of the period.

38. "linguistic structure is *the realization of* social structure, actively symbolizing it in a process of mutual creativity. Because it stands as a metaphor for society, language has the property of not only transmitting the social order but also maintaining and potentially modifying it. . . . Variation in language is the symbolic expression of

variation in society: it is created by society, and helps to create society in its turn": Halliday, "Language and Social Structure," 184, 186, emphasis in the original.

39. The following discussion is based primarily on Hüllen, *Collected Papers*; *idem*, "Characterization and Evaluation"; Blackall, *Emergence of German*; Burke, *Languages and Communities*; Gardt, *Sprachreflexion in Barock*; *idem*, *Nation und Sprache*; Huber, *Kulturpatriotismus und Sprachbewußtsein*; and Straßner, *Deutsche Sprachkultur*.

40. Burke, *Languages and Communities*, 69–70.

41. Quotation in Blackall, *Emergence of German*, 145.

42. On language standardization see Joseph, *Eloquence and Power*; and Milroy and Milroy, *Authority in Language*, chap. 1.4.

43. The following discussion is based primarily on Gardt, *Nation und Sprache*; Stukenbrock, *Sprachnationalismus*, pt. 3; Huber, *Kulturpatriotismus und Sprachbewußtsein*; Koselleck, "Volk, Nation, Nationalismus, Masse"; and Townson, *Mother-Tongue and Fatherland*.

44. On early modern German nationalism see in particular Hardtwig, *Nationalismus und Bürgerkultur*, intro. and chaps. 1 and 2; Blitz, *Aus Liebe zum Vaterland*.

45. Hardtwig, *Nationalismus und Bürgerkultur*, 8–9.

46. On "holy languages" see Fishman, *Beloved Language*, 11–12. In other parts of the book Fishman also elaborates on the close conceptual connection between a "holy language" and a "holy people."

47. See e.g. Hastings, *Construction of Nationhood*, esp. chap. 8. On the claims of early modern European nations to be "holy nation" or "the elected nation" see also the relevant papers in Almog and Heyd, *Ra'ayon ha-behirah be-Yisra'el u-ve-amim*.

48. Leibniz, *Ermahnung an die Teutsche*; *idem*, *Unvorgreiffliche Gedancken*; and see Blackall, *Emergence of German*, chap. 1.

49. Hastings, *Construction of Nationhood*, 108–10.

50. Burke, *Art of Conversation*, 70.

51. [Thirsch], *Nützliches Handlexikon*, 5; and Gerson, *Des Jüdischen Thalmuds*, 208.

52. Quotation from Schudt, *Jüdische Merckwürdigkeiten*, 2:291.

53. Guggenheim, "Meeting on the Road," 131n23.

54. Callenberg, *Bericht*, Andere Fortsetzung (1731), 8.

55. See Bibliophilus, *Jüdischer Sprach-Meister*, 110; and Reizenstein, *Der vollkommene Pferde-Kenner*, Yiddish Appendix, n.p.

56. Schudt, *Jüdische Merckwürdigkeiten*, 2:291; in this passage Schudt cites from the work of Hosmann, "Das schwer zu bekehrende Juden-Hertz," from 1711.

57. Example is from [Einert], *Acten-mäßige Designation*, cited in Glanz, *Geschichte des niederen jüdischen Volkes*, 201.

58. See e.g. Bierbrauer, *Beschreibung*, 15; and [Einert], *Entdeckter Jüdischer Baldober*, 309, 435, 461–62. See also Glanz, *Geschichte des niederen jüdischen Volkes*, 199–201.

59. Freud, *Civilization and Its Discontents*, 114; see also Block, "Narcissism of Minor Differences."

60. Smith, "What a Difference a Difference Makes," 4–5, 15, 47.

61. *Ibid.*, 4.

62. Joseph, *Eloquence and Power*, 72.

63. In the words of the French sociologist Pierre Bourdieu: "Social identity lies in difference, and difference is asserted against what is closest, which represents the greatest threat": Bourdieu, *Distinction*, 479. See also Block, "Narcissism of Minor Differences."

64. Barth's intro. to *Ethnic Groups and Boundaries*, 9–38.

65. See e.g. Barbour, "'der Sprache heilig Band'"; and Townson, *Mother-Tongue and Fatherland*.

66. The notion of the Jew as the constitutor of Christian identity has also gained popularity in recent research. See e.g. Limor, "Christian Sacred Space"; and the relevant essays in Neusner and Frerichs, *"To See Ourselves."*

67. In the sources, Yiddish is often opposed not only to "our German" but also to "*die gantze Teutsche Sprach*" (the whole/entire German language), "*unser gewöhnlich Teutsch*" (our common German), "*das wahre, reine Hochteutsch*" (the true, pure High-German), and the like.

68. Chrysander, *Unterricht vom Nutzen*, 5–6, 27.

69. For the entire quotation see above in this chapter; see also Schudt, *Jüdische Merckwürdigkeiten*, 2:290–91.

70. Quoted in English in Weinberg, "Language Questions," 238.

71. Wagenseil, *Belehrung der Jüdisch-Teutschen*, intro., n.p. As we have seen, not everyone agreed with Wagenseil on this point. Johann Schudt, for example, claimed that Jews did have the opportunity to educate their children in German and other European languages, as some of them in fact did (see Chapter 5 above).

72. In Friedrich, *Unterricht in der Judensprache*.

73. Wagenseil, *Belehrung der Jüdisch-Teutschen*, 88; and Callenberg, *Kurtze Anleitunng*, 2.

74. Calvör, *Gloria Christi*, intro., n.p.

75. Selig, *Kurze und gründliche Anleitung*, 35. See also *idem*, *Lehrbuch*, 37–38.

76. Buxtorf, *Thesaurus grammaticus*, 652.

77. Selig, *Kurze und gründliche Anleitung*, 35.

78. *Idem*, *Lehrbuch*, 37.

79. Calvör, *Gloria Christi*, intro., n.p.; Chrysander, *Jüdisch-Teutsche Grammatick*, 3. It is interesting to note that similar complaints about the Yiddish of the Polish *melamdim* were raised by eighteenth-century German Jews as well, whose language was already much closer to the German of their time. For examples see Shochat, *Im hillufei tekufot*, 63, 135.

80. Calvör, *Gloria Christi*, intro., n.p.

81. Chrysander, *Jüdisch-Teutsche Grammatick*, 3. English trans. from Baumgarten, *Old Yiddish Literature*, 16n48.

82. Chrysander, *Unterricht vom Nutzen*, 5; see also Bibliophilus, *Jüdischer Sprach-Meister*, 79.

83. Chrysander, *Jüdisch-Teutsche Grammatick*, 3. English trans. from Baumgarten, *Old Yiddish Literature*, 17.

84. On this point see Chapter 1 above.

85. Wagenseil, "Rabbi Mose Stendels," intro., n.p.

86. *Idem*, *Belehrung der Jüdisch-Teutschen*, intro., n.p.

87. Bodenschatz, *Kirchliche Verfassung*, pt. 4, 93–94 (quotation from 94); and Buxtorf, *Synagoga Judaica*, 151–52.

88. Haselbauer, *Fundamenta grammatica*, 237, 242. English trans. from Frakes, *Cultural Study of Yiddish*, 235, 241.

89. [Thirsch], *Nützliches Handlexikon*, 4–5. English trans. partially from Grossman, *Discourse on Yiddish*, 130–31. Even authors like Elias Schadeus or Johann Ernesti, whose depictions of Yiddish are by and large free from pejorative statements, do not fail to mention the wish to maintain secrecy as a reason for the Jewish practice of mixing Hebrew words inside the German: Schadeus, *Mysterium*, Yiddish Appendix, n.p.; and Ernesti, *Die wol-eingerichtete Buchdruckerey*, 2nd ed., 146.

90. Quotations from Selig, *Lehrbuch*, viii; and Schudt, *Jüdische Merckwürdigkeiten*, 2:292, 2(b):315. Using a more metaphoric language, Chrysander asserted that not few of the German words in Yiddish were "hammered out arbitrarily on their [the Jews'] own anvil": Chrysander, *Unterricht vom Nutzen*, 32.

91. Fishman, *Sociology of Language*, 6.

Chapter Eight

1. See Chapter 1 above.

2. Since Yiddish is in fact written with the Hebrew alphabet, the difference between the two, referred to here, is only in the type-font: between the sixteenth and the eighteenth centuries Yiddish was printed in the special type-font known as *mashkit* or "Ashkenazi semicursive" (and designated by the Christian authors as "cursive"), whereas Hebrew texts were set in square characters.

3. This is suggested, for example, by Ave-Lallemant, *Das deutsche Gaunertum*, 3:212–13, 220–22.

4. Secular literature translated from German, for example, was either very much adapted to the German literary language or simply transliterated using the Hebrew alphabet. See Baumgarten, *Old Yiddish Literature*, esp. chap. 6. For an interesting discussion on the wide range of Yiddish literary styles in the early modern period, encompassing texts that are basically German on one side, and texts that no speaker of German would have understood on the other, see Aptroort, "Writing 'Jewish' not 'German,'" esp. 121–26.

5. Schadeus, *Mysterium*, intro., n.p.; and Wagenseil, *Belehrung der Jüdisch-Teutschen*, intro., n.p.

6. See esp. Weinreich, *History of the Yiddish Language*; Timm, *Graphische und phonische Struktur*; *eadem*, *Historische jiddische Semantik*; and Jacobs, *Yiddish*.

7. See Chapter 1 above.

8. The fact that Helic did provide Hebrew translations to certain German ex-

pressions at the margins of the text or even used Hebraisms in the text itself, but did so only sparingly and inconsistently, suggests that he was aware of the difficulties that the German text posed for the Jewish reader, but did not consider it important enough to take the trouble and fully adjust the text to Yiddish conventions.

9. Wagenseil, *Belehrung der Jüdisch-Teutschen*, intro., n.p.

10. *Idem*, "Hoffnung der Erlösung Israelis," 55. Tutors could and often did incorporate Christian teachings in their German language classes, frequently giving their pupils Christian works in this language as reading material. For examples see Shochat, *Im hillufei tekufot*, 62n109.

11. Ammersbach, *Neues ABC Buch*, intro., n.p.

12. Fagius, *Die fünff bücher Mosis*, intro., n.p.

13. As Erika Timm notes, Fagius' Bible was in many cases influenced by German; see Timm, *Historische jiddische Semantik*, 701.

14. Schadeus, *Mysterium*, intro., n.p.

15. Moller, *Novum Testamentum Hebraeo-Teutonicum*, intro., n.p.

16. All quotations in the following paragraph are from Calvör, *Gloria Christi*, intro., n.p.

17. Fagius, *Die fünff bücher Mosis*, intro., n.p.; for similar notions see also Wagenseil, *Belehrung der Jüdisch-Teutschen*, intro., n.p. In 1705 Wagenseil referred to Mose Stendel's Yiddish translation of the psalms as a work that "to tell the truth, should be called gibberish rather than German": *idem*, "Rabbi Mose Stendels," intro., n.p.

18. Buxtorf, *Thesaurus grammaticus*, 652. English trans. from Frakes, *Cultural Study of Yiddish*, 161.

19. See also Chapter 7 above.

20. Carpzov, *Critica Sacra*, 751–53, referring to the translation of Joseph ben Alexander Witzenhausen (1679); on p. 759 he directs the same criticism towards the translation of Jekuthiel ben Isaac Blitz (1676–79).

21. Willemer, *Gebet-Buch derer heutigen Jüdinnen*, intro., 57–59, 63, quotation from 57.

22. See e.g. Wagenseil, "Rabbi Mose Stendels," intro., n.p.; and Callenberg's intro. to [Müller], *Licht am Abend*, n.p., referring to the translation of the biblical quotations incorporated in the work.

23. Buxtorf, *Thesaurus grammaticus*, 652. English trans. from Frakes, *Cultural Study of Yiddish*, 161.

24. Calvör, *Gloria Christi*, intro., n.p.

25. Callenberg, *Bericht*, Dritte Fortsetzung (1732), intro., n.p.

26. Calvör, *Casparis Calvoerii catechetica institutio*, Callenberg's intro., n.p.

27. Anon., *Nachrichten von einer Hallischen Bibliothek*, 112.

28. On this point see Rymatzki, *Hallischer Pietismus*, 168–69.

29. Moller, *Evangelium Matthaei*, Callenberg's intro., n.p.

30. See Callenberg, *Bericht*, Neunte Fortsetzung (1734), 182; Eilfte Fortsetzung (1735), 27; Vierte Fortsetzung (1733), 8, 33; and Dritte Fortsetzung (1732), 61–62.

31. *Idem*, *Kurtze Anleitunng*, 2.

32. *Idem*, *Jüdischteutsches Wörterbüchlein*, intro., n.p.

33. Calvör, *Gloria Christi*, intro., n.p. By "*fruchtbringende Gesellschafften*" (fruit-bearing societies) Calvör means the language societies of the Baroque *Sprachpatriotismus*, which were established with the explicit aim of cultivating the German language and purifying it of foreign influences. The "*Fruchtbringende Gesellschaft*," the first and most prominent of these societies, was established in 1617 in Weimar by Fürst Ludwig I. von Anhalt-Köthen, and its linguistic and literary activities lasted for almost a century.

34. Warneck, *Evangelische Missionslehre*, 1:299–304, 3:55; on "holy languages" see Fishman, *Beloved Language*, 11–12.

35. On this point see Clark, *Politics of Conversion*, chap. 2.

36. Carlebach, *Divided Souls*, 157–61.

37. For examples see *ibid*., 160–61.

38. See e.g. Helicz, *Elemental oder lesebuechlein*, *passim*; Gerson, *Des Jüdischen Thalmuds*, 198, 216; Anton, *Einleitung in die rabbinischen Rechte*, 292 (cited by Carlebach, *Divided Souls*, 161n27); and the works of Johann Gottfried and Gottfried Selig, discussed in Chapter 7 above.

39. Carlebach, *Divided Souls*, 42–46.

40. On this point see also Grossman, *Discourse on Yiddish*, 122, 136.

41. Clark, *Politics of Conversion*, 77–78; and Grossman, *Discourse on Yiddish*, 155–56. For later missionary revivals in Germany see e.g. Clark, *Politics of Conversion*, 83ff.

Chapter Nine

1. On Münster's work in the field of Yiddish see Chapter 4 above.

2. Münster, *Chaldaica grammatica*, 4.

3. Fagius, *Die fünff bücher Mosis*, intro., n.p. It is interesting to note that both Münster and Fagius were disciples of the great German Jewish Hebraist Elia Levita, and owed him much of their own knowledge in Hebrew. See Geiger, *Das Studium der hebräischen Sprache*, 55–88; Weil, *Élie Lévita*, esp. 133–51, 221–34, 238–43.

4. For more statements that Hebrew is no longer the language of the Jews, see e.g. Buxtorf, *Synagoga Judaica*, 152; Meelführer, *Grammaticae hebraeae*, 262; Gerson, *Des Jüdischen Thalmuds*, 211, 215–16; Schudt, *Jüdische Merckwürdigkeiten*, 2:281–83; Bodenschatz, *Kirchliche Verfassung*, pt. 4, 94; [Thirsch], *Nützliches Handlexikon*, 3–4; and Callenberg, *Bericht*, esp. Andere Fortsetzung (1731), 187–88; Siebente Fortsetzung (1734), 19, 190; Vierzehnte Fortsetzung (1736), 35; and Fünfzehnte Fortsetzung (1736), 1.

5. Schudt, *Jüdische Merckwürdigkeiten*, 2:281–82.

6. *Ibid*., 2:284.

7. [Thirsch], *Nützliches Handlexikon*, 8, and also at the beginning of his first register.

8. Interestingly enough, many of the "Yiddish" examples for the corrupting of Hebrew nouns and verbs, provided by Christian authors, were either not used in

Yiddish at all or did not enter Yiddish from Hebrew: see Weinreich, *Geschichte der jiddischen Sprachforschung*, esp. 141, 150–51, 160–61, 191.

9. See e.g. Buxtorf, *Thesaurus grammaticus*, 657–58; Schudt, *Jüdische Merckwürdigkeiten*, 2:285, 288, 4:113; Bodenschatz, *Kirchliche Verfassung*, pt. 4, 94; Dilherr, *Atrium linguae sanctae*, 61–62; Wagenseil, *Sota*, 88; Meelführer, *Grammaticae hebraeae*, intro., n.p.; Haselbauer, *Fundamenta grammatica*, 241–42; [Thirsch], *Nützliches Handlexikon*, 5, 8; and Bibliophilus, *Jüdischer Sprach-Meister*, 38, 82–86, and intro., n.p. At the end of his Yiddish tutorial chapter (1543), Fagius warns his readers to be very careful of the way they pronounce their Hebrew, emphasizing the importance of its correct articulation: Fagius, *Compendiaria isagoge*, n.p.

10. Wagenseil, "Hoffnung der Erlösung Israelis," 41. See also Schudt, *Jüdische Merckwürdigkeiten*, 2, 281–82; [Fagius], *Khamishe khumshey toyre*, intro., n.p.; Wagenseil, "Rabbi Mose Stendels," intro., n.p.; Bodenschatz, *Kirchliche Verfassung*, pt. 4, 94; Callenberg, *Neue summarische Nachricht*, 65–66; and *idem*, *Bericht*, esp. Dreyzehnte Fortsetzung (1735), 36, 54–55. An exception to this rule is presented in Chrysander's work, where the author recommends Yiddish Bibles for theology students, not only because of their word-for-word translation but also because the Jews can still contribute from their Hebrew knowledge to other people; see Chrysander, *Unterricht vom Nutzen*, 6.

11. Fagius, *Die fünff bücher Mosis*, intro., n.p.

12. On early modern Yiddish Bibles see esp. Baumgarten, *Old Yiddish Literature*, chap. 5; and the relevant references in Chapters 3 and 4 above.

13. Callenberg, *Genesis germanice litteris judaicogermanicis*, intro., n.p. On Christian criticism of Jewish biblical translations into Yiddish see also Chapters 3, 4, and 8 above.

14. Rambach's intro. to Willemer, *Gebet-Buch derer heutigen Jüdinnen*, n.p.; Schudt, *Jüdische Merckwürdigkeiten*, 2:281, 4:113; Wagenseil, *Tela Ignea Satanae*, 119; and Callenberg, *Bericht*, esp. Siebente Fortsetzung (1734), 19, 31–51, 162, 190; Achte Fortsetzung (1734), 30, 120–21; Dreyzehnte Fortsetzung (1735), 54–55, 151, 230–31; and Fünfzehnte Fortsetzung (1736), 32–33.

15. Schudt, *Jüdische Merckwürdigkeiten*, 2:281.

16. *Ibid.*, 4:113; for a very similar argument see Callenberg, *Bericht*, Neunte Fortsetzung (1734), 313.

17. Schudt, *Jüdische Merckwürdigkeiten*, 4:113; and Callenberg, *Bericht*, Dreyzehnte Fortsetzung (1735), 151; and Neunte Fortsetzung (1734), 45.

18. For similar examples see also Schudt, *Jüdische Merckwürdigkeiten*, 2:281; Willemer, *Gebet-Buch derer heutigen Jüdinnen*, intro., 49–50; Callenberg, *Bericht*, Neunte Fortsetzung (1734), 313; and Bodenschatz, *Kirchliche Verfassung*, pt. 4, 94.

19. For examples of the criticism of early modern Jewish scholars on the state of education in general, and Hebrew education in particular, among the German Jews see Güdemann, *Geschichte des Unterrichts*; see also the discussion in Turniansky, "Ha-limmud ba-heder," esp. 10–20.

20. See e.g. Burnett, *From Christian Hebraism*, 55ff.; and Deutsch, "View of the

Jewish Religion," esp. 276–77, 284–85. On the medieval roots of Christian perception of post-biblical Judaism as a heretical, Talmudic religion, which deviated from the true, biblical one, see Cohen, *Friars and the Jews*, 60–76; and *idem*, *Living Letters*, chap. 8.

21. On this point see e.g. Kalmar and Penslar, *Orientalism and the Jews*, editors' intro.

22. That "historically, Jews have been seen in the Western world variably and often concurrently as occidental and oriental" is well demonstrated in the articles gathered in *ibid*. Quotation from editors' intro., xiii.

23. See esp. Chapters 1 and 4 above.

24. Until the beginning of the nineteenth century, Oriental studies were usually confined to the study of what would be later termed Semitic languages. In addition to Hebrew, the group of "Oriental languages" included mainly Aramaic, Syriac, and Arabic, which due to their linguistic affinity with Hebrew, were considered useful for biblical philology and exegesis. On Oriental studies in early modern Germany see the items listed in Chapter 4, n22, above.

25. On this point see also Chapter 7 above.

26. Wagenseil, *Belehrung der Jüdisch-Teutschen*, intro., n.p. For the entire quotation see Chapter 7 above. Similar notions regarding the corrupting and foreignizing effect of Hebrew loan words in Yiddish are found in almost all the Christian writings on the language.

27. Quotations from Carpzov, *Critica Sacra*, 751, 759.

28. Doederlein, *Theologische Bibliothek*, vol. 3, pt. 1, 3.

29. Calvör, *Gloria Christi*, intro., n.p. See also Selig, *Lehrbuch*, intro., x.

30. Wagenseil, *Belehrung der Jüdisch-Teutschen*, intro., n.p.

31. Quotation from Fagius, *Die fünff bücher Mosis*, intro., n.p.; See also Chapter 8 above.

32. Fecht, *De praecipuis oratoris*, 29.

33. Buxtorf, *Thesaurus grammaticus*, 652.

34. See Burke, "Cultures of Translation," 24ff.

35. See Chapter 2 above.

36. Reuchlin's two famous Hebrew teachers were the Italian Jews Jacob ben Jehiel Loans and Obadiah Sforno. The fact that Reuchlin probably started his Hebrew studies with a German Jew by the name of Kalman is not mentioned in these sources. It remains unclear if Reuchlin preferred to study Hebrew with Italian Jews because he considered their language "better" than that of the German Jews, as was claimed by his Christian successors, or because German Jews were reluctant to teach Christians, a fact he himself noted more than once. On Reuchlin's study of Hebrew see Price, *Johannes Reuchlin*, esp. chap. 4.

37. See e.g. Schudt, *Jüdische Merckwürdigkeiten*, 2:284–85; Wagenseil, *Belehrung der Jüdisch-Teutschen*, intro., n.p.; and Chrysander, *Unterricht vom Nutzen*, 23. A visual example of the notion that there are in fact two kinds of Hebrew—a correct, Christian Hebrew and a corrupt, Jewish Hebrew—can be found in the Yiddish

tutorials of Wagenseil and Moller, in which they present two parallel columns of words in Hebrew; the first is labeled "The Christians read," and the other, "The Jews read": Wagenseil, *Belehrung der Jüdisch-Teutschen*, 85; and Moller, *Novum Testamentum Hebraeo-Teutonicum*, Yiddish instruction, n.p.

38. Calvör, *Gloria Christi*, intro., n.p.; Schudt, *Jüdische Merckwürdigkeiten*, 2:294–95; Wagenseil, "Hoffnung der Erlösung Israelis," 32–34, 39–40; and Callenberg, *Bericht*, esp. Neunte Fortsetzung (1734), 111, 164–65; Zehnte Fortsetzung (1735), 212–13; Zwölfte Fortsetzung (1735), 16; Dreyzehnte Fortsetzung (1735), 102, 198; Vierzehnte Fortsetzung (1736), 108; and Fünfzehnte Fortsetzung (1736), 140. On Reuchlin's "concerted effort to Christianize Hebrew"—which would turn eventually into a fully fledged project by Reuchlin's Protestant successors—see Price, *Johannes Reuchlin*, esp. 68ff. (quotation from *ibid.*, 72). On the Protestant scholars' ambition to gain hegemony over the Hebrew language, beginning with Luther, see also Gilman, *Jewish Self-Hatred*, 60–61, 69–70.

39. Wagenseil, "Hoffnung der Erlösung Israelis," 41–42. The superiority of Protestants over Jews in their knowledge of Hebrew, as well as the Jews' amazement at, and admiration for, Hebrew-speaking Christians, is repeated many times in the reports of the traveling missionaries, with strong, triumphant overtones: see Callenberg, *Bericht*, esp. Sechste Fortsetzung (1734), 45, 66–67; Siebente Fortsetzung (1734), 125, 201; Achte Fortsetzung (1734), 178–79, 322; and Neunte Fortsetzung (1734), 164, 196, 374.

40. Said, *Orientalism*, 42.

41. *Ibid.*, 79.

42. Hsia, "Christian Ethnographies," 229, 233. Hsia demonstrates, for instance, the construction of the image of evangelical Germans as the New Israelites in sixteenth-century Old Testament histories: *idem*, "The Usurious Jew," 173–76. On the Protestants' claim to be the new "Chosen People" (*das neue Gottesvolk*) see also Müller, "Protestantische Orthodoxie," 468ff.

43. An illuminating example for the association made by Protestant scholars between their knowledge of Hebrew and their understanding of themselves as the *real* Jews can be seen in the words of one of Callenberg's traveling students, who were sent to conduct mission in Jewish communities. In his report about a conversation he had with a Jewish man, the student describes how he addressed the latter in Hebrew. The amazed Jew, who knew the student to be a Christian, asked him, "where have you learned Hebrew?" To which the student answered, "We are true Jews, circumcised at the heart" (*wir sind rechte Juden, beschnitten am Hertzen*): Callenberg, *Bericht*, Sechste Fortsetzung (1734), 66–67.

44. Gilman, *Jewish Self-Hatred*, 70.

45. For interesting discussions on the rivalry that took place at the time between Christian Hebraists and Jewish converts regarding the hegemony over the knowledge of Judaism, including that of Hebrew, see Carlebach, *Divided Souls*, 200ff.; Seidman, *Faithful Renderings*, 121–23. The rivalry between Jews and Christian Hebraists over the knowledge of Hebrew is evident in informal disputations as early

as the late fifteenth and early sixteenth centuries: see Ben-Sasson, "Jewish-Christian Disputation," 381–83.

46. In a letter to Wolfgang Capito, 26 Feb. 1517. English trans. in Erasmus, *Correspondence of Erasmus*, 267–68.

47. Friedman, *Most Ancient Testimony*; and *idem*, "Sebastian Münster," esp. 238–39, 252–58. On the history of the term "Judaization," beginning in antiquity, see Dan, "'Judaizare.'"

Conclusion to Part III

1. Schudt, "Appendix of Old and New Jewish Riddles," in *Jüdische Kleider-Ordnung*.

2. *Ibid.*, quotation from 60.

3. The most relevant works are Herder, *Über die Würkung der Dichtkunst*; *idem*, *Vom Geist der Ebräischen Poesie*; and *idem*, "Bekehrung der Juden." See also Grossman, *Discourse on Yiddish*, 32–51.

4. On the concept of "civilizing mission" and its underlying secular ideologies see Osterhammel, *Europe and the Civilizing Mission*.

5. Volkov, "Sprache als Ort der Auseinandersetzung"; *eadem*, *Germans, Jews, and Antisemites*, 181–89; Gilman, *Jewish Self-Hatred*, 81ff.; Grossman, *Discourse on Yiddish*, 163–65.

6. Citation from Joseph II's *Toleranzpatent*, 2 Jan. 1782. The edict is reprinted in Pribram, *Urkunden und Akten*, 1:494–500. English trans. in Mahler, *Jewish Emancipation*, 18–20.

7. An illuminating discussion on the Enlightenment project of "internal colonization," directed at the Jewish population in the German territories, is offered by Hess, *Germans, Jews*.

8. Christian Wilhelm von Dohm (1751–1820): a German scholar and councillor in the Department of Foreign Affairs in the Prussian government, and the author of *Über die bürgerliche Verbesserung der Juden* (1781–83); Johann David Michaelis (1717–91): a prominent German Orientalist and Bible scholar, and professor of Oriental languages at the University of Göttingen. On the Dohm-Michaelis debate and its nineteenth-century aftermath see in particular Hess, *Germans, Jews*; Pasto, "Islam's 'Strange Secret Sharer,'" 450ff.

9. Dohm, *Verbesserung der Juden*, 1:8.

10. See e.g. the examples in Pasto, "Islam's 'Strange Secret Sharer,'" 452ff.

11. Volkov, "Sprache als Ort der Auseinandersetzung," 234.

12. *Ibid.*, 227; see also Toury, "Die Sprache als Problem."

13. Two prominent examples, Julius von Voss's *Der travestirte Nathan der Weise* (ca. 1802) and K.A.B. Sessa's *Unser Verkehr* (1813), are discussed in Grossman, *Discourse on Yiddish*, 137–56.

14. Quoted in English in Volkov, *Germans, Jews, and Antisemites*, 185–86; see also Grossman, *Discourse on Yiddish*, 171–72.

15. For an elaborate discussion on this point see Chapter 7 above.

16. Penslar, *Shylock's Children*, 22ff.

17. Wagenseil, *Belehrung der Jüdisch-Teutschen*, intro., n.p. For the entire citation see Chapter 7 above.

18. Calvör, *Gloria Christi*, intro., n.p. This passage is also cited in Callenberg, *Jüdischteutsches Wörterbüchlein*, intro., n.p.

Conclusion

1. For elaborate discussion on these historiographical currents with regard to early modern Christian-Jewish relations in general, and in the field of Christian Hebraism in particular, see esp. Coudert and Shoulson, *Hebraica veritas?*, editors' intro.

2. *Ibid.*, 7. For earlier examples of this approach see Ettinger, "Change in Attitude," and Zimmer, "Jewish and Christian Hebraist Collaboration."

3. Heschel, "Revolt of the Colonized"; Hess, *Germans, Jews*. For an elaborate discussion on this approach, as well as other interesting examples, also with regard to earlier periods in Jewish history, see the editors' intro. and the relevant papers in Kalmar and Penslar, *Orientalism and the Jews*.

4. Quotation from Heschel, "Revolt of the Colonized," 62.

5. On the "dialectics of assimilation," i.e. the question whether Yiddish is a testimony for isolation of the Jews from their foreign surroundings or rather a testimony for a Jewish assimilation process that has been going on since the Middle Ages; as well as on the fact that each of these concepts stems from very specific ideologies, see Funkenstein, "Dialectics of Assimilation."

6. On the relation between Yiddish and German in the early modern period see esp. Weinreich, *History of the Yiddish Language*.

7. The assertion is from Halliday, "Language and Social Structure."

8. On Eisenmenger and Brenz see Chapter 3 above; the report on the Jewish reaction to Moller's New Testament is provided in Wolf, *Bibliotheca Hebraea*, 4:206.

9. On this topic see Baumgarten, *Old Yiddish Literature*, esp. chaps. 2–4.

10. On the *Haskalah*, including its earlier stages, see Feiner, *Jewish Enlightenment*. On the attitudes of *maskilim* towards Yiddish see esp. Grossman, *Discourse on Yiddish*, chap. 2; Gilman, *Jewish Self-Hatred*, 87ff.; Römer, *Tradition und Akkulturation*; Lässig, "Sprachwandel und Verbürgerlichung."

Bibliography

Primary Sources

[Aemilius, Paulus, ed.]. *Khamishe khumshey toyre im khamesh megiles . . . gam ha-haftoyres be-loshn Ashkenaz*. Augsburg, 1544.

Altshuler, Moses H. Yerushalmi. *Seyfer brantshpigl*. Basel, 1602.

Ammersbach, Heinrich. *Neues ABC Buch*. Magdeburg, 1702 [1689; inside: "Anweisung, Wie man die Rabbinischen Teutschen Bücher und Brieffe, wie auch die Contracte, Hand-Schrifften und Wechsel-Zettul der heutigen Juden, ohne Puncten recht lesen und verstehen soll," 29–40].

Anon. *Nachrichten von einer Hallischen Bibliothek*. Vol. 3. Halle, 1749.

———. *Actenmäßige Nachricht von einer zahlreichen Diebs-Bande. . . .* Hildburghausen, 1753 [inside: "Verzeichniß vorgekommener Wörter von der Spitzbuben-Sprache. NB. Die mit einen [*sic*] Sterngen bemerckte Wörter sind unter den Juden-Spitzbuben gewöhnlich," 73–83].

Anton, Carl. *Einleitung in die rabbinischen Rechte*. Braunschweig, 1756.

Ben Goryon, Yosef. *Yosifon*. Translated by Michael Adam. Zurich, 1546 [inside: Yiddish instruction (in Yiddish), n.p.].

Bibliophilus [pseud.]. *Jüdischer Sprach-Meister, oder Hebräisch-Teutsches Wörter-Buch*. Frankfurt am Main and Leipzig, 1742.

Bierbrauer, J. J. [Johann Jacob]. *Beschreibung Derer Berüchtigten Jüdischen Diebes-Mörder- und Rauber-Banden*. Cassel, 1758.

Bodenschatz, Johann Christoph. *Kirchliche Verfassung der heutigen Juden sonderlich derer in Deutschland*. Frankfurt am Main and Leipzig, 1749.

Boeschenstein, Johannes. "Elementale introductorium in hebreas litteras teutonice & hebraice legendas." Augsburg, 1514 [in an untitled collection of various texts, n.p.].

Brant, Sebastian. *Das Narrenschiff*. Basel, 1494.

Brenz, Samuel Friedrich. *Jüdischer abgestreiffter Schlangen-Balg*. Nuremberg, 1614.

Buxtorf, Johann. *Synagoga Judaica: Das ist Juden Schul*. Basel, 1603.

———. *Thesaurus grammaticus linguae sanctae hebraeae*. Basel, 1609 [inside: "Lectionis Hebraeo-Germanicae usus & exercitatio," 648–71].

——. *Bibliotheca rabbinica nova*. Basel, 1640 [1613].

Callenberg, Johann Heinrich. *Bericht an einige Christliche Freunde von einem Versuch, das arme Jüdische Volck zur Erkäntniß und Annehmung der Christlichen Wahrheit anzuleiten*. Halle, 1730 [with sixteen supplementaries, Halle 1730–38].

——. *Kurtze Anleitunng zur Jüdischteutschen Sprache*. Halle, 1733.

——. *Neue summarische Nachricht von einem Versuch, das arme jüdische Volck zur Erkäntniss und Annehmung der christlichen Wahrheit anzuleiten*. Halle, 1735.

——. *Jüdischteutsches Wörterbüchlein*. Halle, 1736.

——, ed., [and H.C.I. Frommann, trans.]. *Augustana confessio in Germanicum Judaeorum idioma* . . . . Halle, 1732.

——, ed., [and H.C.I. Frommann, trans.]. *Pauli apostoli epistola ad Romanos in germanicum iudaeorum Idioma*. . . . Halle, 1733.

——, ed., [and H.C.I. Frommann, trans.]. *Pauli apostoli posterior epistola ad Corinthios in Germanicum Iudaeorum Idioma*. . . . Halle, 1735.

——, ed. and trans. *Genesis germanice litteris judaicogermanicis*. Halle, 1737.

Calvör, Caspar. *Gloria Christi, oder Herrligkeit Jesu Christi*. Leipzig, 1710 [inside: "Anleitung wie das Jüdisch-Teutsche zu lesen," n.p.].

——. *Casparis Calvoerii catechetica institutio in usum Iudaicae gentis scripta, Recudi & huius nationis captui accommodatiorem reddi curavit Io. Henr. Callenberg*. Halle, 1733.

Carpzov, Johann Gottlob. *Critica Sacra Veteris Testamenti*. Leipzig, 1728.

C.G.C., and L.L.O. [Christian, Christoph Gustav, and?]. *Jüdischer Dolmetscher, oder Hebräisch- u. Teutsche Vocabula*. Nuremberg, 1735.

Chrysander, Wilhelm Christian Just. *Jüdisch-Teutsche Grammatick*. Leipzig and Wolfenbüttel, 1750.

——. *Unterricht vom Nutzen des Juden-Teutschen*. Wolfenbüttel, 1750.

de Sunde, Janus Hercules [Daniel Schwenter]. *Steganologia et Steganographia aucta: Geheime, Magische, Natürliche Red unnd Schreibkunst*. Nuremberg, [ca. 1620].

Dilherr, Johann Michael. *Atrium linguae sanctae Ebraicae*. Nuremberg, 1659 [inside: "Modus legendi & scribendi Germanice, literis Ebraicis," 56–62].

Doederlein, Joh. Christoph. *Theologische Bibliothek*. Vol. 3. Leipzig, 1784.

Dohm, Christian Wilhelm. *Über die bürgerliche Verbesserung der Juden*. 2 vols. Berlin and Stettin, 1781–83 [reprint: Hildesheim, 1973].

[Einert, Paul Nicol]. *Actenmäßige Designation Derer von einer Diebischen Juden-Bande verübten Kirchen-Raubereyen und gewaltsamen mörderischen Einbrüche*. Coburg, 1735 [inside the 3rd ed. (1735/6): "Jüdische Diebsausdrücke," n.p.].

——. *Entdeckter Jüdischer Baldober oder Sachsen-Coburgische Acta Criminalia wider eine Jüdische Diebs- und Rauber-Bande*. Coburg, 1758 [1737; inside: "Anhang. I. Verzeichniß vorgekommener Wörter von der Spitzbuben-Sprache, welche unter den Juden-Spitzbuben gewöhnlich," 591–95].

Eisenmenger, Johann A. *Entdecktes Judenthum*. 2 vols. Königsberg, 1711 [Frankfurt am Main, 1700].

Erasmus, Desiderius. *The Correspondence of Erasmus*. Vol. 4. Translated by R.A.B.

Mynors and D.F.S. Thomson. Edited by James K. McConica. Toronto: University of Toronto Press, 1977.

Ernesti, Johann Heinrich Gottfried. *Die wol-eingerichtete Buchdruckerey*. Nuremberg, 1721 [inside: "Kurze Unterweisung wie man alle Teutsch-Hebräische Buchstaben im Teutschen schreiben und aussprechen solle," 137–38; "Unterricht wie man alle Buchstaben des Teutschen Alphabets mit Hebräischen Buchstaben schreiben, und ganze Wörter formieren solle," 138–39. Inside the 1733 edition: "Von dem Teutsch-Hebräischen," 145–51].

Fagius, Paulus. *Compendiaria isagoge in linguam hebraeam*. Constance, 1543 [inside: "De variis literarum figuris seu notulis," n.p.].

——. *Prima quatuor capita Geneseos hebraice*. Constance, 1543 [inside: "Succincta ratio legendi Hebraeo-Germanica," n.p.].

——, ed., [and Michael Adam, trans.?]. *Khamishe khumshey toyre im khamesh megiles veha-haftoyres . . . mi-loshn ivri le-loshn ashkenazi / Die fünff bücher Mosis sampt dem Hohen lied Salomonis. . . .* Constance, 1544 [inside the German edition: "Ein kurzer Bericht wie man die Jüdische teutsche schrifft, der sich die Juden gemainlich gebrauchen, lesen solle," n.p.].

Fecht, Johann. *De praecipuis oratoris ecclesiastici inperorando virtutibus exercitatio sacra*. Rostock, [1700].

Friedrich, Carl Wilhelm. *Unterricht in der Judensprache und Schrift. Zum Gebrauch für Gelehrte und Ungelehrte*. Prentzlow, 1784.

Gerson, Christian. *Des Jüdischen Thalmuds fürnehmster Inhalt und Widerlegung*. Leipzig, 1685.

[Glüsing, Johann Otto, ed.]. *Biblia Pentapla, Das ist: Die Bücher der Heiligen Schrift . . . , Nach Fünf-facher Deutscher Verdolmetschung*. 3 vols. Wandsbeck and Schiffbeck, 1710–12.

Goethe, Johann Wolfgang. "Anweisung zur teutsch-hebräischen Sprache" [1761?]. In *Der junge Goethe: Neue Ausgabe in sechs Bänden besorgt von Max Morris*. Vol. 1. Leipzig: Insel-Verlag, 1909.

——. *Aus meinem Leben: Dichtung und Wahrheit* (1811–33). In *Goethes Werke. Abt. 1: Werke im engern Sinne*. Vol. 26. Weimar, 1889.

Gottfried, Johann Adam. *Anweisung zum Jüdischdeutschen*. Tübingen, 1753.

Güdemann, Moritz, ed. *Quellenschriften zur Geschichte des Unterrichts und der Erziehung bei den deutschen Juden von den ältesten Zeiten bis auf Mendelssohn*. Berlin: Hofmann, 1891.

Haselbauer, Franciscus. *Gründlicher Bericht von dem Christenthum: Allen Kindern Israel zur Erkanntnus der Wahrheit vorgetragen*. 2 vols. Prague, 1719–22.

——. *Fundamenta grammatica duarum praecipuarum linguarum orientalium, scilicet: Hebraicae et Chaldaicae*. Prague, 1742 [inside: "Appendix De Idiotismo Germanico Judaeorum," 237–44].

Helicz [also: Helic], Paul. *Elemental oder lesebuechlein*. Hundesfeld, 1543.

——, ed., [and Johann Harzuge, trans.?]. *Dos nay testiment dos do vert ginent Evanyelyon . . . dos ist . . . bsure toyve*. Cracow, 1540.

Helvicus, Christoph, ed. and trans. *Jüdische Historien oder Thalmuhdische, Rabbinische, wunderbarliche Legenden. . . .* 2 vols. Giessen, 1612.

Herder, Johann Gottfried. *Herders Sämmtliche Werke*. 33 vols. Berlin: Weidmann, 1877–1913.

———. *Über die Würkung der Dichtkunst auf die Sitten der Völker in alten und neuen Zeiten* (1781). In *Herders Sämmtliche Werke*, vol. 8.

———. *Vom Geist der Ebräischen Poesie* (1782–83). In *Herders Sämmtliche Werke*, vols. 11, 12.

———. "Bekehrung der Juden." *Adrastea* (1802). In *Herders Sämmtliche Werke*, vol. 24.

Hirsch, Salman Zvi of Aufhausen. *Yudisher teryak*. Hanau, 1615.

Hosmann, Sigismund. "Das schwer zu bekehrende Juden-Hertz." In *Fürtreffliches Denck-Mahl der Göttlichen Regierung*. 4th ed. Cell, 1711.

J.W. *Jüdischer Sprach-Meister, oder Erklärung was zwischen zweyen Juden . . . auf ihre gewöhnliche Redens-Art, abgehandelt wird*. N.p., [ca. 1714].

Koch, Johann Michael. *Brevis manuductio ad lectionem scriptorum judaeorum germanicorum*. Frankfurt am Main, 1709.

Kortholt, Christian. *De variis scripturae editionibus tractatus theologico-historico-philologicus*. Kiel, 1686.

Krackherr, Christoph Friedrich. *Bequemes, nützliches, nothwendiges, und für jedermann dienliches Handlexicon. . . .* Nuremberg, 1766 [2nd ed.: *Des Klugen Beamten tägliches Hand-Lexicon. . . .* Nuremberg, 1768; inside: "Anhang eines jüdisch teutschen und rothwelschen Wörterbuchs," 492–514].

Kümmet, Caspar. *Schola Hebraica, In qua per duas Grammaticae Partes. . . .* Würzburg and Nuremberg, 1688 [inside: "Appendix III. De Lectione Hebraeo-Germanica," 308–16].

Lebrecht, Philipp Nicodemus. *Der Eckstein des wahren Christlichen Glaubens*. Dresden and Leipzig, 1719 [inside: "Kurtzer Unterricht der Jüdisch-Teutschen Lesung und Schreibens-Art," n.p.].

Leibniz, Gottfried Wilhelm. *Ermahnung an die Teutsche, ihren Verstand und Sprache beßer zu üben, samt beygefügtem Vorschlag einer Teutsch gesinten Gesellschaft* [written probably in 1682/3]. Published in *Wissenschaftliche Beihefte zur Zeitschrift des Allgemeinen Deutschen Sprachvereins* 29 (1907):290–312.

———. *Unvorgreiffliche Gedancken betreffend die Ausübung und Verbesserung der Teutschen Sprache* [written probably in 1697]. Published in *Wissenschaftliche Beihefte zur Zeitschrift des Allgemeinen Deutschen Sprachvereins* 30 (1908):327–56.

Luther, Martin. *D. Martin Luthers Werke. Kritische Gesamtausgabe. Schriften*. 68 vols. Weimar, 1883–.

———. *Daß Jesus Christus ein geborner Jude sei* (1523). In *D. Martin Luthers Werke*, vol. 11.

———. *Wider die Sabbather* (1538). In *D. Martin Luthers Werke*, vol. 50.

———. *Von den Juden und ihren Lügen* (1543). In *D. Martin Luthers Werke*, vol. 53.

———, ed. *Von der falschen Betler büberey* (1528). In *D. Martin Luthers Werke*, vol. 26.

Meelführer, Johann. *Grammaticae hebraeae compendiosa institutio*. Ansbach, 1607 [inside: "De Scriptura Judaeorum, qua utuntur, tum in Epistolis, tum in Commentariis, pro lingua Germanica exp rimenda," 262–67].

Mendelssohn, Moses. *Gesammelte Schriften: Jubiläumsausgabe*. Edited by Fritz Bamberger, Bruni Strauss, Alexander Altmann, and Eva J. Engel. Vol. 7. Stuttgart-Bad Cannstatt: Frommann-Holzboog, 1974.

Moller, Christian, ed. and trans. *Novum Testamentum Hebraeo-Teutonicum*. Frankfurt an der Oder, 1700 [inside: "Bericht, wie das Jüdisch-Teutsche zu lesen," n.p.].

——, trans. *Evangelium Matthaei ductu Iohannis Mulleri* [i.e. Christiani Molleri] *Sandov literis iudaicogermanicis exscribi curavit Jo. Henr. Callenberg*. Halle, 1736.

Moscherosch, Hanß-Michael [also: Johann Michael]. *Gesichte Philanders von Sittewald, Das ist Straff-Schrifften. Ander Theil*. Strasbourg, 1650.

[Müller, Johannes]. *Or le'eys erev . . . Dos likht kegn abend tsayt*. Halle, 1728.

[——.] *Das Licht am Abend*. Halle, 1736.

Münster, Sebastian. *Dictionarium Hebraicum*. Basel, 1523.

——. *Institutiones Grammaticae in Hebraeam linguam*. Basel, 1524 [inside: "Institutio brevis, quomodo vernacula quaeque lingua Hebraicis characteribus scribi possit," n.p.].

——. *Chaldaica grammatica*. Basel, 1527.

——. *Dictionarium Chaldaicum*. Basel, 1527.

Oppenheimer, Eberhard Carl Friedrich. *Hodegus ebraeo-rabbinicus, das ist: . . . Anweisung wie . . . die Rabbinischen Bücher und Briefe, Contracte . . . u. derer heutigen Jüden teutsch zu lesen und zu verstehen*. Leipzig, 1731.

Osterchrist, Friedrich. *Hebräisch- und Teutsches Sprach-buch, oder sehr leichte Methode. . . .* Regensburg, 1754.

Pfefferkorn, Johannes. *Ich bin ein buchlein, der Juden veindt ist mein namen*. Augsburg, 1509.

Pfeiffer, August. *Critica Sacra*. Leipzig, 1688 [Dresden, 1680; inside: "De lectione Ebraeo-Germanica," 377–83].

PhilogLottus [J.P. Lütke?]. *Kurtze und gründliche Anweisung zur Teutsch-Jüdischen Sprache*. Freiberg, 1733.

Reizenstein, Wolf Ehrenfried von. *Der vollkommene Pferde-Kenner*. Uffenheim, 1764 [inside: "Anhang, woraus diejenigen Redens-Arten können erlernet werden, deren sich die Juden in ihrem Umgang gegen einander und sonderlich auf Roß-Märkten bedienen," n.p.].

Reyher, Samuel. *Mathesis Mosaica*. Kiel, 1679.

Sammlung Tychsen: Die Hebraica und Judaica der Sammlung Tychsen und der Universitätsbibliothek Rostock: die altjiddische (jüdisch-deutsche) Literatur, hrsg. von der Universitätsbibliothek Rostock, bearbeitet von Hermann Süß und Heike Tröger. Erlangen: Harald Fischer Verlag; microfiche edition, 2001; online edition, 2010.

Saubert, Johann. *Codicis . . . in quo Paraphrases, commentaria, & receptissimae apud Judaeos explicationes. . . .* Helmstedt, 1660.

Schadeus, Elias. *Mysterium, Das ist Geheimnis S. Pauli Röm. am II. Von bekehrung der Juden*. Strasbourg, 1592 [inside: "Ein gewisser Bericht von der Teutsch Hebreischen Schrifft deren sich die Juden gebrauchen," n.p.].

——, ed. and trans. *Fünff Bücher des Newen Testaments*. Strasbourg, 1592.

Scherffer, Wencel. *Geist- und weltlicher Gedichte: Erster Theil*. Briege, 1652.

Schudt, Johann Jacob. *Jüdische Merckwürdigkeiten*. 4 vols. Frankfurt am Main and Leipzig, 1714–18 [inside: "Caput XVI: Von der Franckfurter und anderer Juden Teutsch-Hebräischen Sprache," 2:281–96; Supplement: 4:113–23].

——, ed. and trans. *Neue Franckfurter Jüdische Kleider-Ordnung . . . Aus dem Hebräischen ins Hochteutsche übersetzt*. Frankfurt am Main, 1716 [inside: "Anhang von alten und neuen jüdischen Rätzeln," 54–62].

Schwab, Dietrich. *Detectum velum Mosaicum Iudaeorum nostri temporis, Das ist: Jüdischer Deckmantel deß Mosaischen Gesetzes . . . auffgehoben und entdecket*. Mainz, 1619.

Selig, Gottfried. *Kurze und gründliche Anleitung zu einer leichten Erlernung der Jüdischdeutschen Sprache*. Leipzig, 1767.

——. *Lehrbuch zur gründlichen Erlernung der jüdischdeutschen Sprache*. Leipzig, 1792.

Sennert, Andreas. *Rabbinismus: h. e. Praecepta Targumico-Talmudico-Rabbinica*. Wittenberg, 1666 [inside: "Appendix: De scriptura ebraeo-germanica," 63–65].

Thiele, A. F. *Die jüdischen Gauner in Deutschland: ihre Taktik, ihre Eigenthümlichkeiten und ihre Sprache*. 2 vols. Berlin, 1841–42.

[Thirsch, Leopold]. *Nützliches Handlexikon der jüdischen Sprache*. Prague, 1773.

Tychsen, Oluf Gerhard. *Bützowische Nebenstunden: verschiedenen zur morgenländischen Gelehrsamkeit gehörigen Sachen gewidmet*. Vol. 1. Bützow and Rostock, 1766.

Wagenseil, Johann Christoph. *Sota, hoc est: liber mischnicus de uxore adulterii suspecta*. Altdorf, 1674.

——. *Tela Ignea Satanae*. Altdorf, 1681.

——. *Buch von der Meister Singer holdseligen Kunst*. In *De sacri rom. Imperii libera civitate Noribergensi commentatio*. Altdorf, 1697.

——. *Belehrung der Jüdisch-Teutschen Red- und Schreibart*. Königsberg, 1699.

——. *Benachrichtigungen wegen einiger die Judenschafft angehenden wichtigen Sachen*. Leipzig, 1705.

——. "Die Hoffnung der Erlösung Israelis." In *Benachrichtigungen*, 1–125.

——. "Rabbi Mose Stendels nach Jüdisch-Teutscher Red-Art vorlängst in Reimen gebrachte Psalmen Davids." In *Benachrichtigungen*, n.p.

Willemer, Philipp Helfrich, ed. and trans. *Gebet-Buch derer heutigen Jüdinnen . . . aus dem Hebräischen und Jüdisch-Teutschen in das Hoch-Teutsche übersetzt und mit Anmerckungen beleuchtet*. Schweidnitz and Leipzig, 1734.

Wolf, Johann Christoph. *Bibliotheca Hebraea*. 4 vols. Hamburg and Leipzig, 1715–33.

Wucherfeind, Christlieb. *Der verdammliche Juden-Spieß*. N.p., 1688.

Wülfer, Johann. *Theriaca Judaica ad examen revocata*. Nuremberg, 1681.

Secondary Literature

Almog, Shmuel, and Michael Heyd, eds. *Ra'ayon ha-behirah be-Yisra'el u-ve-amim*. Jerusalem: Merkaz Zalman Shazar, 1991.

Althaus, Hans Peter. "Die Erforschung der jiddischen Sprache." In *Germanische Dialektologie: Festschrift für Walther Mitzka*. Zeitschrift für Mundartforschung NF 5, edited by Ludwig E. Schmitt, 1:224–63. Wiesbaden: Steiner, 1968.

Aptroot, Marion. "'In *galkhes* they do not say so, but the *taytsh* is as it stands here': Notes on the Amsterdam Yiddish Bible Translations by Blitz and Witzenhausen." *Studia Rosenthaliana* 27 (1993):136–58.

———. "Jiddischforschung—eine deutsche Tradition." *Jahrbuch der Heinrich-Heine-Universität* 1994–97 (2001):207–20.

———. "Yiddish Bibles in Amsterdam." In Berger, *Bible in/and Yiddish*, 42–60.

———. "Writing 'Jewish' not 'German': Functional Writing Styles and the Symbolic Function of Yiddish in Early Modern Ashkenaz." *Leo Baeck Institute Year Book* 55 (2010):115–28.

Ave-Lallemant, Friedrich Ch. B. *Das deutsche Gaunertum in seiner social-politischen, literarischen und linguistischen Ausbildung zu seinem heutigen Bestande*. 4 vols. Leipzig: Brockhaus, 1858–62 [reprinted in 3 vols., Hildesheim and New York: Olms, 1980].

Barbour, Stephen. "'*Uns knüpft der Sprache heilig Band*': Reflections on the Role of Language in German Nationalism, Past and Present." In *"Das unsichtbare Band der Sprache": Studies in German Language and Linguistic History in Memory of Leslie Seiffert*, edited by John L. Flood, Paul Salmon, Olive Sayce, and Christopher Wells, 313–32. Stuttgart: Heinz, 1993.

Barth, Fredrik, ed. *Ethnic Groups and Boundaries: The Social Organization of Culture Difference*. Bergen-Oslo and London: Universitetsforlaget, 1969.

Baumgarten, Jean. "Hybridité, corruption et mélange: sur quelques représentations du yiddish (XVIe-XIXe siècles)." In *L'inconscient du yiddish*, edited by Max Kohn and Jean Baumgarten, 181–204. Paris: Anthropos, 2003.

———. *Introduction to Old Yiddish Literature*. Edited and translated by Jerold C. Frakes. New York: Oxford University Press, 2005.

Bell, Dean Phillip, and Stephen G. Burnett, eds. *Jews, Judaism, and the Reformation in Sixteenth-Century Germany*. Leiden: Brill, 2006.

Ben-Sasson, Haim Hillel. "Jewish-Christian Disputation in the Setting of Humanism and Reformation in the German Empire." *Harvard Theological Review* 59 (1966):369–90.

Berger, Shlomo, ed. *The Bible in/and Yiddish*. Amsterdam: Menasseh ben Israel Institute, 2007.

Blackall, Eric. *The Emergence of German as a Literary Language 1700–1775*. Ithaca, NY, and London: Cornell University Press, 1978 [Cambridge, UK: Cambridge University Press, 1959].

Blastenbrei, Peter. *Johann Christoph Wagenseil und seine Stellung zum Judentum.* Erlangen: Fischer, 2004.

Blitz, Hans-Martin. *Aus Liebe zum Vaterland: die deutsche Nation im 18. Jahrhundert.* Hamburg: Hamburger Ed., 2000.

Block, Anton. *Honour and Violence.* Cambridge, UK: Polity Press, 2001.

Bobzin, Hartmut. "Vom Sinn des Arabischstudiums im Sprachenkanon der Philologia Sacra." *Hallesche Beiträge zur Orientwissenschaft* 24 (1997):21–32.

Bok, Sissela. *Secrets: On the Ethics of Concealment and Revelation.* New York: Pantheon Books, 1982.

Borochov, Ber. "Di bibliotek funem yidishn filolog: fir hundert yor yidishe shprakh-forshung" (1913). In *Shprakh-forshung un literatur-geshikhte*, collected and edited by Nachman Meysil, 76–136. Tel Aviv: Y. L. Perets farlag, 1966.

Bourdieu, Pierre. *Distinction: A Social Critique of the Judgement of Taste.* Translated by Richard Nice. Cambridge, MA: Harvard University Press, 1984.

Bourel, Dominique. "Die deutsche Orientalistik im 18. Jahrhundert: von der Mission zur Wissenschaft." In *Historische Kritik und biblischer Kanon in der deutschen Aufklärung*, edited by Henning Reventlow, Walter Sparn, and John D. Woodbridge, 113–26. Wiesbaden: Harrassowitz, 1988.

Brenner, Michael, ed. *Jüdische Sprachen in deutscher Umwelt: Hebräisch und Jiddisch von der Aufklärung bis ins 20. Jahrhundert.* Göttingen: Vandenhoeck & Ruprecht, 2002.

Burke, Peter. *The Historical Anthropology of Early Modern Italy.* Cambridge, UK: Cambridge University Press, 1987.

——. *The Art of Conversation.* Ithaca, NY: Cornell University Press, 1993.

——. *Languages and Communities in Early Modern Europe.* Cambridge, UK: Cambridge University Press, 2004.

——. "Cultures of Translation in Early Modern Europe." In *Cultural Translation in Early Modern Europe*, edited by Peter Burke and R. Po-chia Hsia, 7–38. Cambridge, UK: Cambridge University Press, 2007.

——, and Roy Porter, eds. *Languages and Jargons: Contributions to a Social History of Language.* Cambridge, UK: Polity Press, 1995.

Burnett, Stephen G. *From Christian Hebraism to Jewish Studies: Johannes Buxtorf (1564–1629) and Hebrew Learning in the Seventeenth Century.* Leiden: Brill, 1996.

——. "A Dialogue of the Deaf: Hebrew Pedagogy and Anti-Jewish Polemic in Sebastian Münster's *Messiahs of the Christians and the Jews* (1529/39)." *Archiv für Reformationsgeschichte* 91 (2000):168–90.

——. *Christian Hebraism in the Reformation Era (1500–1660): Authors, Books, and the Transmission of Jewish Learning.* Leiden: Brill, 2012.

Carlebach, Elisheva. "Attribution of Secrecy and Perceptions of Jewry." *Jewish Social Studies* 2, no. 3 (1996):115–36.

——. *Divided Souls: Converts from Judaism in Germany, 1500–1750.* New Haven, CT, and London: Yale University Press, 2001.

———. "The Anti-Christian Element in Early Modern Yiddish Culture." *Braun Lectures in the History of the Jews in Prussia* 10. Ramat-Gan: Bar-Ilan University, 2003.

Clark, Christopher. *The Politics of Conversion: Missionary Protestantism and the Jews in Prussia 1728–1941*. Oxford: Clarendon Press, 1995.

Cohen, Jeremy. *The Friars and the Jews: The Evolution of Medieval Anti-Judaism*. Ithaca, NY: Cornell University Press, 1982.

———. *Living Letters of the Law: Ideas of the Jew in Medieval Christianity*. Berkeley: University of California Press, 1999.

Coudert, Allison P., and Jeffrey S. Shoulson, eds. *Hebraica veritas? Christian Hebraists and the Study of Judaism in Early Modern Europe*. Philadelphia: University of Pennsylvania Press, 2004.

Dan, Robert. "'Judaizare'—The Career of a Term." In *Antitrinitarianism in the Second Half of the 16th Century*, edited by Robert Dan and Antal Pirnat, 25–34. Budapest: Akadémiai Kiadó, 1982.

Danker, Uwe. "Bandits and the State: Robbers and the Authorities in the Holy Roman Empire in the Late Seventeenth and Early Eighteenth Centuries." In Evans, *German Underworld*, 75–107.

———. *Räuberbanden im Alten Reich um 1700: ein Beitrag zur Geschichte von Herrschaft und Kriminalität in der Frühen Neuzeit*. Frankfurt am Main: Suhrkamp, 1988.

Dauber, Jeremy. *In the Demon's Bedroom: Yiddish Literature and the Early Modern*. New Haven, CT, and London: Yale University Press, 2010.

Degani, Ben-Zion. "Eduyot al hofa'at ha-markiv 'ha-plili' ba-stereotip ha-yhudi be-Germanyah be-shilhei yemei ha-beynayim u-vreshit ha-et ha-hadashah." In *Tarbut ve-hevra be-toldot Yisra'el bi-ymei ha-beynayim: kovetz ma'amarim le-zikhro shel Hayyim Hillel Ben-Sasson*, edited by Reuven Bonfil, Menahem Ben-Sasson, and Joseph Hacker, 655–86. Jerusalem: Merkaz Zalman Shazar, 1989.

Deutsch, Yaacov. "A View of the Jewish Religion: Conceptions of Jewish Practice and Ritual in Early Modern Europe." *Archiv für Religionsgeschichte* 3 (2001):273–95.

———. "Polemical Ethnographies: Descriptions of Yom Kippur in the Writings of Christian Hebraists and Jewish Converts to Christianity in Early Modern Europe." In Coudert and Shoulson, *Hebraica veritas?*, 202–33.

———. "*Von der Iuden Ceremonien*: Representations of Jews in Sixteenth-Century Germany." In Bell and Burnett, *Jews, Judaism, and the Reformation*, 335–56.

———. "Jewish Anti-Christian Invectives and Christian Awareness: An Unstudied Form of Interaction in the Early Modern Period." *Leo Baeck Institute Year Book* 55 (2010):41–61.

———. *Judaism in Christian Eyes: Ethnographic Descriptions of Jews and Judaism in Early Modern Europe*. New York: Oxford University Press, 2012.

Dickmann, Friedrich. "Judenmissionsprogramm Johann Christoph Wagenseils." *Neue Zeitschrift für systematische Theologie und Religionsphilosophie* 16 (1974):75–92.

Ebert, Hans-Georg, and Thoralf Hanstein, eds. *Johann Jacob Reiske: Leben und Wirkung: Ein Leipziger Byzantinist und Begründer der Orientalistik im 18. Jahrhundert*. Leipzig: Evang. Verl.-Anst., 2005.

Eibach, Joachim. "Stigma Betrug: Delinquenz und Ökonomie im jüdischen Ghetto." In *Kriminalität und abweichendes Verhalten: Deutschland im 18. und 19. Jahrhundert*, edited by Helmut Berding, Diethelm Klippel, and Günther Lottes, 15–38. Göttingen: Vandenhoeck & Ruprecht, 1999.

Ettinger, Shmuel. "The Beginnings of the Change in the Attitude of European Society Towards the Jews." *Scripta Hierosolymitana* 7 (1961):193–219.

Evans, Richard J., ed. *The German Underworld: Deviants and Outcasts in German History*. London and New York: Routledge, 1988.

Feiner, Shmuel. *The Jewish Enlightenment*. Translated by Chaya Naor. Philadelphia: University of Pennsylvania Press, 2003.

Finkin, Jordan D., ed. and trans. *The Eighteenth-Century Language Text of Jüdischer Sprach-Meister: A West-Yiddish Dialogue Together with an English Translation and Introduction*. Lewiston, NY: Edwin Mellen Press, 2010.

Fishman, Joshua A. *The Sociology of Language: An Interdisciplinary Social Science Approach to Language in Society*. Rowley, MA: Newbury House, 1972.

——. *In Praise of the Beloved Language*. Berlin and New York: Mouton de Gruyter, 1997.

Frakes, Jerold C. *The Politics of Interpretation: Alterity and Ideology in Old Yiddish Studies*. Albany: State University of New York Press, 1989.

——. *The Cultural Study of Yiddish in Early Modern Europe*. New York: Palgrave Macmillan, 2007.

——, ed. *Early Yiddish Texts, 1100–1750*. Oxford: Oxford University Press, 2004.

Freud, Sigmund. *Civilization and Its Discontents*. Translated by Joan Riviere. London: Hogarth Press and the Institute of Psycho-analysis, 1930.

Friedman, Jerome. "Sebastian Münster, the Jewish Mission, and Protestant Antisemitism." *Archiv für Reformationsgeschichte* 70 (1979):238–59.

——. *The Most Ancient Testimony: Sixteenth-Century Christian-Hebraica in the Age of Renaissance Nostalgia*. Athens: Ohio University Press, 1983.

Friedrich, Martin. *Zwischen Abwehr und Bekehrung: Die Stellung der deutschen evangelischen Theologie zum Judentum im 17. Jahrhundert*. Tübingen: Mohr, 1988.

Funkenstein, Amos. "The Dialectics of Assimilation." *Jewish Social Studies* 1, no. 2 (1995):1–14.

Gardt, Andreas. *Sprachreflexion in Barock und Frühaufklärung*. Berlin: de Gruyter, 1994.

——, ed. *Nation und Sprache: die Diskussion ihres Verhältnisses in Geschichte und Gegenwart*. Berlin and New York: de Gruyter, 2000.

Geiger, Ludwig. *Das Studium der hebräischen Sprache in Deutschland vom Ende des XV. bis zur Mitte des XVI. Jahrhunderts*. Breslau: Schletter, 1870.

——. *Geschichte der Juden in Berlin*. 2 vols. Berlin: Guttentag, 1871.

Gilman, Sander L. *Jewish Self-Hatred: Anti-Semitism and the Hidden Language of the Jews*. Baltimore and London: Johns Hopkins University Press, 1986.

Glanz, Rudolf. *Geschichte des niederen jüdischen Volkes in Deutschland*. New York: Leo Baeck Institute, 1968.

Grafton, Anthony, and Joanna Weinberg. *"I have always loved the Holy Tongue": Isaac Casaubon, the Jews, and a Forgotten Chapter in Renaissance Scholarship*. Cambridge, MA: Belknap Press of Harvard University Press, 2011.

Grossman, Jeffrey A. *The Discourse on Yiddish in Germany: From the Enlightenment to the Second Empire*. Rochester, NY: Camden House, 2000.

Guggenheim, Yacov. "Meeting on the Road: Encounters Between German Jews and Christians on the Margins of Society." In Hsia and Lehmann, *In and Out of the Ghetto*, 125–36.

Guggenheim-Grünberg, Florence. "The Horse Dealers' Language of the Swiss Jews in Endingen and Lengnau." In *The Field of Yiddish*, edited by Uriel Weinreich, 48–62. London: Mouton, 1954.

Guri, Yosef. *Let's Hear Only Good News: Yiddish Blessings and Curses*. Jerusalem: Hebrew University of Jerusalem, 2004.

Habermann, A. M. "Sebastian Minster un yidish." *Yivo-bleter* 3 (1932):190.

Habersaat, Karl. "Materialien zur Geschichte der jiddischen Grammatik." *Orbis* 11 (1962):352–68.

——. "Zur Geschichte der jiddischen Grammatik. Eine bibliographische Studie." *Zeitschrift für deutsche Philologie* 84 (1965):419–35.

Halliday, Michael A.K. *Language as Social Semiotic: The Social Interpretation of Language and Meaning*. London: E. Arnold, 1978.

——. "Antilanguages." In *Language as Social Semiotic*, 164–82.

——. "An Interpretation of the Functional Relationship between Language and Social Structure." In *Language as Social Semiotic*, 183–92.

Hardtwig, Wolfgang. *Nationalismus und Bürgerkultur in Deutschland: 1500–1914*. Göttingen: Vandenhoeck & Ruprecht, 1994.

Hastings, Adrian. *The Construction of Nationhood: Ethnicity, Religion and Nationalism*. Cambridge, UK: Cambridge University Press, 1997.

Haugen, Einar. *The Ecology of Language: Essays by Einar Haugen*. Stanford, CA: Stanford University Press, 1972.

——. "Dialect, Language, Nation." In *The Ecology of Language*, 237–54.

——. "The Ecology of Language." In *The Ecology of Language*, 325–39.

Heschel, Susannah. "Revolt of the Colonized: Abraham Geiger's *Wissenschaft des Judentums* as a Challenge to Christian Hegemony in the Academy." *New German Critique* 77 (1999):61–85.

Hess, Jonathan M. *Germans, Jews and the Claims of Modernity*. New Haven, CT, and London: Yale University Press, 2002.

Hobsbawm, Eric. *Bandits*. London: Weidenfeld & Nicolson, 2000 [1969].

Hodge, Robert, and Gunther Kress. *Social Semiotics*. Cambridge, UK: Polity Press, 1988.

Horodowich, Elizabeth. *Language and Statecraft in Early Modern Venice*. Cambridge, UK: Cambridge University Press, 2008.

Hsia, R. Po-chia. *The Myth of Ritual Murder: Jews and Magic in Reformation Germany*. New Haven, CT, and London: Yale University Press, 1988.

———. "Christian Ethnographies of Jews in Early Modern Germany." In *The Expulsion of the Jews: 1492 and After*, edited by Raymond B. Waddington and Arthur H. Williamson, 223–35. New York: Garland, 1994.

———. "The Usurious Jew: Economic Structure and Religious Representations in an Anti-Semitic Discourse." In Hsia and Lehmann, *In and Out of the Ghetto*, 161–76.

———, and Hartmut Lehmann, eds. *In and Out of the Ghetto: Jewish-Gentile Relations in Late Medieval and Early Modern Germany*. Cambridge, UK: Cambridge University Press, 1995.

Huber, Wolfgang. *Kulturpatriotismus und Sprachbewußtsein: Studien zur deutschen Philologie des 17. Jahrhunderts*. Frankfurt am Main: Peter Lang, 1984.

Hüllen, Werner. "Characterization and Evaluation of Languages in the Renaissance and in the Early Modern Period." In *Language Typology and Language Universals: An International Handbook*, edited by Martin Haspelmath, 1:234–49. Berlin: de Gruyter, 2001.

———. *Collected Papers on the History of Linguistic Ideas*. Edited by Michael M. Isermann. Münster: Nodus-Publ., 2002.

Israel, Jonathan I. *European Jewry in the Age of Mercantilism: 1550–1750*. Oxford: Clarendon Press, 1985.

Jacobs, Neil G. *Yiddish: A Linguistic Introduction*. Cambridge, UK: Cambridge University Press, 2005.

Jersch-Wenzel, Stefi. "Jewish Economic Activity in Early Modern Times." In Hsia and Lehmann, *In and Out of the Ghetto*, 91–101.

Jones, William Jervis. *Images of Language: Six Essays on German Attitudes to European Languages from 1500 to 1800*. Amsterdam: Benjamins, 1999.

Joseph, John E. *Eloquence and Power: The Rise of Language Standards and Standard Languages*. New York: Blackwell, 1987.

Jütte, Robert. *Abbild und soziale Wirklichkeit des Bettler- und Gaunertums zu Beginn der Neuzeit: sozial-, mentalitäts-, u. sprachgeschichtl. Studien zum Liber Vagatorum (1510)*. Cologne and Vienna: Böhlau, 1988.

———. *Poverty and Deviance in Early Modern Europe*. Cambridge, UK: Cambridge University Press, 1994.

Kalmar, Ivan Davidson, and Derek J. Penslar, eds. *Orientalism and the Jews*. Hanover, NH, and London: Brandeis University Press, 2005.

Katz, Dovid. "On Yiddish, in Yiddish and for Yiddish: 500 Years of Yiddish Scholarship." In *Identity and Ethos: A Festschrift for Sol Liptzin*, edited by Mark H. Gelber, 23–36. New York: Peter Lang, 1986.

Katz, Jacob. *From Prejudice to Destruction: Anti-Semitism, 1700–1933*. Cambridge, MA: Harvard University Press, 1980.

Kaufmann, Thomas. "Die theologische Bewertung des Judentums im Protestantismus des späteren 16. Jahrhunderts (1530–1600)." *Archiv für Reformationsgeschichte* 91 (2000):191–237.

———. "Luther and the Jews." In Bell and Burnett, *Jews, Judaism, and the Reformation*, 69–104.

Kerler, Dov-Ber. *The Origins of Modern Literary Yiddish*. Oxford: Clarendon Press, 1999.

Klayman-Cohen, Israela. *Die hebräische Komponente im Westjiddischen am Beispiel der Memoiren der Glückel von Hameln*. Hamburg: Buske, 1994.

Koch, Ludwig. *Jesuiten-Lexikon*. 2 vols. Löwen-Heverlee: Verl. der Bibliothek SJ, 1962 [Paderborn: Bonifacius-Druckerei, 1934].

Koselleck, Reinhart. "Volk, Nation, Nationalismus, Masse." In *Geschichtliche Grundbegriffe: historisches Lexikon zur politisch-sozialen Sprache in Deutschland*, edited by Otto Brunner, Werner Conze, and Reinhart Koselleck, 7:141–431. Stuttgart: Klett-Cotta, 1992.

Kracauer, Isidor. *Geschichte der Juden in Frankfurt: 1150–1824*. 2 vols. Frankfurt am Main: I. Kauffmann, 1927.

Kraemer, Hendrik. *The Christian Message in a Non-Christian World*. London: Edinburgh House Press, 1938.

———. *The Communication of the Christian Faith*. London: Lutterworth, 1957.

Krauss, Samuel. *Das Leben Jesu nach jüdischen Quellen*. Berlin: Calvary, 1902.

———. *The Jewish-Christian Controversy: From the Earliest Times to 1789*. Vol. 1: *History*. Edited and revised by William Horbury. Tübingen: Mohr, 1995.

Kühn, Christoph. *Jüdische Delinquenten in der Frühen Neuzeit: Lebensumstände delinquenter Juden in Aschkenas und die Reaktionen der jüdischen Gemeinden sowie der christlichen Obrigkeit*. Potsdam: Universitätsverlag Potsdam, 2008.

Küther, Carsten. *Räuber und Gauner in Deutschland: Das organisierte Bandenwesen im 18. und frühen 19. Jahrhundert*. Göttingen: Vandenhoeck & Ruprecht, 1976.

Landau, Alfred. "Bibliographie des Jüdisch-Deutschen." *Deutsche Mundarten* 1, no. 2 (1897):126–32, 208–9.

Landmann, Salcia. *Der jüdische Witz: Soziologie und Sammlung*. 5th ed. Olten: Walter-Verlag, 1962.

Lässig, Simone. "Sprachwandel und Verbürgerlichung: Zur Bedeutung der Sprache im innerjüdischen Modernisierungsprozeß des frühen 19. Jahrhunderts." *Historische Zeitschrift* 270 (2000):617–67.

Levy, Leonard W. *Blasphemy: Verbal Offense Against the Sacred, from Moses to Salman Rushdie*. New York: Knopf, 1993.

Liberles, Robert. "On the Threshold of Modernity: 1618–1780." In *Jewish Daily Life in Germany, 1618–1945*, edited by Marion A. Kaplan, 9–92. Oxford: Oxford University Press, 2005.

Limor, Ora. "Christian Sacred Space and the Jew." In *From Witness to Witchcraft: Jews and Judaism in Medieval Christian Thought*, edited by Jeremy Cohen, 55–77. Wiesbaden: Harrassowitz, 1997.

Loetz, Francisca. *Mit Gott handeln: Von den Züricher Gotteslästerern der Frühen Neuzeit zu einer Kulturgeschichte des Religiösen*. Göttingen: Vandenhoeck & Ruprecht, 2002.

Mahler, Raphael, ed. and trans. *Jewish Emancipation: A Selection of Documents*. New York: American Jewish Committee, 1941.

Mangold, Sabine. *Eine "weltbürgerliche Wissenschaft": die deutsche Orientalistik im 19. Jahrhundert*. Stuttgart: Steiner, 2004.

Manuel, Frank E. *The Broken Staff: Judaism Through Christian Eyes*. Cambridge, MA: Harvard University Press, 1992.

Marchand, Suzanne L. *German Orientalism in the Age of Empire: Religion, Race, and Scholarship*. Washington, DC: German Historical Institute; New York: Cambridge University Press, 2009.

Matisoff, James A. *Blessings, Curses, Hopes, and Fears: Psycho-Ostensive Expressions in Yiddish*. Stanford, CA: Stanford University Press, 2000 [Philadelphia: Institute for the Study of Human Issues, 1979].

Milroy, James, and Lesley Milroy. *Authority in Language: Investigating Language Prescription and Standardisation*. London: Routledge & Kegan Paul, 1985.

Montagu, Ashley. *The Anatomy of Swearing*. New York and London: Macmillan, 1967.

Montgomery, Martin. *An Introduction to Language and Society*. London: Routledge, 1995 [1986].

Müller, Gerhard. "Protestantische Orthodoxie." In *Kirche und Synagoge: Handbuch zur Geschichte von Christen und Juden*, edited by Karl H. Rengstorf and Siegfried von Kortzfleisch, 1:453–504. Munich: Dt. Taschenbuchverl., 1988 [Stuttgart: Klett, 1968].

Neusner, Jacob, and Ernest S. Frerichs, eds. *"To See Ourselves As Others See Us": Christians, Jews, "Others" in Late Antiquity*. Chico, CA: Scholars Press, 1985.

Ohm, Thomas. *Machet zu Jüngern alle Völker: Theorie der Mission*. Freiburg im Breisgau: Wewel, 1962.

Osterhammel, Jürgen. *Europe, the "West" and the Civilizing Mission*. London: German Historical Institute, 2006 (Annual Lecture GHI London, 2005).

Pasto, James. "Islam's 'Strange Secret Sharer': Orientalism, Judaism, and the Jewish Question." *Comparative Studies in Society and History* 40 (1998):437–74.

Penslar, Derek J. *Shylock's Children: Economics and Jewish Identity in Modern Europe*. Berkeley: University of California Press, 2001.

Pribram, Alfred, ed. *Urkunden und Akten zur Geschichte der Juden in Wien*. 2 vols. Vienna: Braumüller, 1918.

Price, David H. *Johannes Reuchlin and the Campaign to Destroy Jewish Books*. New York: Oxford University Press, 2011.

Röll, Walter. "Die Bibelübersetzung ins Jiddische im 14. und 15. Jahrhundert." In *Die Vermittlung geistlicher Inhalte im deutschen Mittelalter: internationales Symposium, Roscrea 1994*, edited by Timothy R. Jackson, Nigel F. Palmer, and Almut Suerbaum, 183–95. Tübingen: Niemeyer, 1996.

Römer, Nils. *Tradition und Akkulturation: Zum Sprachwandel der Juden in Deutschland zur Zeit der Haskalah*. Münster and New York: Waxmann, 1995.

———. "Sprachverhältnisse und Identität der Juden in Deutschland im 18. Jahrhundert." In Brenner, *Jüdische Sprachen in deutscher Umwelt*, 11–18.

Rymatzki, Christoph. *Hallischer Pietismus und Judenmission: Johann Heinrich Callenbergs Institutum Judaicum und dessen Freundeskreis (1728–1736)*. Tübingen: Niemeyer, 2004.

Said, Edward W. *Orientalism*. New York: Vintage Books, 1979.

Schrader, Hans-Jürgen. "Lesarten der Schrift: die 'Biblia Pentapla' und ihr Programm einer 'herrlichen Harmonie Göttlichen Wortes' in 'Fünffacher Deutscher Verdolmetschung.'" In *Zwiesprache: Beiträge zur Theorie und Geschichte des Übersetzens*, edited by John E. Jackson and Ulrich Stadler, 199–218. Stuttgart: Metzler, 1996.

Schröder, Konrad. *Biographisches und bibliographisches Lexikon der Fremdsprachenlehrer des deutschsprachigen Raumes: Spätmittelalter bis 1800*. 7 vols. Augsburg: Univ. Augsburg, 1987–2001.

———. *Die skandinavischen und baltischen Sprachen sowie Jiddisch und Rotwelsch: ein Verzeichnis der Lehr- und Lernmaterialien 1500–1800*. Augsburg: Univ. Augsburg, 2001.

Schwerhoff, Gerd. "Blasphemie zwischen antijüdischem Stigma und kultureller Praxis: Zum Vorwurf der Gotteslästerung gegen die Juden in Mittelalter und beginnender Frühneuzeit." *Aschkenas* 10, no. 1 (2000):117–55.

Scott, James C. *Domination and the Arts of Resistance: Hidden Transcripts*. New Haven, CT, and London: Yale University Press, 1990.

Seidman, Naomi. *Faithful Renderings: Jewish-Christian Differences and the Politics of Translation*. Chicago and London: University of Chicago Press, 2006.

Shandler, Jeffrey. *Adventures in Yiddishland: Postvernacular Language and Culture*. Berkeley: University of California Press, 2006.

Shmeruk, Chone. *Sifrut yidish: perakim le-toldoteihah*. Tel Aviv: Tel Aviv University, 1978.

Shochat, Azriel. *Im hillufei tekufot: reshit ha-Haskalah be-Yahadut Germanyah*. Jerusalem: Mosad Bialik, 1960.

Shtif, N. "Mikhael Adams dray yidishe bikher." *Filologishe shriftn* 2 (1928):135–68.

———. "Poyl Helices 'elemental oder lesbikhlen' (Hundsfeld 1543) (tsu der geshikhte fun yidish-shtudium in 16 yorhundert)." *Filologishe shriftn* 3 (1929):515–24.

Smith, Jonathan Z. "What a Difference a Difference Makes." In Neusner and Frerichs, *"To See Ourselves As Others See Us,"* 3–48.

Stobbe, Otto. *Die Juden in Deutschland während des Mittelalters in politischer, socialer und rechtlicher Beziehung*. Braunschweig: Schwetsche, 1866.

Straßner, Erich. *Deutsche Sprachkultur*. Tübingen: Niemeyer, 1995.

Stukenbrock, Anja. *Sprachnationalismus: Sprachreflexion als Medium kollektiver Identitätsstiftung in Deutschland (1617–1945)*. Berlin: de Gruyter, 2005.

Teter, Magda, and Edward Fram. "Apostasy, Fraud, and the Beginnings of Hebrew Printing in Cracow." *AJS Review* 30, no. 1 (2006):31–66.

Timm, Erika. *Graphische und phonische Struktur des Westjiddischen*. Tübingen: Niemeyer, 1987.

——. "Blitz and Witzenhausen." In *Studies in Jewish Culture in Honour of Chone Shmeruk*, edited by Israel Bartal, Ezra Mendelsohn, and Chava Turniansky, 39*–66*. Jerusalem: Merkaz Zalman Shazar, 1993.

——. *Historische jiddische Semantik: Bibelübersetzungssprache als Faktor der Auseinanderentwicklung des jiddischen und des deutschen Wortschatzes*. Tübingen: Niemeyer, 2005.

Toury, Jacob. "Die Sprache als Problem der jüdischen Einordnung im deutschen Kulturraum." *Jahrbuch des Instituts für deutsche Geschichte, Universität Tel-Aviv* 4 (1982):75–95.

Townson, Michael. *Mother-Tongue and Fatherland: Language and Politics in German*. Manchester: Manchester University Press, 1992.

Trachtenberg, Joshua. *The Devil and the Jews: The Medieval Conception of the Jews and Its Relation to Modern Antisemitism*. Philadelphia: Jewish Publ. Soc. of America, 1983 [New Haven, CT: Yale University Press, 1943].

Turniansky, Chava. "Le-toldot ha-'taytsh-khumesh': 'khumesh mit khibur.'" In *Iyyunim be-sifrut: devarim she-ne'emru be-erev li-khvod Dov Saddan bi-mlot lo 85 shanah*, edited by Chone Shmeruk, 21–51. Jerusalem: Israeli Academy for Sciences, 1988.

——. "Yiddish Literature in Frankfurt am Main." In *Jüdische Kultur in Frankfurt am Main*, edited by Karl E. Grözinger, 273–85. Wiesbaden: Harrassowitz, 1997.

——. "Reception and Rejection of Yiddish Renderings of the Bible." In Berger, *Bible in/and Yiddish*, 7–20.

——. "Ha-limmud ba-heder ba-et ha-hadashah ha-mukdemet." In *Ha-heder: mehkarim, te'udot, pirkei sifrut ve-zikhronot*, edited by Emanuel Etkes and David Assaf, 3–35. Tel Aviv: Tel Aviv University, 2010.

Ulbricht, Otto. "Criminality and Punishment of the Jews in the Early Modern Period." In Hsia and Lehmann, *In and Out of the Ghetto*, 49–70.

Volkov, Shulamit. "Sprache als Ort der Auseinandersetzung mit Juden und Judentum in Deutschland, 1780–1933." In *Jüdische Intellektuelle und die Philologien in Deutschland, 1871–1933*, edited by Wilfried Barner and Christoph König, 223–38. Göttingen: Wallstein-Verl., 2001.

——. *Germans, Jews, and Antisemites: Trials in Emancipation*. New York: Cambridge University Press, 2006.

Waldman, Mark. "Goethe und das Judendeutsch." *Germanic Review* 4 (1929):123–30.

Warneck, Gustav. *Evangelische Missionslehre: Ein Missionstheoretischer Versuch*. 3 vols. Gotha: F. A. Perthes, 1892–1903.

Warren, Carol, and Barbara Laslett. "Privacy and Secrecy: A Conceptual Comparison." *Journal of Social Issues* 33, no. 3 (1977):43–51.

Weil, Gérard E. *Élie Lévita, Humaniste et massorète (1469–1549)*. Leiden: Brill, 1963.

Weinberg, Werner. "Language Questions Relating to Moses Mendelssohn's Pentateuch Translation." *Hebrew Union College Annual* 55 (1984):197–242.

Weinreich, Max. *Shtaplen: fir etyudn tsu der yidisher shprakhvisnshaft un literaturgeshikhte*. Berlin: Wostock, 1923.

———. "Di yidishe shprakh-forshung in 17tn yorhundert." *Tsaytshrift* 2–3 (1927/8):689–732.

———. "*Yidishkayt* and Yiddish: On the Impact of Religion on Language in Ashkenazic Jewry." In *Readings in the Sociology of Language*, edited by Joshua A. Fishman, 382–413. The Hague and Paris: Mouton, 1968.

———. *Geschichte der jiddischen Sprachforschung*. Edited by Jerold C. Frakes. Atlanta, GA: Scholars Press, 1993 [Diss. Marburg, 1923].

———. *History of the Yiddish Language*. Translated by Shlomo Noble. Edited by Paul Glasser. 2 vols. New Haven, CT, and London: Yale University Press, 2008 [Chicago and London: University of Chicago Press, 1980].

Wenzel, Edith. "Alt-Jiddisch oder Mittelhochdeutsch?" *Aschkenas* 14, no. 1 (2004):31–49.

Yuval, Israel Jacob. *Two Nations in Your Womb: Perceptions of Jews and Christians in Late Antiquity and the Middle Ages*. Berkeley: University of California Press, 2006.

Zimmer, Eric. "Jewish and Christian Hebraist Collaboration in Sixteenth Century Germany." *Jewish Quarterly Review* 71, no. 2 (1980):69–88.

Zinberg, Israel. *A History of Jewish Literature*. Vol. 7: *Old Yiddish Literature from Its Origins to the Haskalah Period*. Translated by Bernard Martin. Cincinnati, OH: Hebrew Union College Press, 1975.

Index

The authorized representative in the EU for product safety and compliance is:
Mare Nostrum Group
B.V Doelen 72
4831 GR Breda
The Netherlands

www.ingramcontent.com/pod-product-compliance
Lightning Source LLC
Chambersburg PA
CBHW060807310726
48980CB00002B/264

* 9 7 8 0 8 0 4 7 8 1 9 3 0 *